I0891847

Especially for

From

Date

The BIBLE PROMISE BOOK®

for *Morning & Evening*

Promises, Devotions & Prayers for Women

BARBOUR
PUBLISHING

YOU are the reason we do what we do here at Barbour Publishing. We promise that we will always use our God-given talents to produce content with you in mind—and that we will remain biblically faithful, no matter what.

Thank you for being the heart of our business.

Compiled by JoAnne Simmons.

ISBN 979-8-89151-286-3

Devotions are from *The Bible Promise Book for Morning and Evening Women's Edition* published by Barbour Publishing, Inc.

Published by Barbour Publishing, Inc., 1810 Barbour Drive, Uhrichsville, Ohio 44683, www.barbourbooks.com

Our mission is to inspire the world with the life-changing message of the Bible.

Member of the Evangelical Christian Publishers Association

Printed in China.

The Bible is full of promises.
And when God makes a promise,
you can trust it.

Evening, and morning...
will I pray, and cry aloud:
and he shall hear my voice.

PSALM 55:17 KJV

This edition of Barbour's bestselling *The Bible Promise Book* features themed Bible promises arranged into morning and evening readings for every day of the year. With Bible promises on topics like God's Word, wisdom, faith, prayer, encouragement, love, joy, and more, each scripture will speak directly to your heart, drawing you ever closer to your heavenly Father.

DAY 1

Gifts

Morning

In his grace, God has given us different gifts for doing certain things well.

ROMANS 12:6 NLT

Out of the generosity of Christ, each of us is given his own gift.

EPHESIANS 4:7 MSG

When you choose to put your faith in God, you receive spiritual gifts. God gives you these special abilities so you can help others see Him more clearly. Ask God to help you understand and use the gifts He has so graciously given to you.

Dear Father, thank You for the unique gifts You have given me. Please develop them in me so I can serve You and glorify You. Amen.

Evening

There are different kinds of gifts, but the same Spirit distributes them. There are different kinds of service, but the same Lord. There are different kinds of working, but in all of them and in everyone it is the same God at work.

1 CORINTHIANS 12:4–6 NIV

God has given each of you a gift from his great variety of spiritual gifts. Use them well to serve one another.

1 PETER 4:10 NLT

The Bible encourages us to use our abilities in ways that honor God. Some abilities may take center stage, while others work quietly in the background. Just do what you can with what you have in ways that make God smile.

Dear Father, may I use the gifts You have given me to honor You and draw others to You. Amen.

DAY 2
Abundant Life

Morning

Has not God chosen those who are poor in the eyes of the world to be rich in faith and to inherit the kingdom he promised those who love him?
JAMES 2:5 NIV

May the God of hope fill you with all joy and peace as you trust in him, so that you may overflow with hope by the power of the Holy Spirit.
ROMANS 15:13 NIV

Being rich in faith is the secret to leading an abundant life, because faith allows us to see life from God's perspective. We begin to appreciate how much we have, instead of focusing on what we think we lack. We understand that what's of eternal worth is more valuable than our net worth.

Dear God, I want the abundant kind of life that comes from You alone. Please fill me up with faith and joy and peace. Amen.

Evening

"But seek first his kingdom and his righteousness, and all these things will be given to you as well."
MATTHEW 6:33 NIV

"I have come that they may have life, and that they may have it more abundantly."
JOHN 10:10 NKJV

In Jesus' day, the people of Israel believed the Savior would restore Israel to its former power and prosperity. Jesus exceeded their expectations. Jesus offered them an abundance of riches that couldn't be stolen or lose value—true treasures like joy, peace, forgiveness, and eternal life. Jesus offers these same treasures to you. All you need to do is put your faith in Him.

Dear Lord, in You are the treasures I long for, the only riches that will satisfy my soul. Thank You for abundant life. Amen.

DAY 3
Complete Acceptance

Morning

The Spirit makes us sure God will accept us because of our faith in Christ.
GALATIANS 5:5 CEV

Then Peter began to speak: "I now realize how true it is that God does not show favoritism but accepts from every nation the one who fears him and does what is right."
ACTS 10:34–35 NIV

God accepts you completely. You don't need to clean up your language, change your lifestyle, or step inside of a church. Once you put your faith in Jesus, things between you and God are made right. Period.

Dear Father, because of Jesus I can come to You in full acceptance, and I am forever grateful. Thank You! Amen.

Evening

"All those the Father gives me will come to me, and whoever comes to me I will never drive away."
JOHN 6:37 NIV

Therefore welcome one another as Christ has welcomed you, for the glory of God.
ROMANS 15:7 ESV

Acceptance is only the first step. As God's Spirit continues working in your heart, He gives you the desire and strength you need to mature into who you were created to be—an amazing woman whose character reflects God's.

Father, now that I am accepted by You, please keep working in me that I might know and love and serve You better. Amen.

DAY 4

Goals

Morning

We remember before our God and Father your work produced by faith, your labor prompted by love, and your endurance inspired by hope in our Lord Jesus Christ.
1 THESSALONIANS 1:3 NIV

If you keep yourself pure, you will be a special utensil for honorable use. Your life will be clean, and you will be ready for the Master to use you for every good work.
2 TIMOTHY 2:21 NLT

Whatever you believe God wants you to do, big or small, don't hold back. Today, take at least one step toward your goal. With God's help, you'll accomplish everything He's set out for you to do.

Dear God, it is only because of You that I can accomplish anything. May my work be pleasing to You and give You all the glory. Amen.

Evening

"Blessed is she who has believed that the Lord would fulfill his promises to her!"
LUKE 1:45 NIV

It is God who works in you to will and to act in order to fulfill his good purpose.
PHILIPPIANS 2:13 NIV

God sees the time, energy, and heart you put into your work. Better yet, He adds His own power to your efforts. This means that with God, you can accomplish things you could never do solely on your own. That's something truly worth celebrating—with God!

Dear God, please give me wisdom to know Your will and the good goals You have for me, and help me to accomplish them with Your power. Amen.

DAY 5

Hope

Morning

We live by faith,
not by sight.
2 CORINTHIANS 5:7 NIV

I pray that God, who gives hope, will bless you with complete happiness and peace because of your faith. And may the power of the Holy Spirit fill you with hope.
ROMANS 15:13 CEV

Faith changes how we see the world. From all appearances, your circumstances may seem daunting. But when you place your faith in God instead of what you see, your heart can't help but overflow with hope.

Dear Father, when I am overwhelmed by my circumstances, please strengthen my faith in You and fill me with hope. Amen.

Evening

But I will hope continually and will praise you yet more and more.
PSALM 71:14 ESV

Commit everything you do to the LORD. Trust him, and he will help you. . . . Be still in the presence of the LORD, and wait patiently for him to act.
PSALM 37:5, 7 NLT

God's power is at work behind the scenes. He's working in both you and your circumstances. He promises to bring something good out of every situation, no matter how things may look on the outside.

Father God, I do trust You; help me to be patient as I wait for You to act in Your perfect timing. Amen.

DAY 6

Spiritual Arsenal

Morning

Put on all the armor that God gives, so you can defend yourself against the devil's tricks.
EPHESIANS 6:11 CEV

Be ready! Let the truth be like a belt around your waist, and let God's justice protect you like armor. Your desire to tell the good news about peace should be like shoes on your feet. Let your faith be like a shield, and you will be able to stop all the flaming arrows of the evil one. Let God's saving power be like a helmet, and for a sword use God's message that comes from the Spirit.
EPHESIANS 6:14–17 CEV

The armor God offers is neither make-believe nor outdated. It's a spiritual arsenal of offensive and defensive gear. It includes weapons such as truth, righteousness, peace, and faith.

Dear God, please equip me with Your powerful armor. Amen.

Evening

Let your faith be like a shield.
EPHESIANS 6:16 CEV

But let us who live in the light be clearheaded, protected by the armor of faith and love, and wearing as our helmet the confidence of our salvation.
1 THESSALONIANS 5:8 NLT

Every day a battle is going on for your mind and heart. But you don't need to be afraid; God has given you everything you need to be victorious.

Almighty God, nothing can come against me that You cannot conquer. Please build my confidence in the armor You have given me and in Your mighty strength. Amen.

DAY 7
Everyday Faith

Morning

Without faith no one can please God. We must believe that God is real and rewards everyone who searches for him.
HEBREWS 11:6 CEV

For by grace you have been saved through faith. And this is not your own doing; it is the gift of God, not a result of works, so that no one may boast.
EPHESIANS 2:8–9 ESV

Some women keep their faith tucked away like a family heirloom, displaying it only on holidays like Easter and Christmas. But if you truly believe what God says is true, faith will be part of your everyday life.

Dear Father, I never want to keep my faith tucked away. Help me to live it out daily. Amen.

Evening

Faith shows the reality of what we hope for; it is the evidence of things we cannot see.
HEBREWS 11:1 NLT

We are shown to be right with God by what we do, not by faith alone. Rahab the prostitute is another example. She was shown to be right with God by her actions when she hid those messengers and sent them safely away by a different road. Just as the body is dead without breath, so also faith is dead without good works.
JAMES 2:24–26 NLT

Faith is more than words of comfort. It's a shield that can protect you from an assault of doubt or the temptation to do something you know goes against God's plan for you. Take faith with you wherever you go.

Dear Father, thank You for being worthy of my faith, the only one who is. I want my faith to be evident in all I do. Amen.

DAY 8

God's Promises

Morning

And because of his glory and excellence, he has given us great and precious promises. These are the promises that enable you to share his divine nature and escape the world's corruption caused by human desires.

2 PETER 1:4 NLT

Christ has become a servant of the Jews on behalf of God's truth, so that the promises made to the patriarchs might be confirmed.

ROMANS 15:8 NIV

Because of God's promises and His faithfulness in keeping them in the past, we have the assurance that He'll come through for us in the future.

Dear God, in the times I start to worry and doubt, please remind me of Your faithfulness to Your promises and give me peace. Amen.

Evening

Christ says "Yes" to all God's promises. This is why we have Christ to say "Amen" for us to the glory of God.

2 CORINTHIANS 1:20 CEV

I have been sent to proclaim faith to those God has chosen and to teach them to know the truth that shows them how to live godly lives. This truth gives them confidence that they have eternal life, which God—who does not lie—promised them before the world began.

TITUS 1:1–2 NLT

God has promised we're loved, forgiven, cared for, and destined for heaven. Rest in the fact that what God promises, He delivers.

Dear God, You have proven over and over that I can trust Your promises. Thank You! Amen.

DAY 9

Jesus' Compassion

Morning

When he went ashore he saw a great crowd, and he had compassion on them, because they were like sheep without a shepherd. And he began to teach them many things.

MARK 6:34 ESV

When he went ashore he saw a great crowd, and he had compassion on them and healed their sick.

MATTHEW 14:14 ESV

Even those who don't believe Jesus is God can agree that He was an extraordinary person. The way Jesus selflessly loved others, reaching out to people society cast aside—including women—demonstrates an attitude of compassion, humility, and service.

Dear Jesus, Your compassion and love are inspiring. I want to be more like You. Amen.

Evening

The LORD answered, "Could a mother forget a child who nurses at her breast? Could she fail to love an infant who came from her own body? Even if a mother could forget, I will never forget you."

ISAIAH 49:15 CEV

But you, O Lord, are a God of compassion and mercy, slow to get angry and filled with unfailing love and faithfulness.

PSALM 86:15 NLT

We're drawn to those who sincerely care for us. That's one reason we're drawn toward Jesus. Believing in a God who believes in us doesn't feel risky. It feels like accepting a free invitation to be loved unconditionally.

Dear Father, Your unconditional, merciful love carries me through the highest highs and lowest lows of life. I am so grateful to be Your child. Amen.

DAY 10

Faith That Does Not Fail

Morning

Faith comes from hearing, that is, hearing the Good News about Christ.

ROMANS 10:17 NLT

Therefore, since we are surrounded by such a great cloud of witnesses, let us throw off everything that hinders and the sin that so easily entangles. And let us run with perseverance the race marked out for us, fixing our eyes on Jesus, the pioneer and perfecter of faith.

HEBREWS 12:1–2 NIV

Faith, in and of itself, is nothing more than trust. If you place your trust in something that isn't trustworthy, your faith is futile. You can have faith that money grows on trees, but ultimately that faith isn't going to help you pay your bills.

Dear Lord, You alone are worthy of my faith and trust, and I praise You! Amen.

Evening

For since the creation of the world God's invisible qualities—his eternal power and divine nature—have been clearly seen, being understood from what has been made, so that people are without excuse.

ROMANS 1:20 NIV

The woman said, "I know that Messiah" (called Christ) "is coming. When he comes, he will explain everything to us." Then Jesus declared, "I, the one speaking to you—I am he."

JOHN 4:25–26 NIV

Putting your faith in Jesus is smart. Historical and biblical eyewitness accounts back up Jesus' claims. Consequently, trusting in Jesus is both logical and powerful. It's a faith that won't fail.

Dear Lord, I want my life to be a testimony that believing in You and living for You are both logical and powerful. Amen.

DAY 11

Heart Changes

Morning

Jesus went to Galilee preaching the Message of God: "Time's up! God's kingdom is here. Change your life and believe the Message."

MARK 1:14–15 MSG

Do not be conformed to this world, but be transformed by the renewal of your mind, that by testing you may discern what is the will of God, what is good and acceptable and perfect.

ROMANS 12:2 ESV

Your beliefs will influence the choices you make. If you believe in gravity, you won't jump from a seventh-story balcony to save time getting to your hair appointment. If you believe what Jesus says, you'll change the way you live.

Dear Lord, in all that I do, help me to make choices that please You. Amen.

Evening

My son, do not forget my teaching, but keep my commands in your heart, for they will prolong your life many years and bring you peace and prosperity.

PROVERBS 3:1–2 NIV

Let love and faithfulness never leave you; bind them around your neck, write them on the tablet of your heart. Then you will win favor and a good name in the sight of God and man.

PROVERBS 3:3–4 NIV

Jesus often talks about the importance of traits such as honesty, purity, and generosity. Though God's Spirit helps change your heart, it's the daily choices you make that help bring traits like these to maturity.

Father God, please develop in me the traits that mature my faith and draw me closer and closer to You. Amen.

DAY 12

Life Letter

Morning

These are written so that you will put your faith in Jesus as the Messiah and the Son of God. If you have faith in him, you will have true life.
JOHN 20:31 CEV

Your word is a lamp for my feet, a light on my path.
PSALM 119:105 NIV

The Bible is like a letter from your best friend. In it, God shares how much He loves you, what He's been up to since the creation of the world, and what He plans to do in the future.

Dear Father, thank You so much for Your Word that teaches, encourages, and guides me through life. Amen.

Evening

All Scripture is God-breathed and is useful for teaching, rebuking, correcting and training in righteousness.
2 TIMOTHY 3:16 NIV

"In the same way, let your light shine before others, so that they may see your good works and give glory to your Father who is in heaven."
MATTHEW 5:16 ESV

You're an important part of God's plans. The life you live through faith is the letter you write in return. But others will also sneak a peek at your "life letter"; in fact, the life you live may be the only Bible some people ever read.

Dear God, I want my life letter to encourage others to know and love and follow You. Please help me to keep a good testimony. Amen.

DAY 13

Into Practice

Morning

Truth, righteousness, peace, faith, and salvation are more than words. Learn how to apply them. You'll need them throughout your life. God's Word is an indispensable weapon.

EPHESIANS 6:14–17 MSG

Do not merely listen to the word, and so deceive yourselves. Do what it says.

JAMES 1:22 NIV

What you do with God's words is ultimately what you decide to do with God. If you read the Bible for inspiration, without application, your faith will never be more than a heartwarming pastime.

God, I don't just want to hear Your Word. I want to be eternally changed by it, and I want to live it out. Please help me. Amen.

Evening

If you hear the message and don't obey it, you are like people who stare at themselves in a mirror and forget what they look like as soon as they leave. But you must never stop looking at the perfect law that sets you free. God will bless you in everything you do, if you listen and obey, and don't just hear and forget.

JAMES 1:23–25 CEV

While it's true the Bible can be a source of comfort, it's also a source of power and an instrument of change. Invite God's Spirit to sear the Bible's words into your heart. Then step out in faith and put what you've learned into practice.

Holy Spirit, I invite You to sear the Word of God into my heart, that I might love it and live it. Amen.

DAY 14

Believing Without Seeing

Morning

Jesus said, "So, you believe because you've seen with your own eyes. Even better blessings are in store for those who believe without seeing."

JOHN 20:29 MSG

Immediately the father of the child cried out and said, "I believe; help my unbelief!"

MARK 9:24 ESV

If you're searching for a pair of shoes, you don't rely on a salesperson's description. You want to see them. Try them on. Walk around in them awhile. The same is true when it comes to trying on faith for size.

Dear God, sometimes I struggle to believe in You, but my own sinful nature is what makes me falter. Please renew and strengthen my faith in You through Your Spirit and Your Word. Amen.

Evening

Jesus said, "Did I not tell you that if you believe, you will see the glory of God?"

JOHN 11:40 NIV

For we walk by faith, not by sight.

2 CORINTHIANS 5:7 ESV

We long to see the one we've chosen to place our faith in. But Jesus says believing without seeing holds its own special reward. Ask Jesus to help you better understand those blessings as you walk in faith today.

Dear Father, please remind me of the special blessings that come from walking by faith and not by sight. You are so good and generous, God! Amen.

DAY 15

All Kinds of Blessings

Morning

"Turn to face God so he can wipe away your sins, pour out showers of blessing to refresh you, and send you the Messiah he prepared for you, namely, Jesus."

ACTS 3:19–20 MSG

The blessing of the LORD *makes a person rich, and he adds no sorrow with it.*

PROVERBS 10:22 NLT

Blessings are gifts straight from God's hand. Some of them are tangible, like the gift of a chance acquaintance leading to a job offer that winds up helping to pay the bills. Others are less concrete.

Heavenly Father, help me to count daily all the blessings You have given me. I am so grateful, and I want to be more aware of all Your blessings and grow in gratitude. Amen.

Evening

Whatever is good and perfect is a gift coming down to us from God our Father, who created all the lights in the heavens.

JAMES 1:17 NLT

Because of all that the Son is, we have been given one blessing after another.

JOHN 1:16 CEV

Blessings may come wrapped in things like faith, joy, clarity, and contentment that appear seemingly out of nowhere amid difficult circumstances. The more frequently you thank God for His blessings, the more aware you'll be of how many more there are to thank Him for.

Heavenly Father, I praise and thank You for all You do in my life and all You have given me. May I never forget that all good things come from You. Amen.

DAY 16

Giving Up Burdens

Morning

Give your burdens to the Lord, and he will take care of you. He will not permit the godly to slip and fall.

PSALM 55:22 NLT

Give all your worries and cares to God, for he cares about you.

1 PETER 5:7 NLT

It's important for us women to do some heavy lifting as we age. Weight-bearing exercise helps keep our bones strong and our muscles toned. But bearing mental and emotional weight is another story. These don't build us up; they break us down.

Father God, please forgive me for all the ways I worry. Your Word tells me to give my anxiety to You in exchange for Your peace. Thank You! Amen.

Evening

"Come to me, all who labor and are heavy laden, and I will give you rest. Take my yoke upon you, and learn from me, for I am gentle and lowly in heart, and you will find rest for your souls."

MATTHEW 11:28–29 ESV

Don't worry about anything; instead, pray about everything. Tell God what you need, and thank him for all he has done. Then you will experience God's peace, which exceeds anything we can understand.

PHILIPPIANS 4:6–7 NLT

Allow faith to become your personal trainer when it comes to what's weighing heavily on your mind and heart. God knows how much weight you can bear. Invite Him to carry what you cannot.

Right now I choose to place my worries, fears, and anxious thoughts into Your loving, all-powerful care, Lord. Amen.

DAY 17

Turning Worries into Prayers

Morning

Don't fret or worry.
Instead of worrying, pray.
Let petitions and praises shape
your worries into prayers,
letting God know your concerns.
PHILIPPIANS 4:6 MSG

And my God will meet all your
needs according to the riches
of his glory in Christ Jesus.
PHILIPPIANS 4:19 NIV

If you can't be assured that all of your loved ones' physical and emotional needs are being met, fretting about them makes you feel involved—like you're loving them, even if you're powerless to help. But you know Someone who does have the power to help.

Dear God, You are the only one
who can provide all our needs.
Your power and provision are
sufficient in any and every
circumstance. I trust You! Amen.

Evening

Don't worry and ask yourselves,
"Will we have anything to eat?
Will we have anything to drink?
Will we have any clothes to
wear?" Only people who don't
know God are always worrying
about such things. Your Father
in heaven knows you need all of
these. But more than anything
else, put God's work first and do
what he wants. Then the other
things will be yours as well.
Don't worry about tomorrow. It
will take care of itself. You have
enough to worry about today.
MATTHEW 6:31–34 CEV

Anytime you feel the weight of worry, whether it's over someone else's problems or your own, let faith relieve you of the burden. Turn your worries into prayers.

Oh Father, it's so hard not to
worry sometimes. Help me to
choose, moment by moment, to let
You lift my anxious burdens as I
come to You in prayer. Amen.

DAY 18

Jesus Loves Little Ones

Morning

By faith Moses' parents hid him for three months after he was born, because they saw he was no ordinary child, and they were not afraid of the king's edict.

HEBREWS 11:23 NIV

You made all the delicate, inner parts of my body and knit me together in my mother's womb. Thank you for making me so wonderfully complex! Your workmanship is marvelous— how well I know it.

PSALM 139:13–14 NLT

No mother's child is "ordinary." Love enables parents to see their children's unique gifts and potential—and instills in them the desire to protect their children at any cost. Your heavenly Father feels the same way about you and your children.

Heavenly Father, I am so blessed to be Your child, and I'm so thankful for Your love and protection of me and the extraordinary children You've given me. Amen.

Evening

But Jesus said, "Let the little children come to me and do not hinder them, for to such belongs the kingdom of heaven."

MATTHEW 19:14 ESV

Don't be cruel to any of these little ones! I promise you their angels are always with my Father in heaven.

MATTHEW 18:10 CEV

When fear for your children's health or happiness threatens your peace of mind, let faith put your mind at ease. God cares for your children in ways that reach far beyond your own abilities.

Father, remind me daily that You love my children even more than I do. Please give me peace as I trust You to care for them. Amen.

DAY 19

God-Confidence

Morning

*Forget about self-confidence;
it's useless. Cultivate
God-confidence.*
1 CORINTHIANS 10:12 MSG

*We don't have the right to claim
that we have done anything
on our own. God gives us
what it takes to do all we do.*
2 CORINTHIANS 3:5 CEV

You have countless reasons to be confident in who you are, what you do, and where you're headed—but those reasons don't rest on your talents, intelligence, accomplishments, net worth, or good looks. They rest solely on God and His faithfulness.

*Almighty God, please humble me
and remind me that everything
I am and everything I can do
comes from You. Amen.*

Evening

*For the LORD will be your
confidence and will keep your
foot from being caught.*
PROVERBS 3:26 ESV

*The Fear-of-GOD builds up
confidence, and makes a world
safe for your children.*
PROVERBS 14:26 MSG

Living a life of faith means trading self-confidence for God-confidence. It means holding your head high because you know you're loved and God's Spirit is working through you.

*Dear God, I want all my confidence
to be in You. You are so good and
loving and gracious to me. Amen.*

DAY 20

Nothing to Fear

Morning

The blood of Jesus gives us courage to enter the most holy place by a new way that leads to life! And this way takes us through the curtain that is Christ himself.

HEBREWS 10:19–20 CEV

Be strong, and let your heart take courage, all you who wait for the LORD!

PSALM 31:24 ESV

Imagine standing before a holy, almighty, and perfect God and being judged for how you've lived your life. Every poor choice, selfish action, and moment of rebellion would be exposed. Sounds downright terrifying, doesn't it? But through our faith in Jesus, we have nothing to fear.

Dear Lord, thank You that Jesus has covered my sin with His precious blood and I have nothing to fear when I stand before You. Amen.

Evening

Be strong in the Lord and in the strength of his might.

EPHESIANS 6:10 ESV

"Be strong and brave. Don't be afraid. . .and don't be frightened, because the LORD your God will go with you."

DEUTERONOMY 31:6 NCV

We stand faultless and forgiven. Through Christ, we can take an honest look at ourselves as we really are, faults and all, without shame. Being wholly loved gives us the courage to fully live.

Dear Lord, I want to live in awe of You and Your power and holiness. Thank You that I can come to You through grace. Amen.

DAY 21

Whatever Needs Done

Morning

When I asked for your help, you answered my prayer and gave me courage.
PSALM 138:3 CEV

"Be strong and courageous, and do the work. Do not be afraid or discouraged, for the LORD God, my God, is with you. He will not fail you or forsake you until all the work for the service of the temple of the LORD is finished."
1 CHRONICLES 28:20 NIV

What do you need courage for today? To apologize? To forgive? To break an old habit? To discipline a child? To love in the face of rejection? Courage isn't just for times when you're facing grievous danger. Anytime you face a difficult, unpredictable situation, it takes courage to move forward.

Father God, please remind me every day that no matter what causes fear and anxiety within me, You can give me the courage and ability to face it and conquer it. Amen.

Evening

Trust in the LORD with all your heart, and do not lean on your own understanding. In all your ways acknowledge him, and he will make straight your paths.
PROVERBS 3:5–6 ESV

I can do all things through him who strengthens me.
PHILIPPIANS 4:13 ESV

When you're tempted to turn away from your problems, let faith help you turn toward God. With Him, you'll find the courage you need to do whatever needs to be done.

Dear Father, it's hard to face my problems head-on. I'd rather just run from them. Please give me strength and courage, and help me to act on them according to Your will. Amen.

DAY 22

Right Here, Right Now

Morning

Better is one day in
your courts than a
thousand elsewhere.
PSALM 84:10 NIV

Teach us to number our
days, that we may gain
a heart of wisdom.
PSALM 90:12 NIV

It's fun daydreaming about places you'd like to visit, goals you'd like to accomplish, or the woman you hope to become—someday. But God has given you just one life on this earth. Chances are, you'll have more dreams than you'll have days.

Heavenly Father, only You know the time I have here on earth, so please show me Your will and how best I can serve You. Amen.

Evening

You make known to me the
path of life; in your presence
there is fullness of joy.
PSALM 16:11 ESV

Show me your ways, LORD,
teach me your paths. Guide me
in your truth and teach me, for
you are God my Savior, and my
hope is in you all day long.
PSALM 25:4–5 NIV

Instead of living for "someday," God challenges you to put your heart into today. Whether you're sunning on vacation or scrubbing the kitchen floor, the God of the universe is right here with you. That's something worth celebrating!

Dear God of the universe, how amazing it is to think You are right here with me every moment of every day. I want to live a life pleasing to You. Amen.

DAY 23

Into His Arms

Morning

"Love the LORD your God, walk in all his ways, obey his commands, hold firmly to him, and serve him with all your heart and all your soul."

JOSHUA 22:5 NLT

Keep steady my steps according to your promise, and let no iniquity get dominion over me.

PSALM 119:133 ESV

Every walk you take is a series of steps that moves you forward. Each day you live is like a single step, moving you closer to—or farther away from—God. That's why it's good to get your bearings each morning.

Please, dear Father, guide my steps to keep me walking closely with You. Amen.

Evening

Your word is a lamp that gives light wherever I walk.

PSALM 119:105 CEV

Walk in obedience to all that the LORD your God has commanded you, so that you may live and prosper and prolong your days in the land that you will possess.

DEUTERONOMY 5:33 NIV

Through reading the Bible and spending time with God in prayer, you'll know which direction to take as you continue your walk of faith. Day by day, God will guide you straight into His arms.

Lord, help me better prioritize my schedule so I'm spending quality time with You. Amen.

DAY 24

Behind the Scenes

Morning

We make our own decisions, but the LORD alone determines what happens.
PROVERBS 16:33 CEV

I will instruct you and teach you in the way you should go; I will counsel you with my loving eye on you.
PSALM 32:8 NIV

From the man you choose to marry to the way you style your hair, decisions are part of your daily life. But that doesn't mean you're totally in control. Much of life is out of your hands and solely in God's. That's where faith provides a place of peace.

Heavenly Father, thank You that I never have to make a decision on my own. You are with me, guiding me on the right path. Amen.

Evening

The LORD makes firm the steps of the one who delights in him; though he may stumble, he will not fall, for the LORD upholds him with his hand.
PSALM 37:23–24 NIV

The LORD will guide you continually.
ISAIAH 58:11 NLT

Rest in the knowledge that God is working behind the scenes to bring about good in your life. The best decision you'll ever make is to trust in His love for you.

Father, I trust You and Your love for me. Help me to come to You for wisdom in all of my choices. Amen.

DAY 25

Free Will

Morning

I pray that your love will keep on growing and you will fully know and understand how to make the right choices.

PHILIPPIANS 1:9–10 CEV

How much better to get wisdom than gold! To get understanding is to be chosen rather than silver.

PROVERBS 16:16 ESV

Free will is a wonderful gift. It allows you to have a say in the storyline of your life. But consequences are tied to every decision you make, big or small. That's why making wise decisions is so important.

Dear Lord, help me to think through each decision I make. I so desperately need Your wisdom. Amen.

Evening

"And if you faithfully obey the voice of the LORD your God, being careful to do all his commandments that I command you today, the LORD your God will set you high above all the nations of the earth."

DEUTERONOMY 28:1 ESV

So whether we are at home or away, we make it our aim to please him. For we must all appear before the judgment seat of Christ, so that each one may receive what is due for what he has done in the body, whether good or evil.

2 CORINTHIANS 5:9–10 ESV

The more you allow your faith to influence the decisions you make, the closer you'll be to living the life God desires for you. Invite God into your decision process. Let your "yes" or "no" be preceded by "amen."

Father, You are welcome into my life and into all of my choices. I know You always want what is best for me. Amen.

DAY 26

Root of Desire

Morning

"Wherever your treasure is, there the desires of your heart will also be."
MATTHEW 6:21 NLT

"But seek first the kingdom of God and his righteousness, and all these things will be added to you."
MATTHEW 6:33 ESV

What does your heart long for? If you look at the root of every deep desire, you'll find a need only God can meet. Love, security, comfort, significance, joy. . .trying to satisfy these desires apart from God will yield only limited success.

Dear Lord, please fill my life. Help me never to look elsewhere for the satisfaction and fulfillment that only You can offer. Amen.

Evening

Delight yourself in the LORD, and he will give you the desires of your heart.
PSALM 37:4 ESV

"I delight to do your will, O my God; your law is within my heart."
PSALM 40:8 ESV

God is the only one whose love for you will never waver. You are His treasure, and He wants to spend eternity with you. As your faith grows, so will your desire to treasure Him in return.

Father God, thank You for Your endless, unwavering love for me. I don't know where I'd be without it. I love You! Amen.

DAY 27

Faith on the Move

Morning

For God is not unjust so as to overlook your work and the love that you have shown for his name in serving the saints, as you still do.

HEBREWS 6:10 ESV

Then you will not become spiritually dull and indifferent. Instead, you will follow the example of those who are going to inherit God's promises because of their faith and endurance.

HEBREWS 6:12 NLT

Your spiritual faith is a commitment to love God. And since the word *love* is a verb, an action word, your devotion to God is faith on the move. Where will faith move you today?

Dear God, I want to show others my devotion to You. Help me to genuinely and actively love those You have placed around me. Amen.

Evening

All the believers devoted themselves to the apostles' teaching, and to fellowship, and to sharing in meals. . .and to prayer.

ACTS 2:42 NLT

But his delight is in the law of the LORD, and on his law he meditates day and night.

PSALM 1:2 ESV

The time we set aside to read the Bible and pray each day is often called "daily devotions." Think about what it means to be devoted to your husband, your kids, or your job. Devotion is your commitment to something or someone you love. The same is true with spiritual devotion.

Father, please remind me daily that true devotion means living my life fully committed to You and sharing Your love. Amen.

DAY 28
Doubts

Morning

When you ask for something, you must have faith and not doubt. Anyone who doubts is like an ocean wave tossed around in a storm.
JAMES 1:6 CEV

"Truly I tell you, if anyone says to this mountain, 'Go, throw yourself into the sea,' and does not doubt in their heart but believes that what they say will happen, it will be done for them."
MARK 11:23 NIV

When you need to ask for help, you ask only those who you believe can actually do what needs done. God can do anything that's in line with His will.

Almighty God, please increase my faith in You. I believe You can do absolutely anything. Amen.

Evening

Immediately the boy's father exclaimed, "I do believe; help me overcome my unbelief!"
MARK 9:24 NIV

Trust in the LORD with all your heart; do not depend on your own understanding.
PROVERBS 3:5 NLT

If you pray without expecting God to answer, doubt is derailing your faith. Ask God to help you understand the origins of your doubts. He can help you erase each one.

Father, please erase my doubts when my faith is faltering. Please fix my eyes on You. Amen.

DAY 29

Growing Friendship and Faith

Morning

*When we get together,
I want to encourage you in
your faith, but I also want to
be encouraged by yours.*
ROMANS 1:12 NLT

*Let no corrupting talk come out
of your mouths, but only such
as is good for building up,
as fits the occasion, that it may
give grace to those who hear.*
EPHESIANS 4:29 ESV

When women get together, usually a whole lot of talking goes on. Conversing, counseling, giggling, and catching up on the latest news are all wonderful ways to build a friendship. But if you want to build your faith, take time to encourage one another.

God, I want the conversations I have to honor You and encourage others. Help me to control my tongue and speak in love so that I can grow closer to others and to You. Amen.

Evening

*Therefore encourage one
another and build one another
up, just as you are doing.*
1 THESSALONIANS 5:11 ESV

*We should keep on encouraging
each other to be thoughtful
and to do helpful things. Some
people have given up the habit
of meeting for worship, but we
must not do that. We should
keep on encouraging each
other, especially since you
know that the day of the Lord's
coming is getting closer.*
HEBREWS 10:24–25 CEV

Tell your friends how you've seen God at work in their lives. Share what God has been teaching you. Ask questions. Pray. Praise. Your friendship will grow right along with your faith.

Dear God, help me to be proactive in encouraging my friends and family. Amen.

DAY 30

Path to Heaven

Morning

God loved the people of this world so much that he gave his only Son, so that everyone who has faith in him will have eternal life and never really die.

JOHN 3:16 CEV

And this is eternal life, that they know you, the only true God, and Jesus Christ whom you have sent.

JOHN 17:3 ESV

Eternal life doesn't begin after you die. It begins the day you put your faith in Jesus' love. Right now, you're in the childhood of eternity. You're learning and growing.

Everlasting God, I am amazed and delighted by the eternal life I have in You. Please keep me growing stronger in You. Amen.

Evening

If we are unfaithful, he remains faithful, for he cannot deny who he is.

2 TIMOTHY 2:13 NLT

No power in the sky above or in the earth below—indeed, nothing in all creation will ever be able to separate us from the love of God that is revealed in Christ Jesus our Lord.

ROMANS 8:39 NLT

If you fall, God helps you get back on your feet again. Once your faith sets you on the path toward heaven, nothing—absolutely nothing—can prevent you from reaching your destination.

Father, thank You that nothing can separate me from Your love or take away the heavenly home You have waiting for me. What hope I have because of You! Amen.

DAY 31

One Worth Following

Morning

Follow the example of the correct teaching I gave you, and let the faith and love of Christ Jesus be your model.

2 TIMOTHY 1:13 CEV

Be imitators of me, as I am of Christ.

1 CORINTHIANS 11:1 ESV

The Bible is a pretty thick book. It looks like there's a lot to learn. But Jesus said that if we love God and others, we've fulfilled everything written there. How do we do that? Look to Jesus' own life as recorded in the Gospels.

Dear Jesus, help me to learn all I can about You through Your Word and to live out what I learn. I want to be like You. Amen.

Evening

Make my joy complete by being like-minded, having the same love, being one in spirit and of one mind. Do nothing out of selfish ambition or vain conceit. Rather, in humility value others above yourselves, not looking to your own interests but each of you to the interests of the others. In your relationships with one another, have the same mindset as Christ Jesus.

PHILIPPIANS 2:2–5 NIV

In the Gospels, Jesus never treats people like an interruption or inconvenience. He listens, comforts, and cares. He spends time with His Father in prayer, regardless of His busy schedule. Jesus' example is one worth following.

Dear Jesus, You are the best example of how to treat others. Help me to have compassion and put others' needs before my own. Amen.

DAY 32

A Glimpse of God

Morning

In the morning, LORD,
you hear my voice;
in the morning I lay
my requests before you
and wait expectantly.
PSALM 5:3 NIV

The LORD is good to those
who wait for him, to the
soul who seeks him.
LAMENTATIONS 3:25 ESV

If you're expecting an important package, you're often on the lookout for the mail carrier. You peek out the window. Listen for footsteps. Check the mailbox. When you pray, are you on the lookout for God's answers?

Dear Father, I know You are good and all-powerful and You hear my prayers. I trust You to act according to Your perfect will. Amen.

Evening

I believe that I shall look
upon the goodness of the
LORD in the land of the living!
Wait for the LORD; be strong,
and let your heart take
courage; wait for the LORD!
PSALM 27:13–14 ESV

"For my thoughts are not your
thoughts, neither are your ways
my ways," declares the LORD.
ISAIAH 55:8 NIV

Not every answer will be delivered when, where, and how you expect. So keep your eyes open and your heart expectant. Don't miss out on the joy of catching a glimpse of God at work.

Dear Father, help me remember that Your ways are not mine. Help me to wait for answers to prayer with hope and confidence that Your plans are always best. Amen.

DAY 33

Perfectly Faithful

Morning

Your kingdom is an everlasting kingdom, and your dominion endures through all generations. The Lord is trustworthy in all he promises and faithful in all he does.

Psalm 145:13 NIV

Your steadfast love, O Lord, extends to the heavens, your faithfulness to the clouds.

Psalm 36:5 ESV

God's faithfulness to you never falters. It began before you were born and will last far beyond the day you die. Nothing you do or don't do can adversely affect His love for you. No one but God can demonstrate this kind of faithfulness.

Dear God, I praise You for Your faithfulness to me, even when I am not faithful to You. Thank You! Amen.

Evening

"Know therefore that the Lord your God is God, the faithful God who keeps covenant and steadfast love with those who love him and keep his commandments, to a thousand generations."

Deuteronomy 7:9 ESV

The steadfast love of the Lord never ceases; his mercies never come to an end; they are new every morning; great is your faithfulness.

Lamentations 3:22–23 ESV

Those who love you may promise they'll never let you down, but they're fallible. Just like you. Only God is perfect—and perfectly trustworthy. What He says, He does. Today, tomorrow, always.

Dear God, I know You and You alone will never let me down. Your love is like no other. Please draw me closer to You. Amen.

DAY 34

Spiritual Leadership

Morning

*A wise woman
strengthens her family.*
PROVERBS 14:1 NCV

*Always set a good example
for others. Be sincere and
serious when you teach.*
TITUS 2:7 CEV

Moms wear many hats. They're called to be chefs, teachers, maids, nurses, mediators, and activity directors—sometimes all in the same twenty-four-hour period. But God has entrusted you with an even more important role in your family. You're a spiritual leader.

*Dear Father, please help me to
be an example to my children
that leads them to You. Amen.*

Evening

*The most important one
of you should be like the least
important, and your leader
should be like a servant.*
LUKE 22:26 CEV

*How joyful are those who fear
the LORD—all who follow his
ways! You will enjoy the fruit
of your labor. How joyful and
prosperous you will be!*
PSALM 128:1–2 NLT

As you live out your faith, share the "whys" behind what you do. Point your children in directions that will lead them closer to God. A strong faith helps build a stronger family.

*Father God, please strengthen my
family's faith in You. Please grow
me and mature me in my walk
with You so that I can serve and
lead my children better. Amen.*

DAY 35

Inside and Out

Morning

God met me more than halfway, he freed me from my anxious fears. Look at him; give him your warmest smile. Never hide your feelings from him.

PSALM 34:4–5 MSG

O Lord, you have examined my heart and know everything about me. You know when I sit down or stand up. You know my thoughts even when I'm far away.

PSALM 139:1–2 NLT

God knows you inside and out. He knows how you feel, right here, right now. So why bother telling Him what's going on in your heart? Because that's how relationships grow.

Dear God, forgive me for the way I ignore You at times. Help me to realize what sweet peace there is when I cultivate and rest in my relationship with You. Amen.

Evening

So humble yourselves under the mighty power of God, and at the right time he will lift you up in honor. Give all your worries and cares to God, for he cares about you.

1 PETER 5:6–7 NLT

Rise during the night and cry out. Pour out your hearts like water to the Lord.

LAMENTATIONS 2:19 NLT

Sharing your personal struggles with a spouse or best friend is a sign of intimacy. It demonstrates your faith in his or her love for you. It also gives the other person an opportunity to offer comfort, help, and hope. God desires that same opportunity in your life.

Father, thank You so much that You care about and want to hear about all my worries and concerns and needs. There is no better friend than You! Amen.

DAY 36

Dollars

Morning

For God is working in you, giving you the desire and the power to do what pleases him.
PHILIPPIANS 2:13 NLT

Remember the LORD your God, for it is he who gives you the ability to produce wealth.
DEUTERONOMY 8:18 NIV

A sense of entitlement comes with a paycheck. You earned it, so you get to choose how to spend it, right? But have you ever stopped to consider how the way God created you impacts your ability to earn a living?

Father, every good thing I am able to do is because You have given me the ability to do it. Everything I have is Yours; please help me to use and share what I have for Your glory. Amen.

Evening

Every desirable and beneficial gift comes out of heaven. The gifts are rivers of light cascading down from the Father of Light.
JAMES 1:17 MSG

"No one can serve two masters. . . . You cannot serve both God and money."
MATTHEW 6:24 NIV

Take a moment right now to thank God for His part in your financial picture. Ask Him to give you wisdom, self-control, and a spirit of generosity as you choose how to use every dollar you receive.

Dear Father, please give me wisdom, self-control, and generosity in using and giving the money and blessings I've received that are not mine in the first place. Amen.

DAY 37

Forgiveness

Morning

If we confess our sins to God, he can always be trusted to forgive us and take our sins away.

1 JOHN 1:9 CEV

How far has the L*ORD taken our sins from us? Farther than the distance from east to west!*

PSALM 103:12 CEV

If you believe Jesus loves you so much that He would pay the penalty for your sins with His own life, then you also must believe that He wouldn't hold those sins against you any longer.

Gracious Lord, thank You, thank You, thank You! I can't possibly say thanks enough for saving me from my sins. Amen.

Evening

"If you forgive those who sin against you, your heavenly Father will forgive you."

MATTHEW 6:14 NLT

"The Lord our God is merciful and forgiving, even though we have rebelled against him."

DANIEL 9:9 NIV

If you're feeling guilty, talk to God. Your feelings are not always truth-tellers. God's forgiveness is what makes spending eternity with Him a true paradise.

Dear Lord, the enemy wants me to remember my sins and let guilt distance me from You. But You forgive and forget my sins. Please erase my guilty feelings and hold me close. Amen.

DAY 38

Immediately, Completely, Eternally

Morning

*Be even-tempered,
content with second place,
quick to forgive an offense.*
COLOSSIANS 3:12–13 MSG

*Be kind to one another,
tenderhearted, forgiving
one another, as God in
Christ forgave you.*
EPHESIANS 4:32 ESV

When you put your faith in God, the very first thing He does is forgive you. He doesn't overlook what you've done. He forgives it. Immediately. Completely. Eternally. Choosing to follow His example isn't always easy. But it's always right.

Dear God, it can be so hard to forgive, and You have set a high standard for how to do it right. Help me to want to forgive like You do. Amen.

Evening

*"For if you forgive others
their trespasses, your heavenly
Father will also forgive you, but
if you do not forgive others their
trespasses, neither will your
Father forgive your trespasses."*
MATTHEW 6:14–15 ESV

*As the Lord has forgiven you,
so you also must forgive.*
COLOSSIANS 3:13 ESV

When others offend you, don't let your forgiveness hinge on their apology or repentance. You can wisely set boundaries and still offer forgiveness. Ask God to help you forgive before another's fault can fester into a painful, distracting grudge.

Lord, please give me wisdom and grace to forgive quickly and completely. Please protect my heart from bitterness. Amen.

DAY 39

The Key to Freedom

Morning

*I will walk in freedom,
for I have devoted myself
to your commandments.*
PSALM 119:45 NLT

*You are free, but still you are
God's servants, and you must
not use your freedom as an
excuse for doing wrong.*
1 PETER 2:16 CEV

God's commandments help us build stronger relationships. We're freer to be ourselves and to love God and others well when we follow His rules.

Dear God, thank You for Your commandments. They are not burdensome but rather offer peaceful freedom because of Your protection and care. Amen.

Evening

*The Scriptures declare
that we are all prisoners
of sin, so we receive God's
promise of freedom only by
believing in Jesus Christ.*
GALATIANS 3:22 NLT

*The Lord and the Spirit are
one and the same, and the
Lord's Spirit sets us free.*
2 CORINTHIANS 3:17 CEV

When you place your faith in Jesus, you're handed the key to freedom. Honor Jesus' gift by living a life worthy of such sacrifice.

Dear Jesus, help me to be worthy of the great sacrifice You made to save me from my sin. You gave me freedom, and I want to honor You with it. Amen.

DAY 40

A Fresh New Start

Morning

The faithful love of the LORD never ends! His mercies never cease. Great is his faithfulness; his mercies begin afresh each morning.

LAMENTATIONS 3:22–23 NLT

Let us then with confidence draw near to the throne of grace, that we may receive mercy and find grace to help in time of need.

HEBREWS 4:16 ESV

Faith can break a cycle of regrettable yesterdays—if we let it. God offers forgiveness and a fresh start to all who ask. He never tires of replacing our brokenness with a new beginning.

Oh Father, I sure tire of my brokenness, but I'm so grateful You never do. Thank You that I can come to You again and again for fresh new mercy. Amen.

Evening

We look inside, and what we see is that anyone united with the Messiah gets a fresh start, is created new. The old life is gone; a new life emerges!

2 CORINTHIANS 5:17 MSG

Let the Spirit change your way of thinking and make you into a new person. You were created to be like God, and so you must please him and be truly holy.

EPHESIANS 4:23–24 CEV

Faith is the ultimate makeover. But it doesn't hide who you are with a lift or tuck here and a fresh coat of foundation there. This makeover isn't external. It's eternal. Let go of yesterday and grab hold of God's promise for today!

Dear God, please make me over every day. Make me more like You! Amen.

DAY 41

Make Time for Authentic Friendship

Morning

Just as lotions and fragrance give sensual delight, a sweet friendship refreshes the soul.
PROVERBS 27:9 MSG

A friend loves at all times.
PROVERBS 17:17 ESV

Jesus' disciples were His closest friends. No matter how busy you get, make time for the friends God brings into your life. They may be God's answers to prayers you're praying today.

Dear Lord, thank You for the friends in my life who encourage me in my walk with You. They are such treasures. Help me to make time with them a priority. Amen.

Evening

Just as iron sharpens iron, friends sharpen the minds of each other.
PROVERBS 27:17 CEV

Giving an honest answer is a sign of true friendship.
PROVERBS 24:26 CEV

A true friend doesn't play games or hide behind masks. She's honest about who she is and open about her strengths, weaknesses, hopes, and fears. Her honesty invites others to be as authentic with her as she is with them.

Dear Father, help me to be authentic in my friendships. I want to be open, honest, and encouraging in my relationships with others. Amen.

DAY 42

Fruitfulness

Morning

"I chose you. I appointed you to go and produce lasting fruit, so that the Father will give you whatever you ask for, using my name."

JOHN 15:16 NLT

A good tree produces good fruit, and a bad tree produces bad fruit. You can tell what a tree is like by the fruit it produces.

MATTHEW 12:33 CEV

Because of your faith in God, you can trust He's growing wholesome, ever-lasting fruit in you. You can nurture this fruit, helping it grow to maturity, by watering it frequently with God's words. Read the Bible. Then watch what God produces in your life.

Dear Lord, thank You for Your Word that nourishes and equips me. Amen.

Evening

The Holy Spirit produces this kind of fruit in our lives: love, joy, peace, patience, kindness, goodness, faithfulness, gentleness, and self-control. There is no law against these things!

GALATIANS 5:22–23 NLT

Jesus said to his disciples: I am the true vine, and my Father is the gardener. He cuts away every branch of mine that doesn't produce fruit. But he trims clean every branch that does produce fruit, so that it will produce even more fruit.

JOHN 15:1–2 CEV

God's Spirit is the only one who can bring spiritual fruit to maturity in you. But you can provide the proper conditions to encourage growth. Have faith that God is at work.

Dear Father, help me to keep my heart and life ready and willing for You to produce good fruit in me. Amen.

DAY 43

Faith for the Future

Morning

Because Jesus was raised from the dead, we've been given a brand-new life and have everything to live for, including a future in heaven—and the future starts now!

1 PETER 1:3–4 MSG

But they who wait for the LORD shall renew their strength; they shall mount up with wings like eagles; they shall run and not be weary; they shall walk and not faint.

ISAIAH 40:31 ESV

Faith changes the course of your future as surely as it changes the landscape of your heart. God is preparing a home for you that will never be torn down, a place where your questions will be answered and your longings fulfilled.

Dear Lord, I am so looking forward to the heavenly home You are preparing for Your children. Help me to wait patiently and do Your will until You call me there. Amen.

Evening

"For I know the plans I have for you," declares the LORD, "plans to prosper you and not to harm you, plans to give you hope and a future."

JEREMIAH 29:11 NIV

I press on toward the goal for the prize of the upward call of God in Christ Jesus.

PHILIPPIANS 3:14 ESV

God holds our future in His hands. He has a plan and a purpose for what lies ahead. We may not know the details of all our tomorrows, but faith assures us that it's well worth waiting for.

Father, Your plans for me are perfect. Please help me to trust You and press on toward the prize You have in store for me. Amen.

DAY 44

Give Big

Morning

I am praying that you will put into action the generosity that comes from your faith as you understand and experience all the good things we have in Christ.

PHILEMON 6 NLT

Remember that our Lord Jesus said, "More blessings come from giving than from receiving."

ACTS 20:35 CEV

God's generosity is incomparable. It can also be motivational. When it comes to your time, your finances, your home—or intangibles like forgiveness, grace, or love—follow God's example. Be bighearted and open-handed.

Father, I can never outgive You, but I can strive to be more like You in Your generosity. Help me to be bighearted and open-handed. Amen.

Evening

Have you ever come on anything quite like this extravagant generosity of God, this deep, deep wisdom? It's way over our heads. We'll never figure it out.

ROMANS 11:33 MSG

Give freely and become more wealthy; be stingy and lose everything. The generous will prosper; those who refresh others will themselves be refreshed.

PROVERBS 11:24–25 NLT

God treasures every speck of His creation—especially His children. Entrusting us with free will and with the job of caring for this planet was a risky venture. Honor God's generosity by treating His gifts with the utmost love and care.

Dear God, Your gifts are so good, and I want to honor You in the way I use and share them. Amen.

DAY 45

Gentleness

Morning

*Let your gentleness
be evident to all.
The Lord is near.*
PHILIPPIANS 4:5 NIV

*He will tend his flock like a
shepherd; he will gather the
lambs in his arms; he will carry
them in his bosom, and gently
lead those that are with young.*
ISAIAH 40:11 ESV

Gentleness is a characteristic of the heart—a trait God honors and exemplifies. Allow God to help bring out the gentlewoman in you.

*God, please help me to be gentle
in all I do and say. Amen.*

Evening

*Always be prepared to give
an answer to everyone who
asks you to give the reason for
the hope that you have. But do
this with gentleness and respect.*
1 PETER 3:15 NIV

*Remind the people to be
subject to rulers and authorities,
to be obedient, to be ready to
do whatever is good, to slander
no one, to be peaceable and
considerate, and always to
be gentle toward everyone.*
TITUS 3:1–2 NIV

Sometimes gentleness is viewed as a sign of weakness. Gentleness is not less powerful or less effective than strength. It's strength released in a controlled, appropriate measure. When you are sharing your faith, gentleness shows you care for others the way God does.

*Dear Lord, the gentleness You desire
in me is not a weakness. It is powerful
and inspiring. I want to love others
with a spirit of gentleness. Amen.*

DAY 46

Let Goodness Flow

Morning

"Give, and it will be given to you. A good measure, pressed down, shaken together and running over, will be poured into your lap. For with the measure you use, it will be measured to you."
LUKE 6:38 NIV

Whenever we have the opportunity, we should do good to everyone—especially to those in the family of faith.
GALATIANS 6:10 NLT

You can't be a good woman without doing good things. That isn't a rule; it's more of a reminder. Goodness flows naturally from a faith-filled heart. Say yes to letting goodness flow freely from your life into the lives of others.

Dear God, I want goodness to flow freely from my life as a testimony to Your goodness. Amen.

Evening

He satisfies the longing soul, and fills the hungry soul with goodness.
PSALM 107:9 NKJV

Oh, how abundant is your goodness, which you have stored up for those who fear you and worked for those who take refuge in you, in the sight of the children of mankind!
PSALM 31:19 ESV

Like a good cook who consistently turns out good meals, our good God consistently bestows good gifts. Sometimes they're delectable delights. Other times they're much needed vegetables. You can trust in God's goodness to serve up exactly what you need.

Father, Your goodness means You'll always be caring and providing for me, not necessarily for all my wants, but always for all my needs. Thank You! Amen.

DAY 47

By Grace Alone

Morning

God saved you by his grace when you believed. And you can't take credit for this; it is a gift from God.

EPHESIANS 2:8 NLT

But by the grace of God I am what I am, and his grace toward me was not in vain.

1 CORINTHIANS 15:10 ESV

When you tell God, "I believe," His grace wipes away everything that once came between you and Him. Lies. Anger. Betrayal. Pride. Selfishness. They're history, by God's grace alone.

Dear Father, when the enemy starts whispering that I need to do more to earn Your favor or atone for my sins, remind me it's Your grace that covers me. Thank You for such an indescribable gift! Amen.

Evening

Even though on the outside it often looks like things are falling apart on us, on the inside, where God is making new life, not a day goes by without his unfolding grace.

2 CORINTHIANS 4:16 MSG

For from his fullness we have all received, grace upon grace.

JOHN 1:16 ESV

You may be God's daughter, but you're still growing. There will be times you'll stumble. Times you'll look to yourself first instead of to God. God's grace continues to cleanse you and draw you closer to Him, reassuring you of His unfailing love.

Heavenly Father, thank You for always catching me when I fall and pulling me back toward You. Amen.

DAY 48

The Right Direction

Morning

Keep your eyes on Jesus, who both began and finished this race we're in. Study how he did it. Because he never lost sight of where he was headed.

HEBREWS 12:2 MSG

Then Jesus told his disciples, "If anyone would come after me, let him deny himself and take up his cross and follow me."

MATTHEW 16:24 ESV

Each morning ask God to help you head in the right direction. Then, throughout the day, get your bearings by asking where and who God wants you to be.

Dear Jesus, I know You're always leading me in the right direction. Help me not to go off course. Amen.

Evening

Each morning let me learn more about your love because I trust you. I come to you in prayer, asking for your guidance.

PSALM 143:8 CEV

For to this you have been called, because Christ also suffered for you, leaving you an example, so that you might follow in his steps.

1 PETER 2:21 ESV

Keep your eyes on Jesus the way you follow a trail. Read what other followers have left behind—the Bible. Watch for signs of God's work in the world. Then keep walking, leaving a "faith trail" others can follow.

Dear Jesus, thank You for all those who have left good examples of following You. I want to follow You too. Help me to keep my eyes fixed on You. Amen.

DAY 49

Healing

Morning

*The prayer offered in faith
will make the sick person well;
the Lord will raise them up.*
JAMES 5:15 NIV

*Therefore, confess your sins to
one another and pray for one
another, that you may be healed.
The prayer of a righteous person
has great power as it is working.*
JAMES 5:16 ESV

Not every prayer for healing is answered in the way and time frame we hope for. Sometimes, emotional or spiritual healing takes place while physical healing does not. God can raise us up in different ways.

*Father God, I pray Your will
be done, not mine. Help me to
trust You for perfect healing in
whatever way You see fit. Amen.*

Evening

*My health may fail,
and my spirit may grow
weak, but God remains the
strength of my heart;
he is mine forever.*
PSALM 73:26 NLT

*The LORD is close to the
brokenhearted and saves those
who are crushed in spirit.*
PSALM 34:18 NIV

When you're ill or in pain, God is near. As any parent who's ever loved a child knows, He aches with you as well as for you. When the hope of healing seems distant, if you've run out of words to pray, picture yourself safe in His arms.

*Dear God, thank You for holding
me when I am hurting. I need You
so much. Please stay near. Amen.*

DAY 50

Reserve of Joy

Morning

Though you have not seen him, you love him; and even though you do not see him now, you believe in him and are filled with an inexpressible and glorious joy.

1 PETER 1:8 NIV

Rejoice in the Lord always; again I will say, rejoice.

PHILIPPIANS 4:4 ESV

Happiness is something that must be pursued constantly. Even if you catch it, you can't hold on to it. Joy, on the other hand, is a gift of dependence. The more you depend on God, the deeper your well of joy.

Dear God, I want to depend on You more each and every day. Thank You for the deep, true joy You give me. Amen.

Evening

When troubles of any kind come your way, consider it an opportunity for great joy. For you know that when your faith is tested, your endurance has a chance to grow.

JAMES 1:2–3 NLT

May the God of hope fill you with all joy and peace in believing, so that by the power of the Holy Spirit you may abound in hope.

ROMANS 15:13 ESV

God works in wonderfully unlikely ways. Regard troubles as opportunities instead of obstacles. As you rely on God, His glory will shine through you—and unexpected joy will be your reward.

God, help me to appreciate the troubles that come my way. It's so much easier said than done, but I know troubles draw me closer to You, and for that I'm thankful. Amen.

DAY 51

Quiet Kindness

Morning

You've had a taste of God.
Now, like infants at the breast,
drink deep of God's pure
kindness. Then you'll grow up
mature and whole in God.
1 PETER 2:2–3 MSG

Be kind to one another,
tenderhearted.
EPHESIANS 4:32 ESV

Kindness is the quiet compassion that flows from a loving heart. It doesn't announce its actions with shouts of "Look at me!" It whispers ever so gently, "Look at you. You're so worthy of love. Caring for you is my pleasure, my delight."

Father, our cruel world needs
kindness so much. Help me to
overflow with Your kindness so
it spills onto others. Amen.

Evening

Everything depends on having
faith in God, so that God's
promise is assured by his
gift of undeserved grace.
ROMANS 4:16 CEV

She opens her mouth with
wisdom, and the teaching of
kindness is on her tongue.
PROVERBS 31:26 ESV

A wise mother schools her children in the ways of kindness not only with her words but through her actions. God works the same way. Through the words of the Bible, God encourages His children to treat each other with respect, generosity, and consideration.

Dear Father, help my actions match
what I'm teaching my children
about kindness. Remind me that
others are always watching me.
Help me to show them You. Amen.

DAY 52

Leading Well

Morning

If God has given you leadership ability, take the responsibility seriously.
ROMANS 12:8 NLT

Set an example for the believers in speech, in conduct, in love, in faith and in purity.
1 TIMOTHY 4:12 NIV

If God places you in a position of leadership, whether at home, at work, at church, or in the community, recognize it for the privilege it is. Ask God to help you love those you lead, guiding them with humility and wisdom.

Dear Lord, I want to view leading others well as a privilege. Please give me the right attitude and the right actions. Amen.

Evening

Good leadership is a channel of water controlled by GOD; he directs it to whatever ends he chooses.
PROVERBS 21:1 MSG

Do nothing from selfish ambition or conceit, but in humility count others more significant than yourselves.
PHILIPPIANS 2:3 ESV

Whether you're leading executives in the boardroom or preschoolers through a lesson in sharing, ask God for the right words, right timing, and right attitude so you can wisely steer others in the right direction.

Dear God, the best way to lead others, no matter who they are, is straight to You. Please help me. Amen.

DAY 53

Loneliness

Morning

Jesus often withdrew to lonely places and prayed.
LUKE 5:16 NIV

Even though I walk through the valley of the shadow of death, I will fear no evil, for you are with me; your rod and your staff, they comfort me.
PSALM 23:4 ESV

Loneliness can make you feel like you're on a deserted island surrounded by a sea of people—yet no one notices you're there. But there is Someone who notices. Someone who'll never leave you. Someone who won't forget you or ignore you, no matter what you've done.

Dear Lord, help me not to fear loneliness when I'm away from other people, knowing that I am never away from You. Draw me closer to You in my lonely moments. Amen.

Evening

"Be sure of this: I am with you always, even to the end of the age."
MATTHEW 28:20 NLT

"Just as I was with Moses, so I will be with you. I will not leave you or forsake you."
JOSHUA 1:5 ESV

You may be lonely, but you're never alone. Find a place of solace in the silence through prayer. Loneliness may be the perfect lifeline to draw you closer to God, the one whose love will never fail.

Dear Lord, help me to feel Your presence. Let me be comforted by Your Spirit and Your Word. I know You are here. Thank You for never leaving me! Amen.

DAY 54

Making the Most of Marriage

Morning

A wife of noble character who can find? She is worth far more than rubies.
PROVERBS 31:10 NIV

He who finds a wife finds a good thing and obtains favor from the LORD.
PROVERBS 18:22 ESV

Focus on loving your spouse by praying for him, helping him, and encouraging him. Be the spouse you'd like to be married to and let God handle the rest.

Dear God, help me to put my husband's needs before my own. I know You will bless this kind of love. Amen.

Evening

Marriage is not a place to "stand up for your rights." Marriage is a decision to serve the other.
1 CORINTHIANS 7:4 MSG

Let marriage be held in honor among all, and let the marriage bed be undefiled.
HEBREWS 13:4 ESV

As you and your spouse communicate with God and with each other, God will help set your pace and direct your course. The more you allow God to quell your pride, the more rewarding your marriage will be.

Dear God, I give my marriage to You to guide and direct. Please help us to honor You and love like You do. Amen.

DAY 55

Finding God in Nature

Morning

By faith we understand that the universe was formed at God's command, so that what is seen was not made out of what was visible.

HEBREWS 11:3 NIV

Then the LORD God formed the man of dust from the ground and breathed into his nostrils the breath of life, and the man became a living creature.

GENESIS 2:7 ESV

It takes both faith and science to appreciate the wonders of nature. Surely a God who cares for the tiniest detail of nature is aware of—and at work in—every detail of your life.

Father, Your creation is amazing, down to the tiniest detail. Thank You for also caring about all of my details. Amen.

Evening

Ever since the world was created, people have seen the earth and sky. Through everything God made, they can clearly see his invisible qualities—his eternal power and divine nature.

ROMANS 1:20 NLT

God created everything in the heavenly realms and on earth. He made the things we can see and the things we can't see.

COLOSSIANS 1:16 NLT

God's story is written in more places than the Bible. It's written in the glory of the setting sun, the faithfulness of the ocean tides, the symphony of a thunderstorm, and the detail of a dragonfly's wing. It's written in every cell of you.

Almighty God, Your creation amazes me and testifies to Your magnificence! You are awesome and worthy of praise! Amen.

DAY 56

Practicing Patience

Morning

Let patience have its perfect work, that you may be perfect and complete, lacking nothing.

JAMES 1:4 NKJV

But if we hope for what we do not see, we wait for it with patience.

ROMANS 8:25 ESV

Impatience pushes us to take short-cuts and settle for second best. It can also rob us of opportunities to grow in our faith. The next time you feel impatience rising up in you, ask God, "What would You like me to learn while I wait?"

Oh Lord, it is so hard to practice patience the way I should. Teach me the value of waiting with the right attitude and learning from You during those times. Amen.

Evening

Remember, our Lord's patience gives people time to be saved.

2 PETER 3:15 NLT

So that you may live a life worthy of the Lord and please him in every way: bearing fruit in every good work, growing in the knowledge of God, being strengthened with all power according to his glorious might so that you may have great endurance and patience.

COLOSSIANS 1:10–11 NIV

Be thankful for God's patience with you. He consistently honors you with time to grow, room to fail, and an end-less supply of mercy and love.

Father, what would I do without Your patience with me? It seems endless, since I fail again and again. Thank You! Please help me to extend patience to others since I've received so much. Amen.

DAY 57

Power Source

Morning

We pray for God's power to help you do all the good things you hope to do and your faith makes you want to do.
2 THESSALONIANS 1:11 CEV

For God gave us a spirit not of fear but of power and love and self-control.
2 TIMOTHY 1:7 ESV

The more you grow in your faith, the more God will stretch your idea of who you are—and what you can do. Through God's power, you can confidently say, "Yes!" to doing anything He asks.

Almighty God, I need Your power so much in a world that is becoming more and more opposed to You and Your Son. Help me to do Your will with Your strength. Amen.

Evening

We are like clay jars in which this treasure is stored. The real power comes from God and not from us.
2 CORINTHIANS 4:7 CEV

"You will receive power when the Holy Spirit comes upon you."
ACTS 1:8 NLT

God's power working through you allows you to accomplish so much more than you could on your own. Staying connected with God by spending time in prayer, obeying His commands, reading the Bible, and loving others well will keep His power flowing freely into your life—and out into the world.

Almighty God, thank You for Your matchless power. There is no one like You, and I praise You for the power You place within me to accomplish good things to build Your kingdom. Amen.

DAY 58

Prayer

Morning

Be joyful in hope, patient in affliction, faithful in prayer.
ROMANS 12:12 NIV

"Call to me and I will answer you, and will tell you great and hidden things that you have not known."
JEREMIAH 33:3 ESV

Prayer is simply talking to your best friend. True, it's harder to understand God's reply than it is to read a friend's text or pick up her phone message. But the more frequently you pray, the easier it is to recognize God's voice.

Dear Lord, what a joy it is to come to You in prayer. Help me to be in constant conversation with You. Amen.

Evening

Everything you ask for in prayer will be yours, if you only have faith.
MARK 11:24 CEV

"And I tell you, ask, and it will be given to you; seek, and you will find; knock, and it will be opened to you."
LUKE 11:9 ESV

If we believe God loves us, believe Jesus is who He said He was, believe God has a plan for our lives, and believe He is good, wise, and just, our prayers will reflect these beliefs. They'll be in line with God's will. These are the kind of prayers God assures us He'll answer in His time and His way.

Dear Lord, help me to align my will with Yours. I want Your best in all things. Amen.

DAY 59

God's Presence

Morning

I walk in the Lord's presence as I live here on earth!
PSALM 116:9 NLT

"My presence will go with you, and I will give you rest."
EXODUS 33:14 ESV

Remind yourself of God's presence each morning as soon as you awake. Breathe in and thank God for His gift of life. Then breathe out, asking Him to make you more aware of His hand at work in your life. Throughout the day, just breathe, drawing near to the one who gave you breath.

Father God, help me to realize You are near in every moment of every day with each breath that I take. Amen.

Evening

Because of Christ and our faith in him, we can now come boldly and confidently into God's presence.
EPHESIANS 3:12 NLT

Let us then with confidence draw near to the throne of grace, that we may receive mercy and find grace to help in time of need.
HEBREWS 4:16 ESV

When we repent of our sins and accept Jesus through faith, all that lingers is God's love. Draw close to God in prayer. Never be afraid to enter His presence. You're always welcome just as you are.

Heavenly Father, You are holy and good, and I'm in awe that because of Jesus, I can come into Your presence. Thank You! Amen.

DAY 60

Priorities

Morning

"Seek the Kingdom of God above all else, and live righteously, and he will give you everything you need."
MATTHEW 6:33 NLT

"For where your treasure is, there will your heart be also."
LUKE 12:34 ESV

Making God's kingdom your top priority simply means that God's way becomes your way. Each day, ask God to help you live and love in a way that makes Him proud. Then watch Him provide what you need to do what He asks.

Dear God, I want to live and love in a way that makes You proud. I want to put You first in everything. Amen.

Evening

Honor Christ and put others first.
EPHESIANS 5:21 CEV

"You shall love the Lord your God with all your heart and with all your soul and with all your strength and with all your mind, and your neighbor as yourself."
LUKE 10:27 ESV

If you're struggling to figure out how to balance all your responsibilities and priorities, allow your faith to help put things in perspective. What is God's priority for you? That you live a life of love and integrity.

Dear Lord, help me to put my priorities in perspective of what You want for me. Amen.

DAY 61

Safe and Secure

Morning

You have faith in God, whose power will protect you until the last day. Then he will save you, just as he has always planned to do.

1 PETER 1:5 CEV

I trust in you, O LORD;
I say, "You are my God."
My times are in your hand.

PSALM 31:14–15 ESV

The Bible tells us God has numbered our days. He has planned the day of our birth and the day we'll die. Nothing and no one can alter those plans. Like your future, your faith is in God's sovereign care.

Sovereign God, help me not to fear but to trust that my times are in Your hands. Amen.

Evening

GOD's a safe-house for the battered, a sanctuary during bad times. The moment you arrive, you relax; you're never sorry you knocked.

PSALM 9:9–10 MSG

I have set the LORD always before me; because he is at my right hand, I shall not be shaken.

PSALM 16:8 ESV

The Bible says you'll face all kinds of storms in this life. But God is your safe place, regardless of what's raging all around you. He's with you in every storm, offering protection and peace.

Father God, regardless of the storms in my life, I know You are my haven. Thank You! Amen.

DAY 62

Provision

Morning

God will generously provide all you need. Then you will always have everything you need and plenty left over to share with others.

2 CORINTHIANS 9:8 NLT

My God will supply every need of yours according to his riches in glory in Christ Jesus.

PHILIPPIANS 4:19 ESV

When God says He'll provide what we need, it's always on His terms, not ours. He provides everything we need to do everything He's asked us to do.

Dear Lord, please give me wisdom to know what are truly needs in my life and what are just wants. Thank You for Your perfect provision. Amen.

Evening

Jesus declared, "I am the bread of life. Whoever comes to me will never go hungry, and whoever believes in me will never be thirsty."

JOHN 6:35 NIV

Delight yourself in the LORD, and he will give you the desires of your heart.

PSALM 37:4 ESV

We have spiritual needs that are just as essential as the air we breathe. We thirst for God's forgiveness and hunger for His love. Only a relationship with God can fill this void.

Dear God, thank You that You are the satisfaction of every true need I have. You fill me up and make me whole, and I praise You! Amen.

DAY 63

Relationships

Morning

God wants us to have faith in his Son Jesus Christ and to love each other. This is also what Jesus taught us to do.

1 JOHN 3:23 CEV

Love is always supportive, loyal, hopeful, and trusting. Love never fails!

1 CORINTHIANS 13:7–8 CEV

It's easy to invest yourself only in relationships that feel comfortable and personally beneficial. Ask God to help you reach beyond your relational comfort zone. You may be surprised by the gift of a friend for life.

Dear Father, help me to reach out to others in friendship even when it might feel uncomfortable to do so. Help me to love all people like You do. Amen.

Evening

You can develop a healthy, robust community that lives right with God and enjoy its results only if you do the hard work of getting along with each other.

JAMES 3:18 MSG

You are better off having a friend than to be all alone, because then you will get more enjoyment out of what you earn.

ECCLESIASTES 4:9 CEV

Going beyond superficiality toward unconditional love is hard work. It's a relational journey that takes patience, perseverance, forgiveness, humility, and sacrifice. It's a journey God willingly took to build a relationship with you. Now it's your turn.

Dear Lord, Your example of loving others seems impossible to follow sometimes, but I can do it with Your Spirit helping me. Thank You! Amen.

DAY 64

Renewal

Morning

You're my place of quiet retreat; I wait for your Word to renew me.

PSALM 119:114 MSG

Create in me a clean heart, O God, and renew a right spirit within me.

PSALM 51:10 ESV

When you're in need of refreshment, take time to sit quietly in God's presence. Push RESTART. Wait patiently and expectantly for a word from the one you love.

Lord, I long for the renewal that comes from spending uninterrupted time alone with You. Please refresh me. Amen.

Evening

Those who hope in the LORD will renew their strength. They will soar on wings like eagles; they will run and not grow weary.

ISAIAH 40:31 NIV

Therefore we do not lose heart. Though outwardly we are wasting away, yet inwardly we are being renewed day by day.

2 CORINTHIANS 4:16 NIV

Welcome weariness as a messenger. It's a reminder you're in need of renewal. Get alone with God and ask, "Is there anything I need to change? What's out of my hands and in Yours alone?" Allow God to do His job.

Father God, I come to You weak and weary. Please take my weariness and replace it with Your energy and strength. Amen.

DAY 65

Resting in God

Morning

"Are you tired? Worn out? Burned out on religion? Come to me. Get away with me and you'll recover your life. I'll show you how to take a real rest."

MATTHEW 11:28–29 MSG

On the seventh day he rested from all his work. Then God blessed the seventh day and made it holy, because on it he rested from all the work of creating that he had done.

GENESIS 2:2–3 NIV

If you're suffering from spiritual burn-out, take time to simply relax in God's presence, enjoying His company the way He enjoys yours.

Dear Lord, You created the Sabbath for a reason. Please remind me to take the time to rest and worship You. Amen.

Evening

It is useless for you to work so hard from early morning until late at night, anxiously working for food to eat; for God gives rest to his loved ones.

PSALM 127:2 NLT

"Be still, and know that I am God."

PSALM 46:10 NIV

You have many important roles to fill in this life. Rest is one of God's gifts that can empower you to accomplish what He's given you to do.

Father, I let busyness run me ragged way too often. Help me to be still and focus on You regularly throughout the day. Amen.

DAY 66

Righteousness

Morning

God, in his grace, freely makes us right in his sight. He did this through Christ Jesus when he freed us from the penalty for our sins.

ROMANS 3:24 NLT

If you know that he is righteous, you may be sure that everyone who practices righteousness has been born of him.

1 JOHN 2:29 ESV

Saying you're righteous is the same as saying you're blameless. And that's what God says about you. Once you put your faith and trust in Jesus, every trace of your past rebellion against God is wiped away.

Oh Father, I could never do anything to deserve the righteousness You offer through Your Son. You are a gracious God, and I praise You! Amen.

Evening

Pursue a righteous life—a life of wonder, faith, love, steadiness, courtesy. Run hard and fast in the faith.

1 TIMOTHY 6:11–12 MSG

Blessed are they who observe justice, who do righteousness at all times!

PSALM 106:3 ESV

With God, the rules never change. What's right is always right. Living a righteous life means consistently choosing to do what's right in God's eyes.

Dear God, thank You for the unchanging stability and peace You offer. I want to live a righteous life. Amen.

DAY 67

Secure and Immovable

Morning

I am sure that nothing can separate us from God's love— not life or death, not angels or spirits, not the present or the future.

ROMANS 8:38 CEV

He drew me up from the pit of destruction, out of the miry bog, and set my feet upon a rock, making my steps secure.

PSALM 40:2 ESV

God's love, His character, His gift of salvation, and every promise He's ever made to you stands firm, immovable. You can lean on Him in any and every circumstance, secure in the fact that He'll never let you down.

Oh Father, I find security and peace in Your loving arms that care for me. Thank You! Amen.

Evening

Fear of the LORD leads to life, bringing security and protection from harm.

PROVERBS 19:23 NLT

"And do not fear those who kill the body but cannot kill the soul. Rather fear him who can destroy both soul and body in hell."

MATTHEW 10:28 ESV

Fearing God isn't the same as being afraid of Him. Fearing God means standing in awe of Him. He's the almighty Creator, our sovereign Master, the righteous Judge of all. But this all-powerful God is for you. He's on your side, fighting on your behalf.

Almighty God, I stand in awe of Your power and might! Who am I that You love and care for me? But You do, and I am so grateful! Amen.

DAY 68

Self-Control

Morning

Better to be patient than powerful; better to have self-control than to conquer a city.

PROVERBS 16:32 NLT

Like a city whose walls are broken through is a person who lacks self-control.

PROVERBS 25:28 NIV

Self-control is attractive to others and to God. That's because self-control reflects God's own character. Is there any area of your life where you wish you had more self-control? God can help.

Dear God, in a world that celebrates selfishness, I need help to control my selfish desires and tendencies. Thank You for giving me Your Spirit to empower me. Amen.

Evening

The Spirit God gave us does not make us timid, but gives us power, love and self-discipline.

2 TIMOTHY 1:7 NIV

Do your best to improve your faith by adding goodness, understanding, self-control, patience, devotion to God, concern for others, and love.

2 PETER 1:5–7 CEV

Have you ever excused your own poor behavior by saying, "That's just the way I am"? Consider the character flaws you see in your life. Ask God to help you get these areas under control, one thought, word, or action at a time.

Dear God, I need Your powerful Holy Spirit so desperately to control my actions and words in ways that honor You. Please help me. Amen.

DAY 69

Serving God

Morning

See how Abraham's faith and deeds worked together. He proved his faith was real by what he did.
JAMES 2:22 CEV

My dear friends, stand firm and don't be shaken. Always keep busy working for the Lord. You know that everything you do for him is worthwhile.
1 CORINTHIANS 15:58 CEV

Serving God isn't always an easy path. You may not see the big picture behind what you're asked to do. But you can trust God's plan for you is good.

Dear Father, taking the road to follow and serve You is hard sometimes, especially when I can't see what's ahead. But You are good and just, and I trust You to care for me and to help me do Your will. Amen.

Evening

Offer your bodies to him as a living sacrifice, pure and pleasing. That's the most sensible way to serve God.
ROMANS 12:1 CEV

"Only fear the LORD and serve him faithfully with all your heart. For consider what great things he has done for you."
1 SAMUEL 12:24 ESV

The most important choice you'll ever make is whether to serve God or yourself. The good news is that by choosing to serve God, you wind up doing what's best for yourself as well.

Dear Father, what an honor and blessing it is to serve You! Please forgive me when I forget that. You are so good to me! Amen.

DAY 70

Refreshing Renewal

Morning

I think about you, God, before I go to sleep, and my thoughts turn to you during the night.

PSALM 63:6 CEV

In peace I will both lie down and sleep; for you alone, O LORD, make me dwell in safety.

PSALM 4:8 ESV

Sleep can be elusive, particularly during certain seasons of a woman's life. Turn your thoughts to God. Pour out your problems or lift up your praises. Ask God for refreshment and renewal. Allow God's voice to become your favorite lullaby.

Father God, please calm my anxious thoughts; take my worries and fears and give me the true rest that comes from trusting in Your almighty power and goodness. Amen.

Evening

The LORD is your protector, and he won't go to sleep or let you stumble.

PSALM 121:3 CEV

If you are tired from carrying heavy burdens, come to me and I will give you rest. Take the yoke I give you. Put it on your shoulders and learn from me. I am gentle and humble, and you will find rest.

MATTHEW 11:28–29 CEV

Knowing God never sleeps can help you sleep more soundly. If you're in the dark about a certain situation, if "monsters" are threatening your peace, take your concerns to God. It's never too late to call out to Him.

Oh Father, thank You for being my protector, my provider, my comforter, and my source of true rest. Amen.

DAY 71

The Power of Words

Morning

It is with your heart that
you believe and are justified,
and it is with your mouth
that you profess your
faith and are saved.
ROMANS 10:10 NIV

Words can bring death or life!
PROVERBS 18:21 CEV

Sharing how God is at work in your life gives others permission to ask spiritual questions. Don't worry about not having all the answers. You can't. An infinite God will always be bigger than our finite minds can comprehend. But saying aloud what you believe is part of living out and growing up in your faith.

Heavenly Father, help me to share with others life-giving words, words that praise You and point others to Your love and saving grace. Amen.

Evening

Let everything you say
be good and helpful, so that
your words will be an
encouragement to those
who hear them.
EPHESIANS 4:29 NLT

Let the words of my mouth and
the meditation of my heart be
acceptable in your sight, O LORD,
my rock and my redeemer.
PSALM 19:14 ESV

It's easy to let whatever pops into our heads pop out of our mouths, but the Bible reminds us that our words have power. We're responsible for how we use that power. Will we hurt or heal? Build up or tear down? Ask God to help you choose wisely.

Father, help me to choose my words carefully. Forgive me and help me to apologize when I fail. I want to please You with my words. Amen.

DAY 72

Spiritual Growth

Morning

The godly will flourish like palm trees. . . . Even in old age they will still produce fruit; they will remain vital and green.

PSALM 92:12, 14 NLT

But grow in the grace and knowledge of our Lord and Savior Jesus Christ.

2 PETER 3:18 ESV

The more time you spend with God, the more your character will begin to resemble His—and the humbler you'll become in His presence. This is exactly the kind of woman God is looking for to do wonderful things in this world.

Dear Lord, I want to be the woman You want me to be, spending time with You daily and growing in my faith. Amen.

Evening

Do your best to improve your faith by adding goodness, understanding, self-control, patience, devotion to God, concern for others, and love.

2 PETER 1:5–7 CEV

We must try to become mature and start thinking about more than just the basic things we were taught about Christ.

HEBREWS 6:1 CEV

Only God can make a seed grow. But you can make conditions favorable to help that seed mature and bear fruit. The same is true with faith. Cultivate the seed of faith God has planted in you through obedience.

Dear God, help me to cultivate the faith You have planted in me. I want to grow and bear good fruit for You! Amen.

DAY 73

Success

Morning

Commit to the Lord
whatever you do, and he
will establish your plans.
Proverbs 16:3 NIV

Commit your way to the Lord;
trust in him, and he will act.
Psalm 37:5 ESV

Committing whatever you do to God isn't asking Him to bless what you've already decided to do. It's inviting Him into the planning process. Make sure your dreams and goals are in line with God's.

Dear Lord, please align my plans and goals with Your will. Remove my selfish agenda, and replace it with the best kinds of plans that come from You alone. Amen.

Evening

"The market is flooded with
surefire, easygoing formulas
for a successful life. . . . The way
to life—to God!—is vigorous
and requires total attention."
Matthew 7:13–14 MSG

I have not yet reached my goal,
and I am not perfect. But Christ
has taken hold of me. So I keep
on running and struggling
to take hold of the prize.
Philippians 3:12 CEV

Whether it's making progress at work, parenting your children, or growing in your faith, success is the result of consistent effort toward reaching a goal. A successful life is made up of successful days—and a truly successful day is one that draws you closer to God and His plans for you.

Dear God, help me to have endurance and joy as I keep on growing in faith, drawing closer to You, and seeking Your will. Amen.

DAY 74

Thankfulness

Morning

Give thanks in all circumstances; for this is God's will for you in Christ Jesus.
1 THESSALONIANS 5:18 NIV

Every good gift and every perfect gift is from above, coming down from the Father of lights, with whom there is no variation or shadow due to change.
JAMES 1:17 ESV

Faith gives you new eyes, along with a new heart. It's good to notice God at work. It's even better to say "thank You" when you do. What will you thank Him for today?

Father, please open my eyes to Your goodness and Your presence in all circumstances and in all of creation. You are amazing, and I'm endlessly grateful for Your love! Amen.

Evening

I have not stopped giving thanks for you, remembering you in my prayers.
EPHESIANS 1:16 NIV

First of all, I ask you to pray for everyone. Ask God to help and bless them all, and tell God how thankful you are for each of them.
1 TIMOTHY 2:1 CEV

Asking for God's blessing on those who've generously touched your life with their love takes thankfulness to the next level—an eternal one. It also reminds you to thank God for bringing these special people into your life.

Dear God, You have blessed me immensely through the people You've brought into my life. Please bless them and guide them, and help me to let them know how much they mean to me. Amen.

DAY 75

Worthy Thoughts

Morning

*Create pure thoughts in me
and make me faithful again.*
PSALM 51:10 CEV

*We destroy arguments and
every lofty opinion raised
against the knowledge of
God, and take every thought
captive to obey Christ.*
2 CORINTHIANS 10:5 ESV

The more time you spend with God, the more aware you'll become of random thoughts that don't line up with your faith. Take those thoughts to God. Ask Him to help change your mind for good.

Dear Lord, when my thoughts begin to wander to things that are not good for me, help me to rein them in and fill my mind with You. Amen.

Evening

*Keep your minds on
whatever is true, pure, right,
holy, friendly, and proper.
Don't ever stop thinking about
what is truly worthwhile
and worthy of praise.*
PHILIPPIANS 4:8 CEV

*So prepare your minds for
action and exercise self-
control. Put all your hope in
the gracious salvation that
will come to you when Jesus
Christ is revealed to the world.*
1 PETER 1:13 NLT

Some trains of thought need to be derailed. If others could read your mind and you'd be embarrassed by what they read, flip the switch. Choose to focus on something worthy of your time and God's praise.

Dear Lord, help me to fix my eyes, my heart, my mind, and my hope on You. When I do, my thoughts and my life can be filled with only good things. Thank You! Amen.

DAY 76

Waiting

Morning

The Lord longs to be gracious to you; therefore he will rise up to show you compassion. For the Lord is a God of justice. Blessed are all who wait for him!

Isaiah 30:18 NIV

But they who wait for the Lord shall renew their strength; they shall mount up with wings like eagles; they shall run and not be weary; they shall walk and not faint.

Isaiah 40:31 ESV

As you grow in your faith, you'll begin to trust God's timing more and more. Expect Him to surprise you with the perfect harvest always delivered at exactly the right time.

Father, please strengthen me in my waiting times. I don't always understand Your schedule, but I know it's perfect. Amen.

Evening

My soul waits for the Lord more than watchmen for the morning.

Psalm 130:6 ESV

Wait for the Lord; be strong, and let your heart take courage; wait for the Lord!

Psalm 27:14 ESV

Waiting time is not wasted time. It's growing time. It's time to stay alert, to keep watch, to look for signs that God is on the move. Whatever you're waiting on God for today, keep watching. He's on the way.

Dear Father, waiting can be hard; please let me see it as a blessing, a time for You to teach me good lessons. Amen.

DAY 77

Wholeness

Morning

God made my life complete when I placed all the pieces before him.
PSALM 18:20 MSG

So you also are complete through your union with Christ, who is the head over every ruler and authority.
COLOSSIANS 2:10 NLT

Your life is a bit like a jigsaw puzzle, made up of multiple pieces. Trusting God fully means placing every piece in His hands. Only God has the power to put you together perfectly.

Dear God, I give every part of my life to You. Please fit them all together to make me whole and able to do Your will. Amen.

Evening

And he is before all things, and in him all things hold together.
COLOSSIANS 1:17 ESV

God is keeping careful watch over us and the future. The Day is coming when you'll have it all—life healed and whole.
1 PETER 1:5 MSG

Scars are signs of healing, a step toward wholeness. Thank God for the healing He has brought your way. Remember that when Jesus returns, He'll wipe away every tear. That's when you'll truly be healed and whole.

Father, thank You for the healing only You can bring to any type of injury, whether internal or external. Thank You for the times You provide healing on this earth. Remind me that one day You will give eternal healing for all the pain of this world. I praise You and wait eagerly for that day! Amen.

DAY 78

Wisdom

Morning

The fear of the Lord is
the beginning of wisdom.
Psalm 111:10 niv

If any of you lacks wisdom,
let him ask God, who
gives generously to all
without reproach, and
it will be given him.
James 1:5 esv

Trusting God with your life shows wisdom. And the more closely you follow where He leads, the more your own wisdom will grow.

Dear God, please fill me with Your wisdom. I trust You and am so thankful to learn from You! Amen.

Evening

There's nothing better than
being wise, knowing how
to interpret the meaning of
life. Wisdom puts light in the
eyes, and gives gentleness
to words and manners.
Ecclesiastes 8:1 msg

Blessed is the one who finds
wisdom, and the one who
gets understanding.
Proverbs 3:13 esv

When you spend time with an all-wise God, His character rubs off on you. As you more clearly see others from God's perspective, you'll learn how best to put your God-inspired love into action. Put your wisdom to work today.

Father God, please rub off on me more and more each day. I want to be like You and to love others like You do. Amen.

DAY 79

Working for God

Morning

Whatever you say or do should be done in the name of the Lord Jesus, as you give thanks to God the Father because of him.

COLOSSIANS 3:17 CEV

Do your best to present yourself to God as one approved, a worker who has no need to be ashamed, rightly handling the word of truth.

2 TIMOTHY 2:15 ESV

Your faith should affect your work—in wonderfully positive ways. Whether you work outside the home or in, whether you love your job or are doing it simply to pay the bills, tackle every task as if you were doing it for God Himself.

Father, help me to remember that You are the one I'm ultimately working for, no matter what the task. I want to praise You with every bit of my efforts. Amen.

Evening

Pay careful attention to your own work, for then you will get the satisfaction of a job well done, and you won't need to compare yourself to anyone else.

GALATIANS 6:4 NLT

Always work enthusiastically for the Lord, for you know that nothing you do for the Lord is ever useless.

1 CORINTHIANS 15:58 NLT

When you're working hard, it can be frustrating to be around people who are not. Instead of taking them to task, take them to God in prayer. Measure your own efforts against what God has asked you to do instead of against the efforts of those around you.

Dear Lord, it's hard not to compare myself and my work to others; please help me keep my eyes fixed on You, doing my best work and simply loving those around me. Amen.

DAY 80

Worship

Morning

Worship GOD *if you want the best; worship opens doors to all his goodness.*

PSALM 34:9 MSG

"Sing praises to the LORD, *for he has done gloriously; let this be made known in all the earth."*

ISAIAH 12:5 ESV

When you focus on God, you see more clearly how closely He's focusing on you. Worship weaves a reciprocal circle of love, one that will never end.

Father God, I am in awe at how much You care for me. Please help me to focus on You in worship every single day. I want to be praising You constantly! Amen.

Evening

God gave Christ the highest place and honored his name above all others. So at the name of Jesus everyone will bow down, those in heaven, on earth, and under the earth.

PHILIPPIANS 2:9–10 CEV

"All the earth worships you and sings praises to you; they sing praises to your name."

PSALM 66:4 ESV

One day, every created being will fall facedown in awe at the mere mention of Jesus' name. But you don't have to wait until then. Each new day delivers a fresh invitation to worship and countless more reasons to lift up your praise.

Dear Lord, I bow before You today in awe of Your glory and majesty. I praise You for all You are and all You do! Amen.

DAY 81

God's Love

Morning

For as high as the heavens are above the earth, so great is his love for those who fear him; as far as the east is from the west, so far has he removed our transgressions from us.

PSALM 103:11–12 NIV

Neither death nor life, neither angels nor demons, neither the present nor the future, nor any powers, neither height nor depth, nor anything else in all creation, will be able to separate us from the love of God that is in Christ Jesus our Lord.

ROMANS 8:38–39 NIV

God's love for us surpasses all boundaries. If we go to the highest high or the lowest low, He will meet us there. No matter where we are in our faith journey, He stands with arms wide, ready to forgive our sins.

Father God, I can't even begin to say how grateful I am for Your love. Thank You that it has no boundaries or conditions. Amen.

Evening

I want you to know all about Christ's love, although it is too wonderful to be measured. Then your lives will be filled with all that God is.

EPHESIANS 3:19 CEV

Your love, LORD, reaches to the heavens, your faithfulness to the skies.

PSALM 36:5 NIV

Have you ever thought about measuring God's love? There's no ruler long enough! No map wide enough. No ocean deep enough. God's love is immeasurable.

Dear Father, Your endless, immeasurable love is what carries me and strengthens me. I praise You and love You so dearly. Amen.

DAY 82

The Greatest Gift

Morning

For God so loved the world, that he gave his only begotten Son, that whosoever believeth in him should not perish, but have everlasting life.

JOHN 3:16 KJV

"Greater love has no one than this: to lay down one's life for one's friends."

JOHN 15:13 NIV

Very few human beings have literally laid down their lives. Yet Jesus, who lived a sinless life, willingly gave Himself as a sacrifice for us, His friends. He laid down His life so that we can have life eternal. Oh, what love!

Dear Jesus, I believe You died and rose again to save me from my sins. Thank You for saving me because of Your great love! Amen.

Evening

This is how we know what love is: Jesus Christ laid down his life for us. And we ought to lay down our lives for our brothers and sisters.

1 JOHN 3:16 NIV

But God showed his great love for us by sending Christ to die for us while we were still sinners.

ROMANS 5:8 NLT

Jesus gave us the ultimate example of sacrificial love when He walked up Calvary's hill and took our place on the cross. When we let go of selfishness and pride and put others first, we're following His lead. What an awesome display of love!

Dear Lord, You paid the price for my sin and I can never repay You, but I choose to live my life in honor of and in gratitude to You. Amen.

DAY 83

Active Love

Morning

"I said, 'Plant the good seeds of righteousness, and you will harvest a crop of love.'"

HOSEA 10:12 NLT

If I had the gift of prophecy, and if I understood all of God's secret plans and possessed all knowledge, and if I had such faith that I could move mountains, but didn't love others, I would be nothing.

1 CORINTHIANS 13:2 NLT

What do you suppose would happen if you neglected love? If you never used it? If you hid it away from others? Love is active. It's meant to be shown. Used. Given. Received. It's not what we feel; it's what we do.

Dear God, help me to have an active and authentic love for others. Amen.

Evening

"Remain in me, as I also remain in you. No branch can bear fruit by itself; it must remain in the vine. Neither can you bear fruit unless you remain in me."

JOHN 15:4 NIV

Beloved, let us love one another, for love is from God, and whoever loves has been born of God and knows God.

1 JOHN 4:7 ESV

Want to know how to have a love that remains? One that will never die? Remain in the Lord. Abide in Him. If you're in a fruitless season of your life, double-check to make sure you're still connected to the life giver.

Father God, please keep me close to You. You are the giver of life and love. Amen.

DAY 84

Love Like God Does

Morning

Live a life filled with love, following the example of Christ. He loved us and offered himself as a sacrifice for us, a pleasing aroma to God.
EPHESIANS 5:2 NLT

"I am giving you a new commandment, that you love one another; just as I have loved you, that you also love one another."
JOHN 13:34 NASB

Those who follow Jesus Christ are called to share His love, and not just with people who seemingly deserve it. Jesus loved the unlovable, and we're called to do the same.

Father, I don't want to love just when it's easy. Please fill me with Your love and show me where and when and how to share it best. Amen.

Evening

We love because he first loved us.
1 JOHN 4:19 NIV

The LORD is compassionate and gracious, slow to anger, abounding in love. He will not always accuse, nor will he harbor his anger forever; he does not treat us as our sins deserve or repay us according to our iniquities.
PSALM 103:8–10 NIV

One way to know you're "abounding" in God's love is to live a life that reflects His character. When you're slow to anger and refuse to knee-jerk when provoked, you're demonstrating His love.

Dear Father, I want to be abounding in Your love, patient with others, and slow to get angry. Help me to love more like You do. Amen.

DAY 85

Faithfulness

Morning

And he said to him, "You shall love the Lord your God with all your heart and with all your soul and with all your mind. This is the great and first commandment."

MATTHEW 22:37–38 ESV

Love the LORD, all you his saints! The LORD preserves the faithful but abundantly repays the one who acts in pride.

PSALM 31:23 ESV

God wants us to be faithful to Him. No straying. No playing the field. We're His bride, linked by love, faithful until He calls us home to heaven.

Father, help me to be faithful to You. Thank You for Your great faithfulness to me. Amen.

Evening

Remember this—a farmer who plants only a few seeds will get a small crop. But the one who plants generously will get a generous crop. You must each decide in your heart how much to give. And don't give reluctantly or in response to pressure. "For God loves a person who gives cheerfully."

2 CORINTHIANS 9:6–7 NLT

Give to everyone who asks and don't ask people to return what they have taken from you. Treat others just as you want to be treated.

LUKE 6:30–31 CEV

The Lord expects us to share. He wants us to be givers. When we're in relationship with others, we give to them—not out of obligation but out of love, for loving equals giving.

Dear God, when I want to tighten my grip on my money and possessions, please remind me that everything I have comes from You, and You have called me to give generously. Amen.

DAY 86

Loving Your Spouse

Morning

Each one of you also must love his wife as he loves himself, and the wife must respect her husband.

EPHESIANS 5:33 NIV

He who finds a wife finds a good thing and obtains favor from the LORD.

PROVERBS 18:22 ESV

Nothing is more motivating to a wife than the genuine love of a godly husband, one who would be willing to lay down his life for her. It propels her to be the best possible wife she can be.

Dear Lord, thank You for my husband. Help me to love him well and be the best wife I can be. Amen.

Evening

Then they can urge the younger women to love their husbands and children.

TITUS 2:4 NIV

"But from the beginning of creation, 'God made them male and female.' 'Therefore a man shall leave his father and mother and hold fast to his wife, and the two shall become one flesh.' So they are no longer two but one flesh. What therefore God has joined together, let not man separate."

MARK 10:6–9 ESV

When you're in love with someone, you often find yourselves staring into each other's eyes. People who've been in love for many years, however, learn that it's far more important to gaze in the same direction—toward the Lord.

Dear Lord, please help my husband and me to love each other to the best of our ability by constantly looking toward You. Amen.

DAY 87

Loving Your Enemies

Morning

"But I say, love your enemies! Pray for those who persecute you!"
MATTHEW 5:44 NLT

If your enemy is hungry, give him bread to eat, and if he is thirsty, give him water to drink, for you will heap burning coals on his head, and the LORD will reward you.
PROVERBS 25:21–22 ESV

What would you do if your mortal enemy was in trouble? Spend some time today asking the Lord to show you His plan for sharing love with those who have become enemies. Before long, the walls will come tumbling down!

Lord, You know my enemies and You know how I need to show them love. I can't possibly do it on my own, so please give me wisdom and fill me with Your supernatural love. Amen.

Evening

"But to you who are listening I say: Love your enemies, do good to those who hate you."
LUKE 6:27 NIV

May the Lord direct your hearts to the love of God and to the perseverance of Christ.
2 THESSALONIANS 3:5 NASB

Love is a powerful force, bringing together mortal enemies and restoring near-impossible relationships. Think of someone you've fallen out of relationship with. Take time to pray for him or her. Ask the Lord to show you how to love that person.

Lord, please destroy the walls in the relationships I've had that ended badly. Please show me how to help restore these relationships with love, according to Your will. Amen.

DAY 88

Loving God's People

Morning

God is always fair. He will remember how you helped his people in the past and how you are still helping them. You belong to God, and he won't forget the love you have shown his people.

HEBREWS 6:10 CEV

"By this all people will know that you are my disciples, if you have love for one another."

JOHN 13:35 ESV

God is watching to see how we treat fellow believers. He's looking down from His throne in heaven, making sure we're bound together by His love. When we love, we extend a hand of kindness and friendship. No, it's not always easy, but it's God's way.

God, when You look on me, I want You to be pleased, especially by the way I treat fellow believers. Help me to encourage them in their faith with kindness and love. Amen.

Evening

We know that we have passed out of death into life, because we love the brothers. Whoever does not love abides in death.

1 JOHN 3:14 ESV

Respect everyone, and love the family of believers. Fear God, and respect the king.

1 PETER 2:17 NLT

Our brothers and sisters in Christ should be like family members to us. And like family members, they're not always easy to love! But loving fellow church members is the best way to show that we love God.

Dear God, I don't want to love others only when it's easy. Help me to love fellow believers well, no matter what the circumstances. Amen.

DAY 89

Love in the Workplace

Morning

Knowledge puffs up
while love builds up.
1 CORINTHIANS 8:1 NIV

Beloved, if God so loved us, we
also ought to love one another.
1 JOHN 4:11 ESV

If you're active in the workforce, then you know how tough it can be to love your fellow workers. Nonetheless, sharing God's love with those in our workplace is God's plan for us. Make a decision today to build up your coworkers by loving them.

Dear Father, help me to love
my coworkers well in a way
that builds them up and
points them to You. Amen.

Evening

Dear brothers and sisters,
we can't help but thank God
for you, because your faith
is flourishing and your love
for one another is growing.
2 THESSALONIANS 1:3 NLT

Whoever pursues
righteousness and love finds
life, prosperity and honor.
PROVERBS 21:21 NIV

In the workplace, we often see the best and the worst in people. Some are almost impossible to get along with. If you're dealing with a "tough case," don't give up. Keep extending love. The payoff may be delayed, but you will be found faithful in the meantime.

Dear Lord, please empower me to
extend Your amazing grace in the
difficult relationships in my life,
especially the ones at work. Amen.

DAY 90

Directed by God's Love

Morning

"The Lord. . .will quiet you by his love; he will exult over you with loud singing."
ZEPHANIAH 3:17 ESV

May the Lord direct your hearts to the love of God and to the steadfastness of Christ.
2 THESSALONIANS 3:5 ESV

It's interesting to read that God occasionally needs to direct our hearts into His love. If we don't willingly accept God's little nudges, our love for others can grow cold. Keep your witness strong by allowing the Lord to direct your heart as He sees fit.

Dear God, help me never to ignore the nudges in my heart when You're directing me how to share Your love. Amen.

Evening

I will sing of the Lord's great love forever; with my mouth I will make your faithfulness known through all generations. I will declare that your love stands firm forever, that you have established your faithfulness in heaven itself.
PSALM 89:1–2 NIV

[Nothing] will be able to separate us from the love of God that is in Christ Jesus our Lord.
ROMANS 8:39 NIV

When you're filled with the love of the Lord, it's hard to contain the song that rises up in your heart. Why stop it? Let it flow! Praise makes even the hardest situation manageable.

Oh Lord, how wonderful it is to be filled with Your love! I never want my praise for You to stop flowing! Amen.

DAY 91

Giving to Those in Need

Morning

If anyone has material possessions and sees a brother or sister in need but has no pity on them, how can the love of God be in that person?

1 JOHN 3:17 NIV

Whoever is generous to the poor lends to the LORD, and he will repay him for his deed.

PROVERBS 19:17 ESV

If we love God, we need to take care of others even if it means reaching into our wallet to do it. Material possessions are meant to be shared. They're a tool for ministering to others. People see our love when we have compassion on them in their need.

Dear God, please show me those who are truly needy and help me know how best to help them. Amen.

Evening

But since you excel in everything—in faith, in speech, in knowledge, in complete earnestness and in the love we have kindled in you—see that you also excel in this grace of giving.

2 CORINTHIANS 8:7 NIV

"In all things I have shown you that by working hard in this way we must help the weak and remember the words of the Lord Jesus, how he himself said, 'It is more blessed to give than to receive.'"

ACTS 20:35 ESV

We want to excel at everything we do, and that takes effort on our part. But what about giving? If we love God and others, we should strive to become excellent givers. Want to excel today? Consider giving of yourself to others.

Dear God, You have given me so much more than I deserve. Help me to be an excellent giver just like You. Amen.

DAY 92

Loving Through Betrayal

Morning

While he was still speaking, there came a crowd, and the man called Judas, one of the twelve, was leading them. He drew near to Jesus to kiss him.

Luke 22:47 ESV

But Jesus said to him, "Judas, would you betray the Son of Man with a kiss?"

Luke 22:48 ESV

Imagine how Jesus must have felt watching one of the disciples He loved turn on Him and sell Him out for thirty pieces of silver. Perhaps you feel as if you've been sold out by a friend or loved one. Follow the example of Jesus, who, even in the face of betrayal, chose to forgive.

Dear Lord, You know well how awful it feels to be betrayed, yet You chose to forgive and keep on loving. Help me to do the same. Amen.

Evening

Hatred stirs up strife,
but love covers all offenses.

Proverbs 10:12 ESV

"For if you forgive others their trespasses, your heavenly Father will also forgive you, but if you do not forgive others their trespasses, neither will your Father forgive your trespasses."

Matthew 6:14–15 ESV

Even when it's hard to trust, we have to keep on loving the person who betrayed us. Why? Because love and trust are two separate things. Trust has to be earned. Love does not. It covers offenses and tears down walls.

Dear Lord, please empower me to let love cover over the offenses that have been done to me. Give me wisdom to know when and how much to trust again. Amen.

DAY 93

Love Forgives

Morning

"For this reason I say to you, her sins, which are many, have been forgiven, for she loved much; but the one who is forgiven little, loves little."
LUKE 7:47 NASB

Above all, love each other deeply, because love covers over a multitude of sins.
1 PETER 4:8 NIV

Love covers all wrongs. It also forgives on a grand scale. To extend this kind of forgiveness, you have to genuinely love the other person in both word and deed. Love big. Forgive big.

Dear Father, thank You for the big way You forgive me again and again. I want to love much and forgive much too. Amen.

Evening

Love prospers when a fault is forgiven, but dwelling on it separates close friends.
PROVERBS 17:9 NLT

Stop being bitter and angry and mad at others. Don't yell at one another or curse each other or ever be rude. Instead, be kind and merciful, and forgive others, just as God forgave you because of Christ.
EPHESIANS 4:31–32 CEV

It's human nature to withhold forgiveness in order to teach the other person a lesson, but that's not God's way. He doesn't want us to wait too long to forgive.

Dear God, You never make me wait for forgiveness—it's immediate when I come to You in repentance. Help me to forgive quickly just like You do. Amen.

DAY 94

The Privilege of Prayer

Morning

I prayed to the Lord my God and confessed: "Lord, the great and awesome God, who keeps his covenant of love with those who love him and keep his commandments."

Daniel 9:4 NIV

"Call to me and I will answer you, and will tell you great and hidden things that you have not known."

Jeremiah 33:3 ESV

Prayer is an awesome privilege. We get to communicate with the Creator of all! We share our sorrows, our joys, and our questions. The Lord responds by speaking to us, whispering words of love and direction.

Almighty God, to be in communication with You is an amazing blessing. Thank You for the gift of Your Son, who saved me and allows me to come before You in prayer and praise. Amen.

Evening

By day the Lord directs his love, at night his song is with me— a prayer to the God of my life.

Psalm 42:8 NIV

Evening and morning and at noon I utter my complaint and moan, and he hears my voice.

Psalm 55:17 ESV

Nighttime prayers are precious. Your last words to God before your head hits the pillow stir your heart to praise Him through the night. What a wonderful gift prayer is.

Dear Father, as I fall asleep each night, I give my worries and cares to You, knowing I can rest secure in all things. Amen.

DAY 95

No Love Withheld

Morning

Praise be to God, who has not rejected my prayer or withheld his love from me!

PSALM 66:20 NIV

The LORD is merciful and gracious, slow to anger and abounding in steadfast love.

PSALM 103:8 ESV

Sometimes we're reluctant to pray because we're upset with the Lord or others. We're afraid that if we get gut honest with God in our prayers, He might reject us. Not so!

Dear Father, I'm so thankful I can be completely honest when I'm talking with You. You know my every thought. Please help me to deal with angry feelings according to Your will. Amen.

Evening

Long ago the LORD said to Israel: "I have loved you, my people, with an everlasting love. With unfailing love I have drawn you to myself."

JEREMIAH 31:3 NLT

This is how God showed his love to us: He sent his one and only Son into the world so that we could have life through him.

1 JOHN 4:9 NCV

God will not withhold His love from us, even when we're mad at Him! He's a big God. He can take it. So get it out. Confess your angst. Then watch as He sets everything right again with His amazing love leading the way!

Dear Lord, remind me that I never need to be afraid to come to You in prayer, no matter how angry I might feel about my circumstances. Thank You for never rejecting me. Amen.

DAY 96

Love Drives Out Fear

Morning

There is no fear in love.
But perfect love drives
out fear, because fear has
to do with punishment.
The one who fears is not
made perfect in love.
1 JOHN 4:18 NIV

When I am afraid,
I put my trust in you.
PSALM 56:3 NIV

When fear grips your heart, God's love drives out that fear. It sends a calming message, one you can rest in. Next time fear slips in, remember it's not from God. He extends perfect love, the only force powerful enough to drive out fear!

Dear God, please drive out the fear that's gripping me. Your love is so much more powerful, and I trust You! Amen.

Evening

"The Lord your God is
with you, the Mighty Warrior
who saves. He will take great
delight in you; in his love he will
no longer rebuke you, but will
rejoice over you with singing."
ZEPHANIAH 3:17 NIV

I can lie down and sleep
soundly because you,
Lord, will keep me safe.
PSALM 4:8 CEV

If you're a parent, you know what it's like to rock a baby in your arms, calming him down so he can sleep. It's the same when we climb into God's arms. He quiets us with His love. We drift off to sleep with His gentle words of love drifting over us.

Heavenly Father, thank You for holding me safe in Your arms, the only place I can find true comfort and peace. Amen.

DAY 97

Obedient Love

Morning

Jesus answered him,
"If anyone loves me,
he will keep my word. . . .
Whoever does not love me
does not keep my words."
JOHN 14:23–24 ESV

"And now, Israel, what does the LORD your God require of you, but to fear the LORD your God, to walk in all his ways, to love him, to serve the LORD your God with all your heart and with all your soul."
DEUTERONOMY 10:12 ESV

If we love God, we will obey Him. Sure, our flesh doesn't always want to do it, but we'll have the best outcome if we stick with the teachings of the Bible and follow God's precepts to the best of our ability.

Father God, I want to obey You. When my flesh and selfish desires make me disobey, please bring me to repentance and get me back on track. Amen.

Evening

"Understand, therefore, that the LORD your God is indeed God. He is the faithful God who keeps his covenant for a thousand generations and lavishes his unfailing love on those who love him and obey his commands."
DEUTERONOMY 7:9 NLT

When a man's ways please the LORD, he makes even his enemies to be at peace with him.
PROVERBS 16:7 ESV

God always follows through on His agreement, even when we fall short. And He continues to lavish us with His unfailing love when we love Him back and obey His commands.

Dear Father, I fall short so many times, but You never do. Thank You! Help me to obey You more and more each day. Amen.

DAY 98

Shaped by God's Love

Morning

The Lord disciplines those he loves, as a father the son he delights in.

PROVERBS 3:12 NIV

For the moment all discipline seems painful rather than pleasant, but later it yields the peaceful fruit of righteousness to those who have been trained by it.

HEBREWS 12:11 ESV

God disciplines us out of love because He wants the very best for us. When we strike out on our own, away from His principles and blessings, He has no choice but to reel us back in. Love always disciplines.

Dear Father, help me to view Your discipline as a blessing, a sign of Your great love for me. Thank You for reeling me back in when I need it. Amen.

Evening

"Love the Lord your God with all your heart and with all your soul and with all your mind."

MATTHEW 22:37 NIV

The Lord your God is testing you to find out whether you love him with all your heart and with all your soul. It is the Lord your God you must follow, and him you must revere.

DEUTERONOMY 13:3–4 NIV

It's so important to love the Lord our God with all our heart. When we love Him, we're shaped and fashioned by His words, His love, and His compassion for humankind.

Dear God, I want to grow in my love for You. Please shape me into the person You want me to become. Amen.

DAY 99

Love Is Patient

Morning

*Love is patient, love is kind.
It does not envy, it does not
boast, it is not proud. It does not
dishonor others, it is not self-
seeking, it is not easily angered,
it keeps no record of wrongs.*
1 CORINTHIANS 13:4–5 NIV

*And the Lord's servant must
not be quarrelsome but kind
to everyone, able to teach,
patiently enduring evil.*
2 TIMOTHY 2:24 ESV

Love doesn't demand immediate service. Instead, love waits patiently on the sidelines. The next time you feel yourself losing your patience, take a deep breath. Remind yourself: Love holds on for the ride.

*Dear Father, help me to wait
patiently, and when I'm losing
my patience, please help me
to hold on—to You. Amen.*

Evening

*Whoever is patient
has great understanding,
but one who is quick-
tempered displays folly.*
PROVERBS 14:29 NIV

*You also, be patient. Establish
your hearts, for the coming
of the Lord is at hand.*
JAMES 5:8 ESV

Love responds with understanding and thoughtfulness, not foolish words or a sharp retort. Take a deep breath, my friend! Let love and patience rule the day!

*Father, help me to stop and
take a deep breath when I'm
losing my patience, before I act
or respond in haste or anger.
In that moment, please fill me
with supernatural patience that
comes only from You. Amen.*

DAY 100

Love Encourages

Morning

You must encourage one another each day.
HEBREWS 3:13 CEV

Anxiety in a man's heart weighs him down, but a good word makes him glad.
PROVERBS 12:25 ESV

Criticism rings loud and clear in our ears, but not praise. That's why it's so important to build others up with your love. Speak positive, affirming words. Encourage. Uplift. Love doesn't tear down. It builds up.

Dear Father, I want my words to be a blessing to others, not a curse. Help me to build up those around me. Amen.

Evening

Do not let any unwholesome talk come out of your mouths, but only what is helpful for building others up according to their needs, that it may benefit those who listen.
EPHESIANS 4:29 NIV

And let us consider how we may spur one another on toward love and good deeds.
HEBREWS 10:24 NIV

God longs for us to guard what we say, dwelling only on what is helpful. That's how love operates. It compels us to build others up, not cut them down. May every word be beneficial.

Dear God, help me to guard my lips and speak words that are helpful, loving, and kind. Amen.

DAY 101

Good Advice on Anger

Morning

My dear brothers and sisters, take note of this: Everyone should be quick to listen, slow to speak and slow to become angry.

JAMES 1:19 NIV

A gentle answer turns away wrath, but a harsh word stirs up anger.

PROVERBS 15:1 NIV

God gives good advice on anger. Often if we listen carefully and hold our tongues, we don't get mad in the first place. So when we feel anger building up inside, let's stop, listen, and keep quiet for a while. That's God's plan for more peaceful relationships.

Dear Father, it takes a huge amount of self-control to hold my tongue when I want to let loose with angry words. Help me to keep a tight rein on my tongue. Amen.

Evening

I want everyone everywhere to lift innocent hands toward heaven and pray, without being angry or arguing with each other.

1 TIMOTHY 2:8 CEV

For the anger of man does not produce the righteousness of God.

JAMES 1:20 ESV

One solution to anger is prayer. It's hard to stay angry with someone you pray for even if that person continues to irritate you. As God's Spirit works in your heart, you give the other person another chance. In Jesus, unrighteous anger cannot linger.

Dear God, help me to rid myself of anger toward others. When I bring them before You in prayer, help me to be filled with Your love for them. Amen.

DAY 102

Anxiety

Morning

Do not be anxious about anything, but in every situation, by prayer and petition, with thanksgiving, present your requests to God.
PHILIPPIANS 4:6 NIV

God cares for you, so turn all your worries over to him.
1 PETER 5:7 CEV

Need a sure cure for anxiety? Start praying. As you trust that God has your best interests at heart, no matter what situation you face, His peace can replace your worry.

Dear God, thank You for wanting to take all my cares and concerns away from me. Help me to give them to You, and fill me with Your precious peace. Amen.

Evening

"Let not your hearts be troubled. Believe in God; believe also in me."
JOHN 14:1 ESV

"Peace I leave with you; my peace I give to you. Not as the world gives do I give to you. Let not your hearts be troubled, neither let them be afraid."
JOHN 14:27 ESV

God says there's nothing you need to worry about. Just put all your troubles in His hands, and He who rules universe upon universe and yet knows each hair on your head will see that everything works out right. Are you ready to trust now?

Father, it's mind-boggling to think that You have even the hairs on my head numbered. How silly I am to ever doubt You! I believe You know me intimately and want what's best for me. Thank You! Amen.

DAY 103

No Worries

Morning

"Therefore do not worry about tomorrow, for tomorrow will worry about itself. Each day has enough trouble of its own."

MATTHEW 6:34 NIV

Cast your burden on the LORD, and he will sustain you.

PSALM 55:22 ESV

Since worry never improves the future and only hurts today, you'll benefit most from trusting in God and enjoying the spot where He's planted you today.

Father, why do I ever think that worry helps anything? Help me to turn all my worries into prayers that draw me closer to You, and help me trust in You more. Amen.

Evening

"Can any one of you by worrying add a single hour to your life?"

MATTHEW 6:27 NIV

When the cares of my heart are many, your consolations cheer my soul.

PSALM 94:19 ESV

Worry is the most self-defeating activity we can engage in. Besides, why should we give in to our worries when God controls our lives? He will always set us on the right path, so we don't have to agonize over life's details.

Dear Father, please forgive me for the many times I give in to anxiety. I know I can trust You. Please help me to remember that You are in control. Amen.

DAY 104
Blessing Others

Morning

We work hard with our own hands. When we are cursed, we bless; when we are persecuted, we endure it.
1 CORINTHIANS 4:12 NIV

Bless those who persecute you; bless and do not curse them.
ROMANS 12:14 ESV

Those who cursed Paul did not receive a cursing in return. Instead, he tried to bless them. Do we follow the apostle's example? When we are cursed by the words of others, what is our response?

Dear Lord, help me to learn from Your example and to bless even those who curse me. Amen.

Evening

May the God of hope fill you with all joy and peace in believing, so that by the power of the Holy Spirit you may abound in hope.
ROMANS 15:13 ESV

"The LORD bless you and keep you; the LORD make his face shine on you and be gracious to you."
NUMBERS 6:24–25 NIV

What Christian wouldn't appreciate these words, committing her to God's care and desiring for her to be close to Him? Who would turn down the good things God has to offer? Can you bless your friends and family with these thoughts today?

Father, please bring to mind all those who need Your special blessing today so that I may pray Your Word and Your blessings over them. Amen.

DAY 105

Hope and Joy

Morning

The prospect of the righteous is joy, but the hopes of the wicked come to nothing.
PROVERBS 10:28 NIV

Why am I discouraged? Why is my heart so sad? I will put my hope in God! I will praise him again—my Savior and my God!
PSALM 43:5 NLT

Trusting in Jesus gave you new life and hope for eternity. So how do you respond when life becomes dark and dull? Does hope slip away? Don't assume that God has deserted you. Hold on to Him even more firmly and trust. He will keep His promises.

Dear Father, forgive me for the times I begin to think You've deserted me. You've promised that will never happen. My hope is in You alone. Amen.

Evening

Blessed are those whose way is blameless, who walk in the Law of the LORD.
PSALM 119:1 NASB

For our heart is glad in him, because we trust in his holy name.
PSALM 33:21 ESV

Blessings belong to those who hear God's Word and take it to heart, living it out in love. Want to be blessed? Obey the Master. You'll live blamelessly and joyfully.

Dear God, please remind me that true hope and joy come from living my life for You. Amen.

DAY 106

The Gift of Children

Morning

Train up a child in the way he should go: and when he is old, he will not depart from it.
PROVERBS 22:6 KJV

The rod and reproof give wisdom, but a child left to himself brings shame to his mother.
PROVERBS 29:15 ESV

When you feel pressured by the task of parenting, take comfort. You are not alone—your Father is with you and promises that the effective witness of your life, as you teach your children His way, will not fail to bless them.

Heavenly Father, parenting seems like the hardest job in the world sometimes, yet it is so very worth it. Please help me to teach my children well. Amen.

Evening

"Let the little children come to Me, and do not forbid them; for of such is the kingdom of heaven."
MATTHEW 19:14 NKJV

Children are a heritage from the LORD, offspring a reward from him.
PSALM 127:3 NIV

Do we shut children out of our lives because we are too busy or have more "important" things on our minds? Then we need to take an example from Jesus. For a new perspective on God's kingdom, spend time with a child today.

Dear Father, please remind me every moment what a gift my children are, what a gift all children are. Thank You for precious little ones. Amen.

DAY 107

Comfort

Morning

[God] comforts us in all our troubles, so that we can comfort those in any trouble with the comfort we. . .receive from God.

2 CORINTHIANS 1:4 NIV

You ought to forgive and comfort him, so that he will not be overwhelmed by excessive sorrow.

2 CORINTHIANS 2:7 NIV

When you hurt, God offers you comfort. But when you have received His strength for the trouble at hand, do you share it in turn? Comfort isn't meant to be hidden away but passed on to those in similar need.

Dear God, You are constantly comforting me. Help me in turn to offer comfort to others when they are hurting. Amen.

Evening

Just as we share abundantly in the sufferings of Christ, so also our comfort abounds through Christ.

2 CORINTHIANS 1:5 NIV

"As one whom his mother comforts, so I will comfort you."

ISAIAH 66:13 NKJV

When trials come your way, God will draw you close and comfort you. If life is always going smoothly, comfort is meaningless, but when you're in the midst of trouble, He comes alongside with tender love that overflows your trials and reaches out to others.

Dear Father, help me to see the blessing in trials, realizing that they allow me to feel Your presence and comfort even more. Amen.

DAY 108

Contentment

Morning

Now godliness with contentment is great gain.
1 TIMOTHY 6:6 NKJV

The fear of the LORD leads to life; then one rests content, untouched by trouble.
PROVERBS 19:23 NIV

Money, which comes and goes, never brings real protection. Our security lies in God's provision. Whether or not we have a large bank account, we can rest content in Jesus.

Dear Lord, help me never to depend on money for my security and contentment. Those can come only from You. Amen.

Evening

The LORD is my shepherd; I shall not want.
PSALM 23:1 ESV

I have learned in whatever state I am, to be content.
PHILIPPIANS 4:11 NKJV

No matter what your physical circumstances, if Jesus is your shepherd, you never have to want spiritually. No matter what the world throws at you, you can be at peace.

Dear Lord, thank You for being my shepherd who cares for me and fulfills me in every way. Amen.

DAY 109

Getting Through Grief

Morning

"Where, O death,
is your victory?
Where, O death,
is your sting?"
1 CORINTHIANS 15:55 NIV

For "everyone who calls on the name of the Lord will be saved."
ROMANS 10:13 ESV

When we lose loved ones, our hearts feel pain. But if they gave their lives to Jesus, He is still victorious. In time, we will meet them again in paradise.

Dear Father, You know how badly I hurt for the loved ones I have lost. Please comfort me and remind me of the hope we have in You and the eternal home we have in heaven. Amen.

Evening

This is the promise that He has promised us—eternal life.
1 JOHN 2:25 NKJV

"Truly, truly, I say to you, whoever hears my word and believes him who sent me has eternal life. He does not come into judgment, but has passed from death to life."
JOHN 5:24 ESV

Today you miss the one you lost, and your heart aches. But in eternity you will be reunited and will share the joy of knowing death has been conquered by the Savior. Until you meet again, simply trust in His unfailing promise.

Dear Father, thank You for the salvation You provide and for Your promise of eternal life. Though my heart is aching, I believe in You and Your promises. Amen.

DAY 110

No Need to Doubt

Morning

"I am the way and
the truth and the life.
No one comes to the Father
except through me."
JOHN 14:6 NIV

"Whoever says to this mountain,
'Be removed and be cast into
the sea,' and does not doubt in
his heart, but believes. . .will
have whatever he says."
MARK 11:23 NKJV

Plenty of people doubt Jesus. But those who have accepted Him as their Savior need not wallow in uncertainty. His Spirit speaks to ours moment by moment, if only we will listen.

Dear God, You are worthy of
my trust, and I have no need to
doubt You. Help me to listen to
and believe in You. Amen.

Evening

Good and upright is the
LORD; therefore he instructs
sinners in his ways.
PSALM 25:8 NIV

Be merciful to those who doubt.
JUDE 22 NIV

Be faithful to God, and you will hear His still, small voice guiding you. Still doubting? Ask God for forgiveness of those sins that are barring your communion with Him. Soon, with a clean heart, you'll be headed in the right direction.

Dear God, please forgive me
for the sin that is blocking my
communication with You. I want
to come into Your presence
cleansed by You and able to hear
Your still, small voice. Amen.

DAY 111

Eternity

Morning

Your throne was established long ago; you are from all eternity.
PSALM 93:2 NIV

He has also set eternity in the human heart; yet no one can fathom what God has done from beginning to end.
ECCLESIASTES 3:11 NIV

There was never a moment when God did not exist, and nothing escapes His powerful reign. That's good news for His children. Whatever we face, now or in our heavenly abode, we know our Father is in control.

Almighty God, my mind can't really comprehend Your eternal existence, but I trust in it, and I'm so thankful for Your sovereign power over all times and places and people. Amen.

Evening

Your word, LORD, is eternal; it stands firm in the heavens.
PSALM 119:89 NIV

He became the source of eternal salvation for all who obey him.
HEBREWS 5:9 NIV

God does not change, and none of His promises pass away unfulfilled. The eternal Lord and all He commands stand firm. To gain eternity, simply receive Christ as your Savior, then trust in Him.

Dear God, in a world that changes daily, I'm so thankful that You are constant and trustworthy. Help me to stand firm and confident in You. Amen.

DAY 112

Rejoicing in God

Morning

You make known to me the path of life; you will fill me with joy in your presence, with eternal pleasures at your right hand.
PSALM 16:11 NIV

Rejoice in the Lord always; again I will say, rejoice.
PHILIPPIANS 4:4 ESV

Rejoicing in God? Those who don't know Jesus cannot imagine it. You have to know Jesus to delight in His presence, just as you cannot enjoy a friend until you come to know each other and share companionship.

Dear God, there is no greater joy than to know You, to be able to come into Your presence because of Jesus. Make me a good testimony of that joy to others so that they will want to know You too. Amen.

Evening

Let all who take refuge in you rejoice; let them sing joyful praises forever. Spread your protection over them, that all who love your name may be filled with joy.
PSALM 5:11 NLT

Rejoice always.
1 THESSALONIANS 5:16 ESV

Knowing and loving God brings us, His children, joy in His presence and the prospect of undefined pleasures at His side. Are you prepared to share in those joys with Jesus for eternity?

Dear Lord, to think I have eternity in paradise with You waiting for me at the end of this earthly life is too wonderful to fully comprehend. Thank You! Amen.

DAY 113

Your Story of Faith

Morning

Looking unto Jesus the
author and finisher of our faith.
HEBREWS 12:2 KJV

Trust in the LORD with all
your heart, and do not lean
on your own understanding.
In all your ways acknowledge him,
and he will make straight your paths.
PROVERBS 3:5–6 ESV

God is writing a story of faith through your life. What will it describe? Will it be a chronicle of challenges overcome, like the Old Testament Joseph's story? Or a near-tragedy turned into joy, like that of the prodigal son?

Heavenly Father, my story of faith won't be perfect, but I want to make the best of it, and I want to encourage others and point them to You as our only source of salvation, our only hope for a perfect eternity. Amen.

Evening

"For I know the plans
I have for you, declares
the LORD, plans for welfare
and not for evil, to give you
a future and a hope."
JEREMIAH 29:11 ESV

"No eye has seen, nor ear heard,
nor the heart of man imagined,
what God has prepared
for those who love him."
1 CORINTHIANS 2:9 ESV

Whatever your account says, if you love Jesus, the end is never in question. Those who love Him finish in heaven, despite their trials on earth. The long, weary path ends in His arms. Today, write a chapter in your faithful narrative of God's love.

Father God, thank You that because I have accepted Jesus as my Savior, the end of my faith story will be spending eternity in a perfect paradise with You. What peace there is in knowing the end of the story! Amen.

DAY 114

Jesus Never Fails

Morning

If we are faithless,
he remains faithful,
for he cannot disown himself.
2 TIMOTHY 2:13 NIV

God is faithful, by whom you
were called into the fellowship of
his Son, Jesus Christ our Lord.
1 CORINTHIANS 1:9 ESV

Sometimes our faith fails, but Jesus never does. When we change for the worse, slip, or make a mistake, He is still the same faithful God He has always been. Though we may falter, He cannot.

Dear Lord, thank You that Your faithfulness is never dependent on mine. Your constant, unchanging, perfect nature is what gives me strength, confidence, and hope. Amen.

Evening

His works are perfect,
and all his ways are just.
A faithful God who does no
wrong, upright and just is he.
DEUTERONOMY 32:4 NIV

Let us hold fast the confession
of our hope without wavering,
for he who promised is faithful.
HEBREWS 10:23 ESV

Many unbelievers, or even weakening believers living in crisis, complain that God is unfair. But Moses, who suffered much for God's people, knew better than that. God is always perfect, faithful, and just—it's rebellious humanity that lacks these qualities.

Holy God, help me to remember that Your ways are not the ways of frail human beings. You are always fair and just, even when I don't understand how. Please give me patient wisdom, trusting that You are working all things together for good. Amen.

DAY 115

Spiritual Certainty

Morning

We live by faith,
not by sight.
2 CORINTHIANS 5:7 NIV

Things that are seen don't last forever, but things that are not seen are eternal. This is why we keep our minds on the things that cannot be seen.
2 CORINTHIANS 4:18 CEV

Those things we "see" by faith cannot be envisioned by our physical eyes. That's why doubters disbelieve them. But when God speaks to our hearts, His words are as real as if we'd viewed the truth plainly in front of us.

Heavenly Father, there is so much to distract my attention here on earth. Please keep my ultimate focus on what is unseen—the glory and truth of You and Your Word. Amen.

Evening

Let them praise the name of the LORD, for His name alone is exalted; His glory is above the earth and heaven.
PSALM 148:13 NKJV

Now faith is the assurance of things hoped for, the conviction of things not seen.
HEBREWS 11:1 ESV

Trusting Jesus gives you a spectacular view of God's power. His work in your life increasingly opens your eyes to this glorious King who loves you.

Almighty God, I know You are at work even when Your actions are not always seen clearly with our physical eyes. Please increase my faith in Your power and good work here on earth until that day when You return and all will see and bow before You. Amen.

DAY 116

The Christian Life

Morning

Clearly no one who relies on the law is justified before God, because "the righteous will live by faith."

GALATIANS 3:11 NIV

For by grace you have been saved through faith. And this is not your own doing; it is the gift of God, not a result of works, so that no one may boast.

EPHESIANS 2:8–9 ESV

Rules and regulations aren't what the Christian life is about—faith is. Obeying God challenges you to trust Him every moment of your life. With that kind of belief, you can't help but share His world-changing message.

Dear God, I don't just want to be following rules; I want to be following You. Help me to obey You out of love. I want to change the world for Your glory. Amen.

Evening

Are you willing to acknowledge, you foolish person, that faith without works is useless?

JAMES 2:20 NASB

"Let your light shine before others, so that they may see your good works and give glory to your Father who is in heaven."

MATTHEW 5:16 ESV

No matter what a person says, unless love, compassion, and kindness accompany her words, it would be foolish to consider her Christian testimony believable. Though works don't save us, they do show what's in our hearts. What are we proving by our works today?

Dear Father, help my words about You and about my faith to match up with my works, which should always be done to honor You. Amen.

DAY 117

Home Building

Morning

Each one of you also must love his wife as he loves himself, and the wife must respect her husband.
EPHESIANS 5:33 NIV

Love isn't selfish or quick tempered. It doesn't keep a record of wrongs that others do.
1 CORINTHIANS 13:5 CEV

If you share house space without the love and respect that make it a home, it quickly becomes an empty existence. But that's not what God had in mind when He created marriage to reflect His own love for His people. He can help your marriage to shine brightly for Him, if only you ask Him and are open to His will.

Dear Father, I want my home and my marriage to shine a light that attracts people to You. Please show me what to do to make our light shine brighter. Amen.

Evening

The wise woman builds her house, but the foolish pulls it down with her hands.
PROVERBS 14:1 NKJV

We must not just please ourselves. We should help others do what is right and build them up in the Lord.
ROMANS 15:1–2 NLT

Every Christian woman has the ability to build up her family with her wisdom, industry, and righteousness. Her faithful Christian character blesses those in her home. Today, are you building your house or tearing it down? Seek God, and He will help you make it strong.

Dear Father, help me to be building a home with a firm foundation on Your Word and a warmth that comes from Your love. Amen.

DAY 118

Honoring Parents

Morning

*"Honor your father
and your mother, that your
days may be long upon the land."*
EXODUS 20:12 NKJV

*If one curses his father or
his mother, his lamp will be
put out in utter darkness.*
PROVERBS 20:20 ESV

Treating our parents well improves our relationship with them and gives our family security. Our Father God has special blessings for those of us who respect our parents. Whether it's Holy Land property or deeper love, He gives us just what we need.

Heavenly Father, I may not always agree with my parents, but I can respect them and show them deep love and appreciation for giving me life and raising me. Please help me to love them well. Amen.

Evening

*But if anyone does not
provide for his relatives,
and especially for members
of his household, he has
denied the faith and is worse
than an unbeliever.*
1 TIMOTHY 5:8 ESV

*Her children arise and call
her blessed; her husband
also, and he praises her.*
PROVERBS 31:28 NIV

Wouldn't every woman like to receive this kind of praise? Has a Christian mother been a wonderful influence on your life? She'd probably like to know that. Feel free to share that praise with others too.

Father, help me show my mother and other women in my life who have helped me just how much they mean to me. Amen.

DAY 119

A Good Kind of Mourning

Morning

"Blessed are those
who mourn, for they
will be comforted."
MATTHEW 5:4 NASB

You are kind, God! Please have pity on me. You are always merciful! Please wipe away my sins. Wash me clean from all of my sin and guilt. I know about my sins, and I cannot forget the burden of guilt.
PSALM 51:1–3 CEV

How often do we think of mourning as a good thing? But when it comes to sin, it is. Those who sorrow over their own sinfulness will turn to God for forgiveness.

Holy Father, please forgive me for all my sin. I don't ask You this often enough. Make me aware of and miserable because of my sin so that I will want to flee from it and run closer to You. Amen.

Evening

Come near to God, and he will come near to you. Clean up your lives, you sinners. Purify your hearts, you people who can't make up your mind. Be sad and sorry and weep. Stop laughing and start crying. Be gloomy instead of glad. Be humble in the Lord's presence, and he will honor you.
JAMES 4:8–10 CEV

For the kind of sorrow God wants us to experience leads us away from sin and results in salvation. There's no regret for that kind of sorrow.
2 CORINTHIANS 7:10 NLT

When God willingly responds to repentance, mourning ends. Comforted by God's pardon, transformed sinners celebrate—and joyous love for Jesus replaces sorrow.

Father, I thank You for the kind of sorrow that brings me to repentance. You pardon me, cleanse me, and comfort me again and again, and I am so grateful. Amen.

DAY 120

The Best Kind of Friendship

Morning

There is a friend that
sticketh closer than a brother.
PROVERBS 18:24 KJV

"You are my friends, since
I have told you everything
the Father told me."
JOHN 15:15 NLT

We choose our friends based on common interests and experiences. Often this "chosen family" seems closer to us than siblings. Yet no one clings closer than our elder Brother, Jesus. He teaches us how to love both blood relatives and those we choose.

Dear Lord, thank You for being the very best kind of friend. Amen.

Evening

Whosoever therefore
will be a friend of the world
is the enemy of God.
JAMES 4:4 KJV

The righteous choose
their friends carefully.
PROVERBS 12:26 NIV

When Christ becomes your best friend, other relationships may become distant. Jesus disconnects you from the world and draws you close to His people—Christian friends who share your love for Him. Together you may begin to reach out to those old friends for Jesus too.

Dear Lord, please give me wisdom in my relationships so that I can choose friendships that honor You. Amen.

DAY 121

Giving Generously

Morning

*Whoever sows sparingly
will also reap sparingly, and
whoever sows generously
will also reap generously.*
2 CORINTHIANS 9:6 NIV

*"Give, and it will be given to you.
Good measure, pressed down,
shaken together, running over,
will be put into your lap.
For with the measure you use it
will be measured back to you."*
LUKE 6:38 ESV

What you give is what you get. That's true in life, and it's also true spiritually. Those who try to hold their finances close will be letting go of spiritual blessings, while those who share generously gain in countless ways.

*Dear God, remind me often that
Your spiritual gifts and blessings
are so much more valuable
than any possession or money I
might try to hold on to. Amen.*

Evening

*Each one must give as he
has decided in his heart, not
reluctantly or under compulsion,
for God loves a cheerful giver.*
2 CORINTHIANS 9:7 ESV

*"It is more blessed to
give than to receive."*
ACTS 20:35 NIV

Paul reminds us that giving is the greater blessing. We know that when we see the delight in a child's eyes at receiving a longed-for item. Our heavenly Father loves to see the same joy in our eyes.

*Dear Father, help me to delight
in the joy of giving to others.
I want to be generous like You
and cheerful about it. Amen.*

DAY 122

Tender Love

Morning

A father to the fatherless,
a defender of widows, is
God in his holy dwelling.
PSALM 68:5 NIV

When he went ashore he
saw a great crowd, and he
had compassion on them,
because they were like sheep
without a shepherd.
MARK 6:34 ESV

God's love is very tender toward those who hurt. Children who have lost their fathers and women who have lost their husbands can count on His compassion.

Dear God, thank You for Your tenderness. You are the one true, almighty God, yet You are gentle and loving too, and I am grateful. Amen.

Evening

God is our merciful Father
and the source of all comfort.
2 CORINTHIANS 1:3 NLT

Bless the LORD, O my soul,
and forget not all his benefits,
who forgives all your iniquity,
who heals all your diseases,
who redeems your life from
the pit, who crowns you with
steadfast love and mercy.
PSALM 103:2–4 ESV

When we lose a loved one, do we focus on the Father's gentleness? We are more likely to complain that He did not extend life than to praise Him for His care. But when we feel the most pain, we also receive the largest portion of God's comfort. What hurts His children hurts Him too.

Gracious Father, please forgive me when I focus on my pain rather than on Your provision and care. Please draw me closer while I'm hurting. Amen.

DAY 123

Our Heavenly Father

Morning

The mighty God,
The everlasting Father.
ISAIAH 9:6 KJV

See what great love the Father has lavished on us, that we should be called children of God! And that is what we are!
1 JOHN 3:1 NIV

Only your heavenly Father will always be there for you, guiding you every step of the way. When you need help, call on your Father; He will never fail.

Dear heavenly Father, I call on You for my every need, and You are always with me. You are so precious to me! Amen.

Evening

"I will be a Father to you, and you shall be My sons and daughters, says the LORD Almighty."
2 CORINTHIANS 6:18 NKJV

Because you are his sons, God sent the Spirit of his Son into our hearts, the Spirit who calls out, "Abba, Father."
GALATIANS 4:6 NIV

God draws His children near, connecting them firmly to Himself through the Son and the Holy Spirit. With the Spirit, we call out, "Abba, Daddy," to the Holy One who loved us enough to call us to Himself despite our sin.

Dear Abba Daddy, thank You for calling me to be Your child. Amen.

DAY 124

Standing Firm

Morning

The Lord has become my fortress, and my God the rock in whom I take refuge.
PSALM 94:22 NIV

It is for freedom that Christ has set us free. Stand firm, then, and do not let yourselves be burdened again by a yoke of slavery.
GALATIANS 5:1 NIV

Are you under attack by friends, family, or coworkers? If persecution comes because of your obedience to the Lord, stand firm in the face of their comments. He will defend you.

Dear Lord, I can't stand up under opposition on my own. Please help me to stand firm when others are speaking against me because of my faith in You. Amen.

Evening

Be strong in the Lord and in the strength of his might.
EPHESIANS 6:10 ESV

"I tell you, on the day of judgment people will give account for every careless word they speak."
MATTHEW 12:36 ESV

If you face harsh words or nasty attitudes, remain kind, and God will assist you. Should your boss do you wrong, don't worry. Those who are against a faithful Christian are also against the Lord, and He will somehow make things right.

Dear God, when I'm trying my best to live for You and everything seems to be going wrong, please remind me that one day You will make all things right. Amen.

DAY 125

Our Refuge

Morning

"The Lord Almighty is the one you are to regard as holy. . . . He will be a holy place."
Isaiah 8:13–14 NIV

Trust in him at all times, O people; pour out your heart before him; God is a refuge for us.
Psalm 62:8 ESV

When you live in awe of God—when He alone is Lord of your life—you have nothing to fear. If fears or enemies assail you, a place of refuge is always nearby.

Dear God, You alone are Lord of my life. I give You all my fears and come to You as my faithful refuge. Amen.

Evening

He will cover you with his feathers. He will shelter you with his wings. His faithful promises are your armor and protection.
Psalm 91:4 NLT

For he will hide me in his shelter in the day of trouble; he will conceal me under the cover of his tent; he will lift me high upon a rock.
Psalm 27:5 ESV

God never throws His children to the wolves. Instead, He protects them in His holy place. With Jesus as your Savior, you always have a peaceful place to go to.

Dear heavenly Father, thank You for Your supernatural protection and for the peaceful haven You always provide for me. Amen.

DAY 126

Nothing Is Impossible

Morning

But Jesus looked at them and said, "With man this is impossible, but with God all things are possible."
MATTHEW 19:26 ESV

"Nothing is impossible for God!"
LUKE 1:37 CEV

God offers aid no matter what we face. Nothing is impossible for the one at work in our lives. What impossibilities can He deal with in your life? Have you trusted Him for help?

Almighty God, I give this impossible situation over to You. Help me to stop fretting over it and truly trust that nothing is too hard for You. I know You are at work here. Amen.

Evening

I will never leave thee, nor forsake thee.
HEBREWS 13:5 KJV

"Ah, Lord God! It is you who have made the heavens and the earth by your great power and by your outstretched arm! Nothing is too hard for you."
JEREMIAH 32:17 ESV

Even when fear or stress challenges you, you don't need to deal with it single-handedly if Jesus rules your life. When all seems in shambles around you, He offers strength and comfort for a hurting heart.

Dear heavenly Father, Your constant presence is such a comfort and strength for me. Thank You for always being near and never leaving me to do things on my own. Amen.

DAY 127

God Will Not Fail You

Morning

Blessed are those whose help is the God of Jacob. . . . He remains faithful forever.
PSALM 146:5–6 NIV

For the word of the LORD is upright, and all his work is done in faithfulness.
PSALM 33:4 ESV

Throughout the years, scores of believers have experienced the Lord's provision. Read the Old Testament accounts of those who have never seen Him fail. Watch His acts in the New Testament that showed the believers of the early church that they could trust Him.

Everlasting God, when I am struggling to trust You, please draw me to Your Word and remind me how You've provided for and protected generation after generation of people who call You Lord. Amen.

Evening

"Know therefore that the LORD your God is God, the faithful God who keeps covenant and steadfast love with those who love him and keep his commandments, to a thousand generations."
DEUTERONOMY 7:9 ESV

If we are faithless, he remains faithful— for he cannot deny himself.
2 TIMOTHY 2:13 ESV

God cannot fail His children, and He will not fail you. Trust in the God of Jacob, and pass on your testimony of His faithfulness.

God of Jacob, You are my God too, and I want to leave a legacy to those after me that I trusted in You and let You work in my life. I'm so thankful to be Your child. Amen.

DAY 128

Ask for Help

Morning

Let us then approach God's throne of grace with confidence, so that we may receive mercy and find grace to help us in our time of need.
HEBREWS 4:16 NIV

My help comes from the LORD, who made heaven and earth.
PSALM 121:2 ESV

Don't feel shy about approaching Jesus with all your cares. As God's child, you have a special place in His heart. When you have failed, you need not fear coming to the King of kings for mercy and grace.

Almighty God, I bow before You, so grateful and amazed that I can come to You with my concerns and to confess my sins. Thank You for Your great mercy and love for me. Amen.

Evening

Now all of us can come to the Father through the same Holy Spirit because of what Christ has done for us.
EPHESIANS 2:18 NLT

Because of Christ and our faith in him, we can now come boldly and confidently into God's presence.
EPHESIANS 3:12 NLT

God is just waiting for you to admit the problem and ask for help. Seek Jesus' aid, whatever your trouble. That's what He wants you to do.

Gracious God, please forgive me of my sins and help me with all my troubles. I can do nothing without You, but anything is possible with You guiding and loving me. Amen.

DAY 129

God's Delight

Morning

The Lord takes delight in his people.
Psalm 149:4 NIV

For the Lord your God is living among you. He is a mighty savior. He will take delight in you with gladness. With his love, he will calm all your fears.
Zephaniah 3:17 NLT

God doesn't just like you—He takes delight in you. You are so special to Him that He brought you into His salvation so He could spend eternity with you. God loves each of His children in a special way.

Dear Father, thank You for Your deep, delightful love for me. It means so much to me. Amen.

Evening

He led me to a place of safety; he rescued me because he delights in me.
Psalm 18:19 NLT

Where is another God like you, who pardons the guilt of the remnant, overlooking the sins of his special people? You will not stay angry with your people forever, because you delight in showing unfailing love.
Micah 7:18 NLT

God knows every bit of you, your faithfulness and your failures, and still loves you "to pieces." We could never earn such love—it is His special gift to each of us. Let's rejoice in that blessing today.

Dear Father, that You love me even though nothing about me is hidden from You feels so incredible. The security and joy I find in Your love are indescribable. Thank You! Amen.

DAY 130
Endurance

Morning

We can rejoice, too, when we run into problems and trials, for we know that they help us develop endurance.
ROMANS 5:3 NLT

And endurance develops strength of character, and character strengthens our confident hope of salvation.
ROMANS 5:4 NLT

Endurance in faith, hard as it may seem, brings happiness. Trials are no sign of God's disfavor or His will to punish His children carelessly. The tenderhearted Savior never acts cruelly.

Almighty God, please give me strength to endure this trial. I trust that eventually it will lead to blessing. I know You are not punishing me but teaching me and building my faith. Amen.

Evening

As you know, we count as blessed those who have persevered. You have heard of Job's perseverance and have seen what the Lord finally brought about. The Lord is full of compassion and mercy.
JAMES 5:11 NIV

For you have need of endurance, so that when you have done the will of God you may receive what is promised.
HEBREWS 10:36 ESV

Through troubles, we draw close to God and see His power at work in our lives. Then when we persevere in faith, God rewards us bountifully.

Heavenly Father, the blessing of trouble is that You hold me ever so close. Let me nestle into Your powerful yet gentle embrace as You carry me through this hard time. Amen.

DAY 131

Love Mercy

Morning

Mercy triumphs
over judgment.
JAMES 2:13 NIV

"Blessed are the merciful,
for they shall receive mercy."
MATTHEW 5:7 ESV

Not only is God merciful to us, but He expects us to pass mercy on to others. Instead of becoming the rule enforcers in this world, we are to paint a picture of the tender love He has for fallen people and to call many other sinners into His love.

Dear Lord, You are so merciful to me, and I want to extend that mercy to others. Thank You for Your tender love that inspires me. Amen.

Evening

"Be merciful, even as
your Father is merciful."
LUKE 6:36 ESV

The Lord has told you what is good, and this is what he requires of you: to do what is right, to love mercy, and to walk humbly with your God.
MICAH 6:8 NLT

When we criticize the world and never show compassion, we lose the powerful witness we were meant to have. As you stand firm for Jesus, may mercy also triumph in your life.

Dear Lord, help me to get my critical attitude under control. Replace it with compassion. I want to do what is right, love mercy, and walk humbly with You. Amen.

DAY 132

Rebirth and Renewal

Morning

"For this is how God loved the world: He gave his one and only Son, so that everyone who believes in him will not perish but have eternal life."

JOHN 3:16 NLT

He saved us, not because of righteous things we had done, but because of his mercy. He saved us through the washing of rebirth and renewal by the Holy Spirit.

TITUS 3:5 NIV

Could we save ourselves? No way! Even our best efforts fall far short of God's perfection. If God had left us on our own, we'd be eternally separated from Him.

Holy God, Your perfection is nothing I could ever attain on my own, so You sacrificed Your Son to make me righteous and able to come before You. I praise You for salvation, dear Lord! Amen.

Evening

Jesus answered him, "Truly, truly, I say to you, unless one is born again he cannot see the kingdom of God."

JOHN 3:3 ESV

Therefore, if anyone is in Christ, he is a new creation. The old has passed away; behold, the new has come.

2 CORINTHIANS 5:17 ESV

Graciously, the Father reached down to us through His Son, sacrificing Jesus on the cross. Then the Spirit touched our lives with rebirth and renewal. Together the three Persons of the Godhead saved us in merciful love.

Heavenly Father, thank You for reaching down to me and giving me rebirth and renewal through Jesus Christ. I'm so grateful I will never be separated from You. Amen.

DAY 133

God Meets Our Needs

Morning

"He has brought down
rulers from their thrones
but has lifted up the humble.
He has filled the hungry with
good things but has sent
the rich away empty."
LUKE 1:52–53 NIV

God will supply every need of
yours according to his riches
in glory in Christ Jesus.
PHILIPPIANS 4:19 ESV

God provides for every one of His children, even the humblest. Wealth cannot gain His favor nor poverty remove it. For the Father looks not at the pocketbook but at the heart.

Dear God, I have such peace in knowing You will always provide for my every need. Thank You! Amen.

Evening

Once I was young,
and now I am old.
Yet I have never seen the
godly abandoned or their
children begging for bread.
PSALM 37:25 NLT

The LORD will guide you
always; he will satisfy your
needs in a sun-scorched land
and will strengthen your
frame. You will be like a well-
watered garden, like a spring
whose waters never fail.
ISAIAH 58:11 NIV

Those who love God, though they lack cash, see their needs fulfilled, but unbelievers who own overflowing storehouses harvest empty hearts. God never ignores His children's needs. What has He given you today?

Loving Father, I want to count my blessings each day, recalling all the good things You give me. You fulfill my every need and add gifts on top. I cannot thank You enough! Amen.

DAY 134

Provided For

Morning

"Not a single sparrow can fall to the ground without your Father knowing it. And the very hairs on your head are all numbered. So don't be afraid; you are more valuable to God than a whole flock of sparrows."
MATTHEW 10:29–31 NLT

You open your hand and satisfy the desires of every living thing.
PSALM 145:16 NIV

Our faithful Lord provides for all His created beings. Will He fail to care for you? How could He satisfy the needs of the smallest birds and beasts yet forget His human child?

Faithful Lord, Your Word promises You care for even the smallest sparrow, and I am even more valuable than a whole flock of them. How good You are to me, dear Lord! I praise You! Amen.

Evening

Don't worry and ask yourselves, "Will we have anything to eat? Will we have anything to drink? Will we have any clothes to wear?" Only people who don't know God are always worrying about such things. Your Father in heaven knows you need all of these.
MATTHEW 6:31–32 CEV

Those who seek the LORD lack no good thing.
PSALM 34:10 ESV

God is always faithful. Though we fail, He will not. He cannot forget His promises of love and will never forget to provide for your every need.

Dear Father, thank You for Your provision in all things. Help me to provide for others because I've been given so much. Amen.

DAY 135

Power and Grace

Morning

For Christ's sake,
I delight in weaknesses,
in insults, in hardships, in
persecutions, in difficulties.
For when I am weak,
then I am strong.
2 CORINTHIANS 12:10 NIV

The Spirit helps us in our
weakness. For we do not
know what to pray for as
we ought, but the Spirit
himself intercedes for us with
groanings too deep for words.
ROMANS 8:26 ESV

Only God can make you strong in the weak places. In those spots of persecution and hardship, His power and grace shine through your fragile vessel as you live as a faithful Christian.

Almighty God, when I realize my weakness, I realize how much I need Your strength. Help me to truly delight in my weaknesses so that I can delight in Your strength and depend on You more. Amen.

Evening

Our sufferings were
so horrible and so unbearable
that death seemed certain.
In fact, we felt sure we were
going to die. But this made us
stop trusting in ourselves
and start trusting God,
who raises the dead to life.
2 CORINTHIANS 1:8–9 CEV

God chose the weak things of
the world to shame the strong.
1 CORINTHIANS 1:27 NIV

When you feel broken and useless, trust in God to fill your flaws, and His light will shine through the cracks of your pain to reach a hurting world.

Father God, please use my pain for good somehow. I don't understand it, but I trust You. Please use my life as a light to help others find You. Amen.

DAY 136

The Living Word

Morning

All Scripture is inspired by God and is useful to teach us what is true and to make us realize what is wrong in our lives. It corrects us when we are wrong and teaches us to do what is right. God uses it to prepare and equip his people to do every good work.

2 TIMOTHY 3:16–17 NLT

The word of God is living and active, and sharper than any two-edged sword, even penetrating as far as the division of soul and spirit.

HEBREWS 4:12 NASB

The Bible is not a dead book. The writer of Hebrews says it lives, and those who trust in Jesus can attest to this truth.

Almighty God, thank You for Your powerful, living Word that guides and directs and brings stability and purpose to my life. Amen.

Evening

Your word is a lamp to my feet and a light to my path.

PSALM 119:105 ESV

The instructions of the LORD are perfect, reviving the soul. The decrees of the LORD are trustworthy, making wise the simple. The commandments of the LORD are right, bringing joy to the heart. The commands of the LORD are clear, giving insight for living.

PSALM 19:7–8 NLT

Have you ever read a scripture and felt God knew just what you needed because it related to your needs in a special way? Then you've experienced the living Word of God that pierces your soul and spirit.

Dear Father, thank You for revealing exactly what I need at just the right time that I need it in Your holy, living Word. Amen.

DAY 137

Doing God's Word

Morning

But don't just listen to God's word. You must do what it says. Otherwise, you are only fooling yourselves.
JAMES 1:22 NLT

If you look carefully into the perfect law that sets you free, and if you do what it says and don't forget what you heard, then God will bless you for doing it.
JAMES 1:25 NLT

Maybe you've had days when you wanted to go in one direction, and God's Word said to go in another. If you were wise, you trusted in its truth instead of following your own way.

Dear God, I don't want to just hear Your Word. That's only the first step. Please help me to listen to, comprehend, and do Your Word. Amen.

Evening

"Every word of God is flawless."
PROVERBS 30:5 NIV

"Make them holy by your truth; teach them your word, which is truth."
JOHN 17:17 NLT

Can you claim that your every word is error-free? No. How much better to follow in the perfect way of your Lord, who willingly shares His wisdom. To avoid many of the pitfalls of this world, trust the flawless Word of God.

Father God, there are so many people and ideas and ways of life I could choose to follow in this world, but only Your way is perfect and leads to eternal life. You have given me the best guide in Your Holy Word. Please give me the faith and endurance to live it out. Amen.

DAY 138

Guidance

Morning

*Your hand will
guide me, your right
hand will hold me fast.*

PSALM 139:10 NIV

*I will instruct you and
teach you in the way you
should go; I will counsel you
with my eye upon you.*

PSALM 32:8 ESV

Allowing God to guide your steps means you won't get off track and land in a nasty situation. For the believer, the best place to be is in the palm of God's hand, safe from harm and in the center of His will.

*Father God, please show me
the steps You want me to take.
Keep me on track for the good
works You want me to do. Amen.*

Evening

*"In your unfailing love
you will lead the people you
have redeemed. In your
strength you will guide them
to your holy dwelling."*

EXODUS 15:13 NIV

*The steps of a man are
established by the LORD, when he
delights in his way; though he
fall, he shall not be cast headlong,
for the LORD upholds his hand.*

PSALM 37:23–24 ESV

Your powerful Lord directs you in His everlasting way. If you start to stray, He will guide you back to the right path. God will never desert His obedient child.

*Dear God, like a small child, I put my
hand in Yours and know You won't
let me go. Please lead me and guide
me according to Your will. Amen.*

DAY 139

Abiding Hope

Morning

May the God of hope fill you with all joy and peace as you trust in him, so that you may overflow with hope by the power of the Holy Spirit.

ROMANS 15:13 NIV

Let your steadfast love,
O LORD, be upon us,
even as we hope in you.

PSALM 33:22 ESV

Where does hope come from? From God. Unbelievers may have moments of wishful thinking or snatches of optimism in their lives, but they cannot exist in an abiding hope. Christians, filled with the Spirit, see hope overflow as they live in Christ, fulfilling the will of the Father.

Almighty God, hope from You is powerful and purposeful and the only kind that satisfies my soul. Thank You for filling me to overflowing! Amen.

Evening

Put your hope in God,
for I will yet praise him,
my Savior and my God.

PSALM 42:5 NIV

We who have fled to him for refuge can have great confidence as we hold to the hope that lies before us. This hope is a strong and trustworthy anchor for our souls. It leads us through the curtain into God's inner sanctuary. Jesus has already gone in there for us. He has become our eternal High Priest.

HEBREWS 6:18–20 NLT

Where should the believer place her hope? No human has power to turn her life around without Jesus. No solution lies beyond Him. Though you wait long and the path seems hard, hold on to Jesus.

Dear Jesus, You and You alone are my only true hope. Nothing and no one else is worthy. I praise You as I live for You and trust in You! Amen.

DAY 140

Strong in Hope

Morning

Be strong and take heart,
all you who hope in the Lord.
Psalm 31:24 NIV

But they who wait for the Lord
shall renew their strength;
they shall mount up with
wings like eagles; they shall
run and not be weary; they
shall walk and not faint.
Isaiah 40:31 ESV

Hope is not some weak, airy-fairy kind of thing. It takes strength to put your trust in God when life batters your heart and soul.

Almighty God, it does take strength to keep on trusting You when life is so painful at times. It takes supernatural strength that comes only from You. Please keep making me stronger. Amen.

Evening

Fear not, for I am with you;
be not dismayed, for I am
your God; I will strengthen you,
I will help you, I will uphold
you with my righteous
right hand.
Isaiah 41:10 ESV

God, the Lord, is my strength;
he makes my feet like the
deer's; he makes me tread
on my high places.
Habakkuk 3:19 ESV

The spiritually strong put their trust in God and let Him lift up their hearts in hope. Battering may come, but it cannot destroy them. Hope makes Christians stronger still.

Dear heavenly Father, please lift my weary head and heart to look to You, the one true source of my strength and hope. Amen.

DAY 141

Joy Will Come

Morning

My lips will shout for joy
when I sing praise to you—
I whom you have delivered.
PSALM 71:23 NIV

Glory in his holy name;
let the hearts of those who
seek the LORD *rejoice!*
PSALM 105:3 ESV

Having trouble finding joy in your life today? Do what the psalmists often did, and remind yourself what God has already done for you. How many ways has following Him blessed you?

Dear Lord, I have countless reasons to praise You and choose joy. Help me to focus on all that You've done and all that You do to bless me. Amen.

Evening

There I will go to
the altar of God, to God—
the source of all my joy.
PSALM 43:4 NLT

Restore to me the joy of
your salvation, and uphold
me with a willing spirit.
PSALM 51:12 ESV

Perhaps sin has overtaken your life, and you long to lean close to God and share His tender love once again. Ask Him to turn your heart away from the barren landscape of transgression and return it to Him. Your sorrow can turn to joy.

Gracious Father, please forgive me for my sin. I long to be close to You again. Please cleanse me and turn me from my sin and fill me with Your presence and joy again. Amen.

DAY 142

Close to Jesus

Morning

"Be still, and
know that I am God."
PSALM 46:10 NIV

Blessed are those who keep
his testimonies, who seek him
with their whole heart.
PSALM 119:2 ESV

So often we seek to do things for God or to prove our Christian witness. But if we become simply caught up in busyness, we lose the distinctiveness of our faith: a close relationship with Jesus.

Heavenly Father, I want to listen
to You, and I can't do that unless
I silence all the worldly voices
vying for my attention. Please
help me to be quiet and still as
I come before You. Amen.

Evening

Draw near to God,
and he will draw near to you.
JAMES 4:8 ESV

"Call to me and I will answer you,
and will tell you great and hidden
things that you have not known."
JEREMIAH 33:3 ESV

Knowing God is not about what we do but about whom we love. Our good works mean little if we disconnect from Him. Spend time being still with God today, and a deepened knowledge of Him will be your blessing.

Dear Father, help me to slow down
my busy pace and reconnect with
You each and every day. Amen.

DAY 143

Sweet Sacrifice

Morning

I will offer to you the sacrifice of thanksgiving and call on the name of the Lord.
PSALM 116:17 ESV

Walk in the way of love, just as Christ loved us and gave himself up for us as a fragrant offering and sacrifice to God.
EPHESIANS 5:2 NIV

We don't think of sacrifice as being sweet. More often, we see it as hardship or drudgery. But when we have experienced the sweetness of Jesus' sacrifice, which brought us into a love relationship with Him, we understand just what Ephesians 5:2 means.

Loving God, I am so grateful to be a recipient of Your great sacrifice. How could I possibly not want to share Your sacrificial love with others? Amen.

Evening

Our sacrifice is to keep offering praise to God in the name of Jesus. But don't forget to help others and to share your possessions with them. This too is like offering a sacrifice that pleases God.
HEBREWS 13:15–16 CEV

"Greater love has no one than this, that someone lay down his life for his friends."
JOHN 15:13 ESV

God calls us not only to receive love but to pass it on to others who also need to understand the sweetness of His sacrifice.

Dear Lord, help me to view sacrifice as a joy to delight in because of the love it shows—love that imitates You. Amen.

DAY 144

How to Love

Morning

And this commandment
we have from him:
whoever loves God must
also love his brother.
1 JOHN 4:21 ESV

"A new commandment I give to you, that you love one another: just as I have loved you, you also are to love one another. By this all people will know that you are my disciples, if you have love for one another."
JOHN 13:34–35 ESV

How do we know how to love? We learn from Jesus. We see it in God's Word and in the lives of faithful believers.

Dear Lord, please train me in love for others. Teach me from Your Word and from the lives of those I know who sincerely follow You. Amen.

Evening

"But love your enemies, and do good, and lend, expecting nothing in return, and your reward will be great, and you will be sons of the Most High, for he is kind to the ungrateful and the evil."
LUKE 6:35 ESV

Anyone who does not love does not know God, because God is love.
1 JOHN 4:8 ESV

In God's power we can take what we know and follow Jesus, living out the words He spoke and the good examples we have seen.

Almighty God, I need Your power to keep following Jesus and trying to be more like Him. Help me to live every part of my life as a testimony for You. Amen.

DAY 145

Spiritual Renewal

Morning

Therefore we do not lose heart. Though outwardly we are wasting away, yet inwardly we are being renewed day by day.

2 CORINTHIANS 4:16 NIV

My body and mind may fail, but you are my strength and my choice forever.

PSALM 73:26 CEV

On the outside, people see us getting older and frailer. But looks are deceiving. As Christians, we are constantly building our belief if we walk consistently with God. We're growing deeper in faith, being spiritually renewed every day.

Dear Lord, aging means nothing in comparison to the refreshing renewal You offer me day by day. Thank You! Amen.

Evening

Our bodies are buried in brokenness, but they will be raised in glory. They are buried in weakness, but they will be raised in strength.

1 CORINTHIANS 15:43 NLT

"He will wipe away every tear from their eyes, and death shall be no more, neither shall there be mourning, nor crying, nor pain anymore, for the former things have passed away."

REVELATION 21:4 ESV

God's glory lies ahead of us, as on earth we learn to appreciate His love and compassion. We look ahead to eternity and a new body made perfect by our Savior.

Everlasting God, I look forward to spending eternity with You with a new and perfect body that will never know pain or sadness. Amen.

DAY 146

Living in the Light

Morning

In him was life,
and that life was the
light of all mankind.
JOHN 1:4 NIV

Jesus spoke to them, saying,
"I am the light of the world.
Whoever follows me will
not walk in darkness, but
will have the light of life."
JOHN 8:12 ESV

Jesus is a Christian's life and light, as anyone who has walked with Him for a while can tell you. Everything is different once He enters a soul.

Dear Lord, everything is brighter and clearer in my life because of Your shining light. I thank You and praise You! Amen.

Evening

For at one time you
were darkness, but now
you are light in the Lord.
Walk as children of light.
EPHESIANS 5:8 ESV

And I will lead the blind in
a way that they do not know,
in paths that they have not
known I will guide them.
I will turn the darkness before
them into light, the rough
places into level ground.
ISAIAH 42:16 ESV

When Jesus enters, the new believer begins to make changes, cleaning out the dark corners of her existence so the bright light shining within her will not fall on dirty places. She's living in the light, following Jesus.

Loving Savior, thank You for Your light that ruins all the dark things in me. Amen.

DAY 147

Obedience and Blessings

Morning

"All these blessings shall come upon you and overtake you, because you obey the voice of the LORD your God."
DEUTERONOMY 28:2 NKJV

Trust in the LORD with all your heart; do not depend on your own understanding. Seek his will in all you do, and he will show you which path to take.
PROVERBS 3:5–6 NLT

Obey God, receive blessings. It seems simple enough, doesn't it? But what if we obey and then have more troubles than we did before? Perhaps we're looking at the situation from our perspective, not His.

Loving Father, remind me every day that I can't lean on my own understanding when it comes to obedience and blessings. I will keep obeying You as I trust that You see me, care for me, and are doing what is best for me. Amen.

Evening

For you have need of endurance, so that when you have done the will of God you may receive what is promised.
HEBREWS 10:36 ESV

Therefore the LORD waits to be gracious to you, and therefore he exalts himself to show mercy to you. For the LORD is a God of justice; blessed are all those who wait for him.
ISAIAH 30:18 ESV

Blessings don't always follow on the heels of obedience; they often take time to appear. But because God has promised, we know they will come if only we wait patiently. Today's blessings may result from long-ago faithfulness.

Father God, remind me daily that Your timing is far different from mine, and Yours is perfect. Please give me patience and peace while I wait for You. Amen.

DAY 148

Blessings Forever

Morning

Blessed are they that do
his commandments,
that they may have right
to the tree of life, and may
enter in through the
gates into the city.
REVELATION 22:14 KJV

"Do not lay up for yourselves
treasures on earth, where
moth and rust destroy and
where thieves break in and
steal, but lay up for yourselves
treasures in heaven."
MATTHEW 6:19–20 ESV

The blessings of obedience not only impact us today but follow us into eternity in God's heavenly city. Whatever we do to please God never goes unrewarded.

Everlasting God, I'm not living for this world; I'm living for eternity with You, where my true treasures are waiting. I choose to obey You here on earth until the day I reach my heavenly home. Amen.

Evening

"Sell your possessions
and give to those in need.
This will store up treasure
for you in heaven!"
LUKE 12:33 NLT

Now all glory to God, who
is able, through his mighty
power at work within us, to
accomplish infinitely more
than we might ask or think.
EPHESIANS 3:20 NLT

Works that demonstrate our faith give us joy now and lead to a future reward. We look forward to life in the New Jerusalem even as we reap God's blessings now.

Heavenly Father, I give my life and possessions and finances to do Your will, and I trust that You are working and blessing in ways that are much bigger than I can imagine. Amen.

DAY 149

Prayer—Give and Receive

Morning

*Brothers and sisters,
pray for us.*
1 THESSALONIANS 5:25 NIV

Dear brothers and sisters, I urge you in the name of our Lord Jesus Christ to join in my struggle by praying to God for me. Do this because of your love for me, given to you by the Holy Spirit.
ROMANS 15:30 NLT

Do you find it hard to ask others to pray for you? Remember how Paul asked the Thessalonians to pray for his ministry, and don't be afraid to take that step in humility.

Dear Father, please make me humble. Let me never be too proud to ask other believers for prayer. Amen.

Evening

Therefore, confess your sins to one another and pray for one another, that you may be healed. The prayer of a righteous person has great power as it is working.
JAMES 5:16 ESV

So Peter was kept in prison, but earnest prayer for him was made to God by the church.
ACTS 12:5 ESV

As church members pray for each other, their spirits connect in a new, caring way. Choose carefully whom you share private concerns with, but never fear to have a mature Christian pray for you.

Father God, may my church know the awesome power of joining together in prayer. Help us to do so regularly for all things so that we might further Your kingdom. Amen.

DAY 150

The Best Answer

Morning

Pray without ceasing.
1 THESSALONIANS 5:17 KJV

Rejoicing in hope, patient in tribulation, continuing steadfastly in prayer.
ROMANS 12:12 NKJV

Haven't received an answer to your prayer? Don't give up. There's no time limit on speaking to God about your needs. It's just that we often work on a different time schedule than God does.

Dear Father, forgive me when I want You to change Your perfect timing to fit my schedule. I trust You with every moment of my life. Amen.

Evening

Pray in the Spirit at all times and on every occasion. Stay alert and be persistent in your prayers for all believers everywhere.
EPHESIANS 6:18 NLT

Continue steadfastly in prayer, being watchful in it with thanksgiving.
COLOSSIANS 4:2 ESV

We want answers to prayer yesterday, while God has something better in mind for tomorrow. So keep praying. God listens to His children and gives them the best answer, not the fastest one.

Sovereign God, I feel so impatient at times when I'm waiting for Your answers. Please remind me that You always respond to my prayers with the best answer at the best time. Amen.

DAY 151

Only by God's Strength

Morning

*"Love your enemies
and pray for anyone
who mistreats you."*
MATTHEW 5:44 CEV

*Do not rejoice when your enemy
falls, and let not your heart
be glad when he stumbles.*
PROVERBS 24:17 ESV

Consistently loving an enemy is a real challenge. If you hurt from pain inflicted by another, you hardly want to pray for her. Without God's strength, could any of us follow Jesus' command to love our enemies?

Father God, only with Your strength can I choose to pray for someone who has hurt me. I want to do Your will in this matter, so please help me. Amen.

Evening

*"If your enemy is hungry,
feed him; if he is thirsty,
give him something to drink.
In doing this, you will heap
burning coals on his head."*
ROMANS 12:20 NIV

*Ask God to bless everyone who
mistreats you. Ask him to bless
them and not to curse them.*
ROMANS 12:14 CEV

Loving actions and prayer can bring peace between two people at odds with each other. When we ask God to bless our enemies, He helps us to rise above the strife.

Loving Father, please change my will to Yours in regard to my enemies. I cannot love them on my own, but I can let You use me to show love. Amen.

DAY 152

Call to Repentance

Morning

I came not to call the righteous, but sinners to repentance.
LUKE 5:32 KJV

"He commands everyone everywhere to repent of their sins and turn to him."
ACTS 17:30 NLT

Repentance isn't meant for "good people" who have only "tiny" sins to confess. Acts 17:30 reminds us that no sin is too awful for God to hear about it. God calls all who are sinful—those who need Him most and who have the most to fear from His awesome holiness.

Dear God, You want all people to see our need for salvation from our sins that separate us from You. Thank You for providing the cleansing blood of Jesus to forgive us and draw us near to You. Amen.

Evening

If we confess our sins, he is faithful and just to forgive us our sins and to cleanse us from all unrighteousness.
1 JOHN 1:9 ESV

People who conceal their sins will not prosper, but if they confess and turn from them, they will receive mercy.
PROVERBS 28:13 NLT

Often we hesitate to admit to wrongs that embarrass us, sins we hate to confess. But when we lay out our sins before God, that one moment of repentance opens the door for His Spirit to cleanse our lives.

Gracious Lord, I confess my sin of ________ to You and ask for Your cleansing from it. Thank You for forgiving me! Amen.

DAY 153

Ready for Good Work

Morning

All Scripture is given by inspiration of God, and is profitable for doctrine, for reproof, for correction, for instruction in righteousness, that the man of God may be complete, thoroughly equipped for every good work.

2 TIMOTHY 3:16–17 NKJV

For we are his workmanship, created in Christ Jesus for good works, which God prepared beforehand, that we should walk in them.

EPHESIANS 2:10 ESV

Did you realize that God has prepared good works for you to do every day of your life? Because you believe in Him, He will lead you to carry out these works, following His special plan for your life.

Dear Lord, help me to know the things You have planned for me to do. I want to accomplish good works for Your glory. Amen.

Evening

Let us think of ways to motivate one another to acts of love and good works.

HEBREWS 10:24 NLT

Let all that you do be done in love.

1 CORINTHIANS 16:14 ESV

Read the Bible, God's guidebook. There you will learn what to believe, how to act, and how to speak with love. Soon you'll be ready to start putting into action all you've learned.

Heavenly Father, please fill me so full of Your love that it overflows into every single thing I do for others. Amen.

DAY 154

You're Equipped

Morning

In Christ you have been brought to fullness. He is the head over every power and authority.
COLOSSIANS 2:10 NIV

Now may the God of peace. . .equip you with everything good that you may do his will, working in us that which is pleasing in his sight, through Jesus Christ, to whom be glory forever and ever.
HEBREWS 13:20–21 ESV

Do you feel incomplete or inadequate, unable to carry out the tasks God has given you? You aren't, you know, if you tap into His Spirit. God equips you to do all things through Him.

Father, please rid my mind of thoughts of inadequacy. You have filled me with Your Spirit, and I can do all things You have called me to do. Amen.

Evening

"I delight to do your will, O my God; your law is within my heart."
PSALM 40:8 ESV

Let God transform you into a new person by changing the way you think. Then you will learn to know God's will for you, which is good and pleasing and perfect.
ROMANS 12:2 NLT

If you feel overwhelmed, make sure you haven't taken on tasks rightfully belonging to someone else. God does not overload your life with busyness. So be certain you're serving in the right place, doing work He planned for you.

Sovereign God, I need Your wisdom to balance all the good things I can get involved in for You. Please show me where I can serve You most effectively. Amen.

DAY 155

Vigilance

Morning

Since everything will be destroyed in this way, what kind of people ought you to be? You ought to live holy and godly lives.

2 PETER 3:11 NIV

So teach us to number our days that we may get a heart of wisdom.

PSALM 90:12 ESV

Knowing this world won't last forever, how should we act? We have no devil-may-care option in which we act as if eternity doesn't matter, because God calls us to live wholly for Him.

Sovereign God, I want to live my life wholly for You, wholly in light of eternity. Amen.

Evening

Live wisely among those who are not believers, and make the most of every opportunity.

COLOSSIANS 4:5 NLT

How do you know what your life will be like tomorrow? Your life is like the morning fog—it's here a little while, then it's gone. What you ought to say is, "If the Lord wants us to, we will live and do this or that."

JAMES 4:14–15 NLT

The world's destruction should not make us careless but rather vigilant to make the most of our time. In the end, all we do here will not be lost but will pass on into eternity.

Heavenly Father, help me to make the most of every moment You give me here on earth. May I be constantly pointing others to You. Amen.

DAY 156

In His Power

Morning

For my life is spent with sorrow, and my years with sighing; my strength fails because of my iniquity, and my bones waste away.

PSALM 31:10 ESV

I can do all things through Christ who strengthens me.

PHILIPPIANS 4:13 NKJV

Need strength? Turn to God for all you need. When your spiritual muscles feel feeble and all your efforts to do good seem to fall short, remember that we aren't called to live the Christian life on our own. Why take on life by yourself when He offers you His mighty power?

Almighty God, forgive me when I try to do everything on my own. You are here to strengthen me and to help me do Your will. I need You! Amen.

Evening

It is God who arms me with strength and keeps my way secure.

PSALM 18:32 NIV

He gives power to the weak and strength to the powerless.

ISAIAH 40:29 NLT

When Christ's Spirit works through us, the Christian life flows smoothly; in His power we accomplish His purposes. Today, is Christ bearing the burden, or are we? Only He has the strength we need in our lives.

Almighty God, I give up this burden to You. Thank You for wanting to carry it for me. I trust in Your power and love. Amen.

DAY 157

Tapping into Strength

Morning

God is our refuge
and strength, a very
present help in trouble.
PSALM 46:1 NKJV

Please, LORD, be kind to us! We
depend on you. Make us strong
each morning, and come to save
us when we are in trouble.
ISAIAH 33:2 CEV

When you rely on God's strength, what are you tapping into? Not some small pool of power that fails at a critical moment. The Christian's strength is mighty because that's what God is.

Almighty God, Your power
never fails and never runs out.
Thank You for Your endless,
awesome strength. Amen.

Evening

The LORD directs the
steps of the godly.
He delights in every
detail of their lives.
PSALM 37:23 NLT

Lift up your eyes and look to
the heavens: Who created all
these? He who brings out the
starry host one by one and
calls forth each of them by
name. Because of his great
power and mighty strength,
not one of them is missing.
ISAIAH 40:26 NIV

The one who created the universe doesn't have a short arm that can't reach down to your situation. Shining stars testify to His authority. Galaxies in space are ordered by His hand. Can He not order your life too?

Dear Father, You set the whole
universe into order and motion.
Forgive me for not letting You order
my life. I ask for Your help now. Amen.

DAY 158

Have Courage

Morning

Be on your guard;
stand firm in the faith;
be courageous; be strong.
1 CORINTHIANS 16:13 NIV

"God is my salvation; I will
trust, and will not be afraid;
for the LORD GOD *is my strength*
and my song, and he has
become my salvation."
ISAIAH 12:2 ESV

Being a Christian takes courage. As the world around us becomes increasingly hostile to God and our personal lives become tense because of our beliefs, we feel the challenge.

Father God, I will choose to trust in You and have courage even as the challenges of being a Christian in this world increase. Please help me to be brave because of Your power. Amen.

Evening

If God is for us,
who can be against us?
ROMANS 8:31 ESV

"He may have a great army,
but they are merely men. We
have the LORD *our God to help*
us and to fight our battles for
us!" Hezekiah's words greatly
encouraged the people.
2 CHRONICLES 32:8 NLT

We are not defenseless. Christians through the ages have faced opposition and triumphed. The Lord who supported them gives us strength too. Let us stand fast for Jesus, calling on His Spirit to strengthen our lives. Then we will be strong indeed.

Almighty God, please remind me every moment that I am never defenseless. You are always on my side helping me in any kind of battle. Amen.

DAY 159

Lift Them Up!

Morning

Welcome all the Lord's followers, even those whose faith is weak. Don't criticize them for having beliefs that are different from yours.

Romans 14:1 CEV

We who are strong ought to bear with the failings of the weak and not to please ourselves.

Romans 15:1 NIV

Likely God has made you strong in a particular area—perhaps by experience, as you have struggled to obey Him. Now how do you respond to others?

Gracious Lord, help me to come alongside those who have struggled in ways that I once struggled. You have brought me through the fight and made me strong; now please use me to help them the same way. Amen.

Evening

Be completely humble and gentle; be patient, bearing with one another in love.

Ephesians 4:2 NIV

The Father is a merciful God, who always gives us comfort. He comforts us when we are in trouble, so that we can share this same comfort with others in trouble.

2 Corinthians 1:3–4 CEV

Don't criticize those who have different experiences or different strengths or carp about the failings of new, weak Christians. Instead, use your God-given strength to lift others up. Come alongside and help. Then God's strength will have helped you both.

Merciful God, You have helped me in so many ways, and I want to comfort and encourage others as You have comforted and encouraged me. May they see Your love in me. Amen.

DAY 160

True Prosperity

Morning

"Do not turn from it. . .that you may prosper. . . . But you shall meditate in it [the Book of the Law] day and night."
JOSHUA 1:7–8 NKJV

And we know that for those who love God all things work together for good, for those who are called according to his purpose.
ROMANS 8:28 ESV

God promised success to Joshua if he would obey Him. That promise works for you too. But sometimes you may not feel that obeying God has brought you great prosperity. Just wait.

Everlasting God, I believe You will make me prosper according to the promises of Your Word. Please give me patience and peace as I wait for You. Amen.

Evening

A thief comes only to rob, kill, and destroy. I came so everyone would have life, and have it fully.
JOHN 10:10 CEV

"Blessed rather are those who hear the word of God and obey it."
LUKE 11:28 NIV

It may take time, the success may not take the form you expect, or you may not see the results until you reach heaven, but God will prosper those who do His will. He promised it, and His promises never fail.

Loving Father, abundant life is found only in You, here on earth and for eternity. True success is found in serving You! Amen.

DAY 161

Escape Hatch

Morning

No temptation has overtaken you except what is common to mankind. And God is faithful. . . . When you are tempted, he will also provide a way out so that you can endure it.
1 CORINTHIANS 10:13 NIV

For because he himself has suffered when tempted, he is able to help those who are being tempted.
HEBREWS 2:18 ESV

No matter how powerful it seems, you need not give in to temptation. God always provides you with an escape hatch.

Almighty God, Your power is always greater than the pull toward sin. Please strengthen me and show me the way out of sin's snare. Amen.

Evening

"Watch and pray that you may not enter into temptation. The spirit indeed is willing, but the flesh is weak."
MATTHEW 26:41 ESV

Submit yourselves therefore to God. Resist the devil, and he will flee from you.
JAMES 4:7 ESV

When temptation pulls at you, turn your eyes to Jesus. Replace that tempting object or activity with Him, and you will not fall.

Loving Savior, please fix my eyes on You when I feel the pull toward sin. I want to honor You, not grieve You. Amen.

DAY 162

God Is Greater

Morning

Each person is tempted when they are dragged away by their own evil desire and enticed.

JAMES 1:14 NIV

Let the Holy Spirit guide your lives. Then you won't be doing what your sinful nature craves. The sinful nature wants to do evil, which is just the opposite of what the Spirit wants.

GALATIANS 5:16–17 NLT

God does not draw us into temptation. He is holy, unable to tempt anyone into wrongdoing. The attraction to sin comes from within us; our evil desires lead us toward sin.

Holy God, I long to be more like You. Help my sinful desires to grow weaker and weaker as my desire for You grows ever stronger. Amen.

Evening

For you know that the testing of your faith produces steadfastness.

JAMES 1:3 ESV

God blesses those who patiently endure testing and temptation. Afterward they will receive the crown of life that God has promised to those who love him.

JAMES 1:12 NLT

When we face situations that encourage our own wickedness, they are not designed by God to make us fall. Instead, they provide opportunities to turn to Him and progressively turn away from iniquity. No evil within us is so great that God is not greater still.

Father God, every temptation I face is an opportunity for Your power to shine through. Sin will not prevail in my life because You are always greater! I choose You! Amen.

DAY 163

You Have Gifts!

Morning

Now to each one the manifestation of the Spirit is given for the common good.
1 CORINTHIANS 12:7 NIV

God has given each of you a gift from his great variety of spiritual gifts. Use them well to serve one another.
1 PETER 4:10 NLT

Did you know that you are a gifted person? God gives each of us spiritual gifts designed to help both us and others—wisdom, knowledge, faith, healing, to name just a few.

Heavenly Father, thank You for the way You've gifted me for Your service. Amen.

Evening

In his grace, God has given us different gifts for doing certain things well.
ROMANS 12:6 NLT

He makes the whole body fit together perfectly. As each part does its own special work, it helps the other parts grow, so that the whole body is healthy and growing and full of love.
EPHESIANS 4:16 NLT

As you grow spiritually, you begin to unwrap new spiritual gifts from God. Over time, you may be surprised and blessed by all the ways He has provided for you. Feeling unimportant? Remind yourself that you're gifted by God!

Dear Lord, please give me wisdom and direction for how best to use my spiritual gifts to share Your love and further Your kingdom. Amen.

DAY 164

Grace Is a Gift

Morning

But unto every one of us is given grace according to the measure of the gift of Christ.

EPHESIANS 4:7 KJV

For by grace you have been saved through faith. And this is not your own doing; it is the gift of God, not a result of works, so that no one may boast.

EPHESIANS 2:8–9 ESV

We don't usually think of grace as a spiritual gift. But consider: It's the basis for all the gifts God gives us. Without His gracious forgiveness, we'd have nothing spiritually.

Loving Savior, Your grace is what has saved me from my sin; it's the greatest gift I've ever been given. I thank You and praise You! Amen.

Evening

But by the grace of God I am what I am, and his grace toward me was not in vain.

1 CORINTHIANS 15:10 ESV

For from his fullness we have all received, grace upon grace.

JOHN 1:16 ESV

Whether we receive a large measure of grace or a smaller one, it is Jesus' perfect gift just for us. Let's appreciate what it cost Him and walk in His grace today.

Dear Savior, You've given me indescribable grace. Please help me to extend grace to others, following Your loving example. Amen.

DAY 165

God's Protection

Morning

The Lord knows how to deliver the godly out of temptations and to reserve the unjust under punishment for the day of judgment.

2 PETER 2:9 NKJV

The Lord will rescue me from every evil deed and bring me safely into his heavenly kingdom. To him be the glory forever and ever.

2 TIMOTHY 4:18 ESV

Feeling surrounded by temptations? God hasn't forgotten you. He knows how to protect His children from harm and will impart His wisdom to you.

Dear Father, please rescue me from the sin and temptations all around me. I want no part of them; I only want You! Amen.

Evening

Don't do as the wicked do, and don't follow the path of evildoers. Don't even think about it; don't go that way. Turn away and keep moving.

PROVERBS 4:14–15 NLT

Be on your guard and stay awake. Your enemy, the devil, is like a roaring lion, sneaking around to find someone to attack. But you must resist the devil and stay strong in your faith.

1 PETER 5:8–9 CEV

Maybe you need to avoid certain places that could lead you into sin—that may mean taking action to find a new job or new friends. When God is trying to protect you, don't resist. Sin is never better than knowing Him.

Loving Savior, help me to let go of those things and relationships from my past that might harm my relationship with You and tempt me to sin. Amen.

DAY 166

Giving Thanks Always

Morning

Giving thanks always and for everything to God the Father in the name of our Lord Jesus Christ.

EPHESIANS 5:20 ESV

Give thanks to the God of gods. His love endures forever.

PSALM 136:2 NIV

Having trouble being thankful? Read Psalm 136. You'll be reminded of the wonders of God's power and His enduring love. The God who protected Israel watches over you too.

Dear Father, please forgive me when I find it hard to be thankful. Remind me of Your love, Your wonders, Your power, and Your many blessings in my life. Amen.

Evening

Praise the LORD! Oh give thanks to the LORD, for he is good, for his steadfast love endures forever!

PSALM 106:1 ESV

Enter his gates with thanksgiving, and his courts with praise! Give thanks to him; bless his name!

PSALM 100:4 ESV

Even when there may not be a lot in your life to rejoice about, you can always delight in the Lord. Give thanks to God. He has not forgotten you—His love endures forever.

Almighty God, I choose to praise You even when I am hurting or confused or in need. You are always good and worthy of honor and glory. Amen.

DAY 167

Eternal Appreciation

Morning

O Lord my God, I will give thanks to you forever!
Psalm 30:12 ESV

"Blessing and glory and wisdom and thanksgiving and honor and power and might be to our God forever and ever! Amen."
Revelation 7:12 ESV

Even in eternity, you will be thanking God. Our appreciation of God's mercy never stops. Without His grace, we would be forever separated from Him, lost in the cares of sin and a hellish existence.

Holy God, I want to thank You forever for who You are and how You have saved me and blessed me. Amen.

Evening

Give thanks to the Lord, for He is good; for His mercy is everlasting.
Psalm 118:1 NASB

I will sing of the steadfast love of the Lord, forever; with my mouth I will make known your faithfulness to all generations.
Psalm 89:1 ESV

Could you thank Jesus too much? Or could you never find enough words to show Him your love? Maybe it's time to get started on your eternal appreciation of your Lord.

Father God, there aren't enough words or prayers or praise songs to ever fully thank You, so I will just continue every day to say how grateful I am for You! Amen.

DAY 168

Appreciation Overflow

Morning

Continue to live your lives in [Jesus], rooted and built up in him, strengthened in the faith as you were taught, and overflowing with thankfulness.
COLOSSIANS 2:6–7 NIV

It is good to give thanks to the LORD, to sing praises to your name, O Most High.
PSALM 92:1 ESV

Strong Christians are thankful Christians. As we realize all Jesus has sacrificed for us and face up to our inability to live the Christian life on our own, we remember to praise our Savior for His grace.

Lord Jesus, Your sacrifice for me is my greatest blessing and treasure. I am forever grateful that You died and rose again for me. Amen.

Evening

You prepare a table before me in the presence of my enemies. You anoint my head with oil; my cup overflows. Surely your goodness and love will follow me all the days of my life, and I will dwell in the house of the LORD forever.
PSALM 23:5–6 NIV

LORD, you alone are my inheritance, my cup of blessing. You guard all that is mine.
PSALM 16:5 NLT

Today we can be rooted in Jesus, strong in our faith, and thankful to the one who has given us countless blessings. Let's overflow with appreciation!

Dear Lord, I want to be rooted in You, growing stronger every day in faith and gratitude for Your salvation and all of Your precious promises. Amen.

DAY 169

Pain and Trials

Morning

For our light and momentary troubles are achieving for us an eternal glory that far outweighs them all.

2 CORINTHIANS 4:17 NIV

Therefore let those who suffer according to God's will entrust their souls to a faithful Creator while doing good.

1 PETER 4:19 ESV

What trouble could you face on earth that will not seem small in heaven? No pain from this life will impede us there. Blessing for faithful service to God will replace each heartache that discourages us today.

Father God, please strengthen me in Your promise that no matter what troubles we have on earth, You will make all things right for eternity in heaven. Amen.

Evening

The genuineness of your faith, being much more precious than gold that perishes, though it is tested by fire, may be found to praise, honor, and glory at the revelation of Jesus Christ.

1 PETER 1:7 NKJV

God will bless you, if you don't give up when your faith is being tested. He will reward you with a glorious life, just as he rewards everyone who loves him.

JAMES 1:12 CEV

Trials have a purpose in our lives. As a smith heats up gold to purify it, God heats up our lives to make spiritual impurities rise to the surface. If we cooperate with Him, sin is skimmed off our lives, purifying our faith.

Holy Father, help me welcome the trials and tests of my life as opportunities to draw closer to You. Help me to endure and succeed through them because of Your power. Amen.

DAY 170

Hope in God Alone

Morning

"It is the LORD who goes before you. He will be with you; he will not leave you or forsake you. Do not fear or be dismayed."
DEUTERONOMY 31:8 ESV

Because of the LORD's great love we are not consumed, for his compassions never fail.
LAMENTATIONS 3:22 NIV

Despite Jeremiah's deep troubles as he sorrowed over Judah's exile, hope remained in his heart. Though he and his nation faced terrible trials, the prophet understood that God would still uphold them.

Loving Father, I trust that You will never fail me. You are always holding me and giving me hope. Amen.

Evening

"I am with you always, to the end of the age."
MATTHEW 28:20 ESV

Our LORD, we belong to you. We tell you what worries us, and you won't let us fall.
PSALM 55:22 CEV

God's compassion never fails His hurting people. No matter how we struggle, we have hope. God alone comforts our hearts as we stumble along a rocky trail.

Father, You alone are my one true source of compassion. Thank You for knowing and relating to my heartaches. Amen.

DAY 171

His Concern

Morning

You keep track of all my sorrows. You have collected all my tears in your bottle. You have recorded each one in your book.

PSALM 56:8 NLT

The righteous cry out, and the LORD hears, and delivers them out of all their troubles.

PSALM 34:17 NKJV

As God's child, you have His ear 24-7, if only you will pray. Every need, trouble, or praise is His concern. And not only will He hear about your trials; He will deliver you from them.

Oh dear Father, knowing You hear my every cry and collect all my tears fills me with such gratitude. I long to be near You, Lord. Please draw me close and deliver me from my troubles. Amen.

Evening

The LORD is close to the brokenhearted; he rescues those whose spirits are crushed.

PSALM 34:18 NLT

The righteous person faces many troubles, but the LORD comes to the rescue each time. For the LORD protects the bones of the righteous; not one of them is broken!

PSALM 34:19–20 NLT

Feel discouraged in your troubles? You need not stay that way. Just spend time with Jesus. His help is on the way.

Father, I feel so discouraged. I need You desperately right now. Please hold me tight and help me to trust You and Your promises more. Amen.

DAY 172

Wisdom in God

Morning

Wisdom is the principal thing; therefore get wisdom: and with all thy getting get understanding.
PROVERBS 4:7 KJV

If any of you lacks wisdom, you should ask God, who gives generously to all without finding fault, and it will be given to you.
JAMES 1:5 NIV

Have you ever thought of yourself as wise? The Bible says you can be. You don't need a lot of education or a certain IQ. Real wisdom is found in God.

Almighty God, I'm amazed and grateful that I can ask for and receive Your awesome wisdom. I believe You give it generously. Please fill me to overflowing with it, that I might live a life that honors You. Amen.

Evening

The wisdom from above is first of all pure. It is also peace loving, gentle at all times, and willing to yield to others. It is full of mercy and the fruit of good deeds. It shows no favoritism and is always sincere.
JAMES 3:17 NLT

Look carefully then how you walk, not as unwise but as wise, making the best use of the time, because the days are evil. Therefore do not be foolish, but understand what the will of the Lord is.
EPHESIANS 5:15–17 ESV

Obey your Lord's commandments and make knowing Him well your first priority. Seek after wisdom, and you will find it in Him. As you daily search for truth in God's Word, your understanding will grow.

Dear Lord, I choose to put You first. I want to obey Your Word, be filled with Your wisdom, and seek You in all I do. Amen.

DAY 173

Wise Humility

Morning

Woe unto them that are wise in their own eyes, and prudent in their own sight!
ISAIAH 5:21 KJV

The way of fools seems right to them, but the wise listen to advice.
PROVERBS 12:15 NIV

Wisdom without humility isn't wisdom at all. When we feel astute under our own power, we are actually in big trouble and heading into foolishness!

Almighty God, Your wisdom and instruction are far, far better than anything I can know on my own. May I humbly listen to and learn from Your Spirit and Your Word and others who are following You. Amen.

Evening

Trust in the Lord with all your heart; do not depend on your own understanding. Seek his will in all you do, and he will show you which path to take.
PROVERBS 3:5–6 NLT

Wisdom's instruction is to fear the Lord, and humility comes before honor.
PROVERBS 15:33 NIV

The truly wise person recognizes that all wisdom comes from God, not frail humans. As we tap into His mind and connect with His insight, we are wise indeed. No one is wiser than our Lord.

Father God, oh how I need Your wisdom to journey well through this life. I want to be connected to You every moment of every day. Amen.

DAY 174

Wise Words

Morning

She speaks with wisdom,
and faithful instruction
is on her tongue.
Proverbs 31:26 NIV

The words of the reckless pierce
like swords, but the tongue
of the wise brings healing.
Proverbs 12:18 NIV

The virtuous woman speaks with kindly wisdom. Hers is no sharp tongue that destroys relationships. As we seek to do God's will, truthful yet caring speech must be ours. Wise words heal hurting hearts.

Dear Lord, I need help choosing what I say. Please give me wisdom with every word I speak. Amen.

Evening

Gracious words are like a
honeycomb, sweetness to the
soul and health to the body.
Proverbs 16:24 ESV

May the words of my mouth
and the meditation of my heart
be pleasing to you, O Lord,
my rock and my redeemer.
Psalm 19:14 NLT

If we have trouble knowing what words will bring God's healing, we need only ask Him to let His Spirit bring wisdom and kindness to our mouths and tongues. When we speak as His Spirit directs, we are wise indeed.

Dear Lord, please give me Your kindness, love, and wisdom every time I open my mouth. May my words bring sweetness and health to those in my life. Amen.

DAY 175

Shine On

Morning

"You are the light of the world. A city set on a hill cannot be hidden."
MATTHEW 5:14 ESV

"In the same way, let your light shine before others, so that they may see your good works and give glory to your Father who is in heaven."
MATTHEW 5:16 ESV

God intends for you to be a light that is set where the world can see it clearly, not a flame hidden behind closed doors with curtains drawn. Being a light isn't easy—people see everything you do, and they don't always like it.

Father, please forgive me when I hide Your light that is within me. I know it won't always be easy, but I want to shine for You. You are the one true Savior, and I want everyone to know about You! Amen.

Evening

Don't be ashamed to speak for our Lord. And don't be ashamed of me, just because I am in jail for serving him. Use the power that comes from God and join with me in suffering for telling the good news.
2 TIMOTHY 1:8 CEV

I will tell everyone about your righteousness. All day long I will proclaim your saving power, though I am not skilled with words.
PSALM 71:15 NLT

Don't let the critics stop you. Your works were ordained to glorify God, not make people comfortable. Knowing that, are you ready to shine?

Almighty God, I want to shine for You. Please fill me with Your light and love, and let me help others find their way to You. Amen.

DAY 176

God's Compassionate Salvation

Morning

Do not repay anyone evil for evil. Be careful to do what is right in the eyes of everyone.
ROMANS 12:17 NIV

Do all that you can to live in peace with everyone. Dear friends, never take revenge. Leave that to the righteous anger of God.
ROMANS 12:18–19 NLT

Tit-for-tat retribution for evil is not a principle of our compassionate God. We know this, if we've received His undeserved salvation. With such a gift, God has opened our hearts to treating our enemies as He has treated us.

Loving Savior, I certainly did not deserve Your grace that has covered my sins, and yet You lavished it on me. Please remind me of Your compassion as I seek to forgive and extend grace to those who have wronged me. Amen.

Evening

Love is patient, love is kind. It does not envy, it does not boast, it is not proud. It does not dishonor others, it is not self-seeking, it is not easily angered, it keeps no record of wrongs.
1 CORINTHIANS 13:4–5 NIV

He has removed our sins as far from us as the east is from the west. The LORD is like a father to his children, tender and compassionate to those who fear him.
PSALM 103:12–13 NLT

If we refuse to count up each wrong and repay it with harshness, lost souls may understand God's compassionate salvation. By doing right, even when we receive wrong in return, we become powerful witnesses.

Dear Lord, You never keep score of all my sins, and I'm so grateful because the number would be astronomical. Help me to be like You and let go of sins that have been done against me. Amen.

DAY 177

Inheritors of the Earth

Morning

Who is wise and understanding among you? By his good conduct let him show his works in the meekness of wisdom.

JAMES 3:13 ESV

Encourage those who are timid. Take tender care of those who are weak. Be patient with everyone.

1 THESSALONIANS 5:14 NLT

In the workplace, meekness isn't often seen as a positive thing. "Looking out for number one" is the theory of many who tout assertiveness as the way to get the most out of life. But God doesn't agree.

Dear God, it's easy to be selfish and want to get ahead of others. Help me to put others before myself, even in the workplace. Amen.

Evening

But the meek shall inherit the land and delight themselves in abundant peace.

PSALM 37:11 ESV

"Blessed are the meek, for they will inherit the earth."

MATTHEW 5:5 NIV

Ultimately, those who follow God faithfully in front of a watching world won't be the "nice guys" who "finish last" but rather the inheritors of this earth. What plot of earth could God have mapped out for you?

Father God, I believe the rewards You have in heaven for following Your Word are so much more than I can dream of. It's an honor to serve You here on earth, Lord, knowing I will spend eternity in paradise with You! Amen.

DAY 178

Mind Your Business

Morning

Make it your ambition to lead a quiet life: You should mind your own business and work with your hands.

1 THESSALONIANS 4:11 NIV

Let the thief no longer steal, but rather let him labor, doing honest work with his own hands, so that he may have something to share with anyone in need.

EPHESIANS 4:28 ESV

Whether we work at a computer or on a factory production line, those of us who work with our hands shouldn't feel unimportant. Manual labor is serious business in God's sight.

Dear Lord, help me to realize that no task is too small or insignificant not to do my best at it as a form of praise and respect for You. Amen.

Evening

Commit your work to the LORD, *and your plans will be established.*

PROVERBS 16:3 ESV

Yet we hear that some of you are living idle lives, refusing to work and meddling in other people's business. We command such people and urge them in the name of the Lord Jesus Christ to settle down and work to earn their own living. As for the rest of you, dear brothers and sisters, never get tired of doing good.

2 THESSALONIANS 3:11–13 NLT

Christians who quietly, faithfully go about their business day by day make an important contribution to this world, bearing God's message to a wide range of people. What a testimony our lives become when we live out God's Word.

Father, please remind me that any task I do, as I do it to the best of my ability for Your glory, is important work for Your kingdom. Amen.

DAY 179

Treasures in Heaven

Morning

Be not afraid when a man becomes rich, when the glory of his house increases. For when he dies he will carry nothing away; his glory will not go down after him.

PSALM 49:16–17 ESV

"One's life does not consist in the abundance of his possessions."

LUKE 12:15 ESV

Luke 12:15 is the Bible's way of saying, "You can't take it with you." When life ends, the only treasures that remain are the works we have done for Jesus.

Dear Father, help me to hold my material possessions loosely and focus on the good things You want me to accomplish for Your kingdom. Amen.

Evening

Don't store up treasures on earth! Moths and rust can destroy them, and thieves can break in and steal them. Instead, store up your treasures in heaven, where moths and rust cannot destroy them, and thieves cannot break in and steal them. Your heart will always be where your treasure is.

MATTHEW 6:19–21 CEV

"Provide yourselves with moneybags that do not grow old, with a treasure in the heavens that does not fail, where no thief approaches and no moth destroys."

LUKE 12:33 ESV

Money and fame cling to earth, soon to be forgotten. So when unbelievers seem to get all the goodies, just remember that the treasures we send ahead to heaven are greater than any temporary gain.

Father God, please decrease my desire for the things of this world and increase my desire for the things of heaven. Amen.

DAY 180

God's Favor

Morning

May the favor of the
Lord our God rest on us;
establish the work of
our hands for us.
PSALM 90:17 NIV

"Don't do your good deeds
publicly, to be admired by others,
for you will lose the reward
from your Father in heaven."
MATTHEW 6:1 NLT

Want your work to be effective? Don't make sure the boss knows every good thing you do. Instead, seek God's favor, and He will see to it that your work really gets the job done.

Father, help me to be humble about my good works. You are always watching, and I seek Your favor above all else. Amen.

Evening

So, whether you eat or
drink, or whatever you do,
do all to the glory of God.
1 CORINTHIANS 10:31 ESV

Whatever you do, work heartily,
as for the Lord and not for men.
COLOSSIANS 3:23 ESV

Whether you're caring for a child, arguing a legal case, or waiting on a customer, our Lord makes you productive for Him as you serve others in His name.

Dear Lord, what an honor it is to serve You in any and every task I undertake. Amen.

DAY 181

Belong to Jesus

Morning

*"If the world hates you,
know that it has hated me
before it hated you."*
JOHN 15:18 ESV

*"If you belonged to the world,
it would love you as its own.
As it is, you do not belong to
the world, but I have chosen
you out of the world. That is
why the world hates you."*
JOHN 15:19 NIV

Don't expect the world to love you for loving Jesus. Because He doesn't accept its evil, and neither do you, the world is at enmity with both of you. That's not such a bad thing.

Almighty God, please strengthen me in a world that is often hostile to You and all who love You. You are all-powerful, and I trust You! Amen.

Evening

*Do not love the world
or the things in the world.
If anyone loves the world,
the love of the Father
is not in him.*
1 JOHN 2:15 ESV

*Don't you realize that friendship
with the world makes you
an enemy of God? I say it
again: If you want to be a
friend of the world, you make
yourself an enemy of God.*
JAMES 4:4 NLT

To whom would you rather belong—Jesus, who holds eternity's joys in His hands, or the world, which offers so much sin and pain?

Dear Jesus, always and forever I'd rather belong to You! Thank You for saving me from this sinful, dying world and giving me eternal life and the hope of heaven. Amen.

DAY 182

Kingdom-Purposed Friendship

Morning

"I tell you, use worldly wealth to gain friends for yourselves, so that when it is gone, you will be welcomed into eternal dwellings."

LUKE 16:9 NIV

Tell them to use their money to do good. They should be rich in good works and generous to those in need, always being ready to share with others.

1 TIMOTHY 6:18 NLT

There is a good way to use the things of the world, and Jesus describes it here. God gives us wealth so that we might share it with others to further His kingdom.

Father God, help me to remember that everything I have is ultimately from You. I want to share it with others as a way to show love and point others to You. Amen.

Evening

"For I was hungry and you gave me something to eat, I was thirsty and you gave me something to drink, I was a stranger and you invited me in."

MATTHEW 25:35 NIV

"The King will reply, 'Truly I tell you, whatever you did for one of the least of these brothers and sisters of mine, you did for me.'"

MATTHEW 25:40 NIV

Though we may not have more than a pot of soup and some bread to offer, those simple things can be the start of a kingdom-purposed friendship. What do you have that God could use in this way?

Dear Father, please loosen my hold on all of my possessions, both big and small. I want to be willing to give anything I can to anyone in need, according to Your will. Amen.

DAY 183

Ability

Morning

There are different kinds of spiritual gifts, but the same Spirit is the source of them all.
1 CORINTHIANS 12:4 NLT

God works in different ways, but it is the same God who does the work in all of us.
1 CORINTHIANS 12:6 NLT

We each have many abilities, and they aren't necessarily related to how well we performed in school or what level of proficiency we reached in music or sports. If that were the case, many of us would have to declare ourselves not able at all!

Father God, please show me the specific gifts and abilities You've given me. I want to have confidence in them and use them to love others and honor You! Amen.

Evening

As each has received a gift, use it to serve one another, as good stewards of God's varied grace.
1 PETER 4:10 ESV

Having gifts that differ according to the grace given to us, let us use them.
ROMANS 12:6 ESV

God has granted everyone the gift of special abilities, and He intends for each of us to develop, share, and enjoy them. The more you use your skills and talents, the more you grow in appreciation for the great kindness God has shown you, and the more willing you become to share your gifts with others.

Dear Lord, thank You for my unique gifts. Please give me more and more opportunities to use them in praise to You! Amen.

DAY 184

Empowered for Kindness

Morning

Understand this, my dear brothers and sisters: You must all be quick to listen, slow to speak, and slow to get angry. Human anger does not produce the righteousness God desires.

JAMES 1:19–20 NLT

When God our Savior revealed his kindness and love, he saved us, not because of the righteous things we had done, but because of his mercy.

TITUS 3:4–5 NLT

When emotions threaten your ability to respond kindly to others, pause and let God's unfailing kindness embrace your heart and mind.

Father God, help me to take the breather I need when I feel stress getting the best of me. I want kindness to be my first response to any situation, not an emotional outburst. Amen.

Evening

I can do everything through Christ, who gives me strength.

PHILIPPIANS 4:13 NLT

Stop being bitter and angry and mad at others. Don't yell at one another or curse each other or ever be rude. Instead, be kind and merciful, and forgive others, just as God forgave you because of Christ.

EPHESIANS 4:31–32 CEV

God restores your peace, enabling you to curb negative feelings and thwart unproductive emotions. The comfort God sends strengthens your confidence and increases your ability to pour out His kindness on others.

Father, with Your strength I can act and react with kindness even when I don't feel like it. Please give me Your love for others. Amen.

DAY 185

The Picture of Kindness

Morning

Let us not love with words or speech but with actions and in truth.
1 JOHN 3:18 NIV

Be sincere in your love for others.
ROMANS 12:9 CEV

The adage "A picture is worth a thousand words" is certainly true as it pertains to kindness. All the kind, well-intentioned words in the world are meaningless unless they're backed up with observable kind actions.

Father, help my words and attitudes about treating others kindly match up with what I actually do to treat others kindly. Amen.

Evening

Suppose someone disagrees and says, "It is possible to have faith without doing kind deeds." I would answer, "Prove that you have faith without doing kind deeds, and I will prove that I have faith by doing them."
JAMES 2:18 CEV

For God is working in you, giving you the desire and the power to do what pleases him.
PHILIPPIANS 2:13 NLT

Kind words can trip easily off the tongue, but kind actions come at the cost of time, effort, and attention to the needs of others. It is God's action in your life that enables you not simply to speak kindly but to act kindly. With His Spirit as your counselor and guide, you are the picture of kindness!

Father God, please give me the motivation and stamina to do the good things and kind deeds I know You want me to do. Amen.

DAY 186

God's Heart and Hands

Morning

*Remember those who
are suffering as if you were
suffering with them.*
HEBREWS 13:3 NCV

*All praise to God, the Father
of our Lord Jesus Christ. God
is our merciful Father and
the source of all comfort.*
2 CORINTHIANS 1:3 NLT

"It's lonely at the top," say some high-level executives, diplomats, and policymakers. An equally lonely place, however, is at the opposite end of society.

*Dear Lord, please show me how
best to serve others and to share
Your love and compassion with
every hurting and lonely person
You bring across my path. Amen.*

Evening

*"When you pass through
the waters, I will be with you;
and through the rivers,
they shall not overwhelm you;
when you walk through fire you
shall not be burned, and the
flame shall not consume you."*
ISAIAH 43:2 ESV

*He comforts us in all our troubles
so that we can comfort others.
When they are troubled, we will
be able to give them the same
comfort God has given us.*
2 CORINTHIANS 1:4 NLT

Those who live in poverty-stricken areas, who have lost their source of income, who are bound by adversity, addiction, or mental illness—all these people may feel alone and forgotten, and they are in need of your compassion and kindness. Allow God to use your heart and your hands to ease the suffering of others.

*Loving Father, use my hands
and feet to show loving-kindness
toward others. I want to do Your
will in caring for others. Amen.*

DAY 187

The Right Response

Morning

We know that all things work together for good to those who love God.

ROMANS 8:28 NKJV

We are pressed on every side by troubles, but we are not crushed. We are perplexed, but not driven to despair. We are hunted down, but never abandoned by God.

2 CORINTHIANS 4:8–9 NLT

When adversity enters your life, you have every reason to feel that God isn't being very kind! You ask yourself why you should have to confront this issue or handle this problem. Yet don't forget that God's wisdom reaches far beyond human understanding.

Almighty God, I am suffering, but I trust in Your wisdom and presence. I know You are walking with me through this trial and will deliver me. Amen.

Evening

Give all your worries and cares to God, for he cares about you.

1 PETER 5:7 NLT

And after you have suffered a little while, the God of all grace, who has called you to his eternal glory in Christ, will himself restore, confirm, strengthen, and establish you.

1 PETER 5:10 ESV

If you are facing a difficult challenge right now, put your burden in God's care. Rely on Him to turn whatever you're going through to your ultimate advantage. Let Him shower you with His comfort, peace, and hope.

Loving God, I put this challenge into Your care. I know You will work out this situation for good in Your perfect timing. Amen.

DAY 188

Good Advice

Morning

Everyone enjoys a fitting reply; it is wonderful to say the right thing at the right time!
PROVERBS 15:23 NLT

Let everything you say be good and helpful, so that your words will be an encouragement to those who hear them.
EPHESIANS 4:29 NLT

When people ask for your advice, you're given both a privilege and a burden. A privilege because they think highly of your experience and perspective and believe you can point them in the right direction. But also a burden, because what you say may influence their decisions and actions. Be sure to choose your words carefully.

Holy Father, I need Your wisdom when others ask for my advice. Please let my words help guide them according to Your holy Word. Amen.

Evening

Where there is no guidance, a people falls, but in an abundance of counselors there is safety.
PROVERBS 11:14 ESV

Listen to advice and accept instruction, that you may gain wisdom in the future.
PROVERBS 19:20 ESV

Good advice kindly given by mature Christians is one of the ways God guides His people when they're at a crossroads in life. Just as you have received the blessing of good advice, so your good advice is a blessing to others.

Heavenly Father, thank You for the godly people You have placed in my life to help guide me toward You. Please help me do the same for others. Amen.

DAY 189

A Good Exchange

Morning

If you are angry,
you cannot do any of the
good things God wants done.
JAMES 1:20 CEV

Stop being angry! Turn from
your rage! Do not lose your
temper—it only leads to harm.
PSALM 37:8 NLT

How quickly anger can get out of control! What might start out as a natural reaction to an offense can quickly flare into a craving for revenge, which leads to a never-ending cycle of punishing words and violent actions. Clearly, this isn't the way God wants you to handle angry feelings.

Dear Lord, please forgive me for my out-of-control anger. I can rein it in and tame it only with Your help. Oh, how I need You! Amen.

Evening

Whoever is slow to anger
is better than the mighty.
PROVERBS 16:32 ESV

Let all bitterness and wrath
and anger and clamor and
slander be put away from you,
along with all malice. Be kind
to one another, tenderhearted,
forgiving one another,
as God in Christ forgave you.
EPHESIANS 4:31–32 ESV

God asks you to exchange anger for self-control, retaliation for forgiveness, and cruelty for kindness. God's Spirit at work in your heart empowers you to make these exchanges.

Loving God, help me to put away the anger and bitterness that threaten to get the best of me at times. I want to be full of Your self-control, forgiveness, and kindness. Amen.

DAY 190

Three Steps to Kindness

Morning

Don't befriend angry people or associate with hot-tempered people, or you will learn to be like them.
PROVERBS 22:24–25 NLT

A hot-tempered man stirs up strife, but he who is slow to anger quiets contention.
PROVERBS 15:18 ESV

Anger is contagious. If someone has ever screamed at you in rage, you know how difficult it is to remain calm, much less respond with kindness and understanding. While it's not always possible to avoid people given to outbursts of anger, you can protect yourself.

Dear Lord, help me not to facilitate anger. Please protect me from it and help me to defuse it. Amen.

Evening

Short-tempered people do foolish things, and schemers are hated.
PROVERBS 14:17 NLT

If a wise man has an argument with a fool, the fool only rages and laughs, and there is no quiet.
PROVERBS 29:9 ESV

When someone confronts you in anger, first, listen without commenting or contradicting. Second, respond in a gentle and kind voice, setting the tone for a productive conversation. Third, and most important, pray for them as you would for any hurting soul in need of God's comfort and love.

Father, please give me wisdom and patience to deal with other people's anger and my own in healthy ways. Amen.

DAY 191

The Attitude of Jesus

Morning

May the God who gives endurance and encouragement give you the same attitude of mind toward each other that Christ Jesus had.

ROMANS 15:5 NIV

In your relationships with one another, have the same mindset as Christ Jesus.

PHILIPPIANS 2:5 NIV

You don't have to delve far into the biblical account of Jesus' earthly ministry to discover how He treated people. Personifying God's attitude, Jesus extended incomparable kindness and compassion to those He encountered.

Jesus, Your example of love and relationship with others is incomparable, and I want to be more and more like You. Amen.

Evening

Beloved, if God so loved us, we also ought to love one another.

1 JOHN 4:11 ESV

"This is my commandment, that you love one another as I have loved you."

JOHN 15:12 ESV

Jesus saw people not as a means to get what He wanted, nor as faceless beings in a crowd, but as individuals, each created in the image of God. Through Him, your loving attitude toward others is a bright reflection of His loving attitude toward you.

Dear Lord, thank You for Your matchless, unconditional love for me and all people. Amen.

DAY 192

Unchanging Style

Morning

Charm is deceptive,
and beauty does not last;
but a woman who fears the
Lord will be greatly praised.
PROVERBS 31:30 NLT

"For man looks at the outward
appearance, but the Lord
looks at the heart."
1 SAMUEL 16:7 NKJV

If you enjoy paging through fashion magazines, you might notice that the standard of beauty changes constantly. What's "in" today is "out" tomorrow! Mercifully, God's standard of beauty has not changed since time began, nor will it ever change.

Dear Father, thank You that Your concern is for the hearts and souls of people. Thank You that I am beautiful in Your eyes. Amen.

Evening

Let your adorning be
the hidden person of the
heart with the imperishable
beauty of a gentle and
quiet spirit, which in God's
sight is very precious.
1 PETER 3:4 ESV

I praise you, for I am fearfully
and wonderfully made.
Wonderful are your works;
my soul knows it very well.
PSALM 139:14 ESV

Graciousness, kindness, generosity, and gentleness continue to please our Lord. A heart filled with patience, love, and joy never fails to receive His favor. The best thing of all? You don't need to buy a thing. The beauty that God gives is yours for the asking!

Dear Jesus, please adorn me with love, joy, peace, patience, kindness, goodness, faithfulness, gentleness, and self-control—these are what make a person truly, deeply beautiful. Amen.

DAY 193

A Test of Faith

Morning

Dear friends, don't be surprised or shocked that you are going through testing that is like walking through fire.
1 PETER 4:12 CEV

However, if you suffer as a Christian, do not be ashamed, but praise God that you bear that name.
1 PETER 4:16 NIV

Every believer faces situations that challenge their faith. Mostly they're little more than dismissive remarks. But sometimes questions about religion or spirituality make you question what you believe and why.

Dear Father, please give me wisdom when my faith in You is challenged. Amen.

Evening

Blessed is the man who remains steadfast under trial, for when he has stood the test he will receive the crown of life, which God has promised to those who love him.
JAMES 1:12 ESV

But if you suffer for doing good and you endure it, this is commendable before God. To this you were called, because Christ suffered for you, leaving you an example, that you should follow in his steps.
1 PETER 2:20–21 NIV

For some of God's people, their faith pits them against entrenched authority and strict social norms. Perhaps you don't face such extreme conditions, but the tests you do confront still pose challenges to your faith. Don't be surprised. Such challenges come with the territory.

Father God, please keep me steadfast and firmly planted in You and Your Word, no matter what test I am going through. Amen.

DAY 194

Take a Challenge

Morning

Don't copy the behavior and customs of this world, but let God transform you into a new person by changing the way you think.
ROMANS 12:2 NLT

You have spent enough time in the past doing what pagans choose to do. . . . They are surprised that you do not join them in their reckless, wild living, and they heap abuse on you. But they will have to give account.
1 PETER 4:3–5 NIV

Living according to God's commandments is certainly a challenge! The views of others—their actions, values, and ambitions—can clash with those God's Spirit puts in your heart. But as the world challenges you, why not challenge the world?

Father, I need Your strength to be up to the challenge of living according to Your Word. Help me to face the world head-on with Your light and love! Amen.

Evening

Do your best to present yourself to God as one approved, a worker who has no need to be ashamed, rightly handling the word of truth.
2 TIMOTHY 2:15 ESV

"Love your enemies, do good to those who hate you, bless those who curse you, pray for those who mistreat you."
LUKE 6:27–28 NIV

Though you might not receive kindness or consideration for acting according to God's standards, respond with kindness and consideration to those who challenge your beliefs and values.

Father, please give me the self-control, patience, and love needed to respond respectfully and gently to those who challenge me because of my love for You and Your Word. Amen.

DAY 195

A New Season

Morning

To everything there
is a season, a time for every
purpose under heaven.
ECCLESIASTES 3:1 NKJV

You number my wanderings;
put my tears into Your bottle;
are they not in Your book?
PSALM 56:8 NKJV

An unwelcome and bitter life change can happen instantly. Confusion and anger are natural responses, yet they can never bring back a season once it has passed.

Father God, I'll be honest that I don't like this bitter life change that has happened, and I don't understand why You allowed it. Please help me to trust in Your love and promises. Amen.

Evening

The LORD is near to the
brokenhearted and saves
the crushed in spirit.
PSALM 34:18 ESV

The LORD is my shepherd, I lack nothing. He makes me lie down in green pastures, he leads me beside quiet waters, he refreshes my soul. He guides me along the right paths for his name's sake. Even though I walk through the darkest valley, I will fear no evil, for you are with me; your rod and your staff, they comfort me.
PSALM 23:1–4 NIV

If change has left you reeling, be kind to yourself. Give yourself time to embrace your new reality with the courage your kind and compassionate God offers to you.

Father, please be patient with me, as I know You are. I'm tempted to blame You for my hurt, but I know that's not right. Please give me courage and comfort and draw me closer to You in this confusing and painful time. Amen.

DAY 196

Colors of Change

Morning

Jesus Christ is the same yesterday and today and forever.
HEBREWS 13:8 ESV

"I am the LORD, and I do not change."
MALACHI 3:6 NLT

Life is like a kaleidoscope, constantly changing! If it didn't change, how quickly you'd slip into a monochromatic pattern, never to have new experiences, meet new people, or welcome new babies into the world. Yet amid change, you likely yearn for certainty and stability.

Father, while I don't always enjoy change, help me not to fear or avoid it. You use change to develop me and draw me closer to You, and You are always the one true constant in my life. I am so thankful. Amen.

Evening

"God is not human, that he should lie, not a human being, that he should change his mind. Does he speak and then not act? Does he promise and not fulfill?"
NUMBERS 23:19 NIV

Whatever is good and perfect is a gift coming down to us from God our Father, who created all the lights in the heavens. He never changes or casts a shifting shadow.
JAMES 1:17 NLT

You want to know there's something you can hold on to now and always, regardless of where you are in your life. That's why God has given you His promise that He will never change. And because He never changes, you can meet the myriad colors of change with acceptance and grace.

Dear Lord, I rest secure in Your promise that You never change. What a relief it is to know that You are always the same and I can always trust You! Amen.

DAY 197

A Question of Character

Morning

"Each tree is recognized by its own fruit. People do not pick figs from thornbushes, or grapes from briers."

LUKE 6:44 NIV

The fruit of the Spirit is love, joy, peace, patience, kindness, goodness, faithfulness, gentleness, self-control.

GALATIANS 5:22–23 ESV

When you want to determine a person's character, you use your eyes. Regardless of what the person says about herself, you watch her actions. Do her choices correspond with her glowing self-assessment?

Father, help me to wisely discern the character of others and develop relationships accordingly. Amen.

Evening

If anyone thinks he is religious and does not bridle his tongue but deceives his heart, this person's religion is worthless.

JAMES 1:26 ESV

If we say we love God and don't love each other, we are liars.

1 JOHN 4:20 CEV

For a quick check of your own character, examine your own actions. Shine a light on any gaps between opinion and fact, imagination and reality. Ask for God's help as you steadily and objectively grow in godly character.

Dear Father, help me to keep my character in check with words that match my actions and vice versa. I want my character to reflect You more and more each day. Amen.

DAY 198

The Core of Character

Morning

Let us not love in word or talk but in deed and in truth.
1 JOHN 3:18 ESV

Stand therefore, having fastened on the belt of truth.
EPHESIANS 6:14 ESV

Truth and kindness form the core of godly character. When truth or kindness is set aside for gain or convenience, ambition or greed, godly character suffers and eventually crumbles. How does it happen? Little by little, with each white lie, unkind comment, and selfish decision.

Dear Lord, please forgive me when little by little I let my character crumble. I ask You to help build it back up. Amen.

Evening

Lead me in your truth and teach me, for you are the God of my salvation; for you I wait all the day long.
PSALM 25:5 ESV

Don't ever forget kindness and truth. Wear them like a necklace. Write them on your heart as if on a tablet.
PROVERBS 3:3 NCV

God gives you this command: Don't ever forget truth and kindness! Practice kindness in real life in real time. Speak the truth to real people in real circumstances. Godly character increases the same way it weakens: bit by bit every day.

Holy God, I need Your kindness and truth in my head and heart, actions and words at all times. Let them become the core of my character. Amen.

DAY 199

He Chose You

Morning

Even before he made the world, God loved us and chose us in Christ to be holy and without fault in his eyes.

EPHESIANS 1:4 NLT

I chose you and sent you out to produce fruit, the kind of fruit that will last.

JOHN 15:16 CEV

During His earthly ministry, Jesus chose each of His disciples with a purpose in mind. They were not simply to talk about belonging to Him but to actually follow in His footsteps. Then as today, being chosen by the Lord calls for action!

Dear Lord, I want to follow You closely and be ready for action according to Your will. Please guide me and equip me for good works that will glorify You. Amen.

Evening

God decided in advance to adopt us into his own family by bringing us to himself through Jesus Christ. This is what he wanted to do, and it gave him great pleasure.

EPHESIANS 1:5 NLT

Put on then, as God's chosen ones, holy and beloved, compassionate hearts, kindness, humility, meekness, and patience.

COLOSSIANS 3:12 ESV

With great kindness, the Lord has chosen you by planting faith in your heart and stirring your desire to make your relationship with Him more tangible and real. Kindness to others is just one of many actions that shows you belong to Him—just one of the many fruits that will last.

Father, I am so blessed to belong to You. Please help me to produce the good fruit You have planned for me. Amen.

DAY 200

You Choose Him

Morning

"Choose for yourselves this day whom you will serve."

JOSHUA 24:15 NKJV

I have chosen the way of faithfulness; I set your rules before me.

PSALM 119:30 ESV

Though God has chosen you to serve Him, He gives you the option to choose other gods and serve them with your time and energy. Many people do. They prefer to chase after fame, money, or status. They place their own thoughts, desires, and understanding above God's commandments and His revealed truth.

Father, please forgive me when I make choices that turn me away from You and Your truth. Please cleanse me and draw me close to You again. Amen.

Evening

Let your hand be ready to help me, for I have chosen your precepts. I long for your salvation, O Lord, and your law is my delight.

PSALM 119:173–174 ESV

"I have set before you life and death, blessing and curse. Therefore choose life, that you and your offspring may live, loving the Lord your God, obeying his voice and holding fast to him, for he is your life and length of days."

DEUTERONOMY 30:19–20 ESV

With unbounded kindness, God loves everyone and welcomes all who return to Him with a repentant heart. He forgives and comforts, and He once again asks the question: Whom will you serve? Choose for yourself.

Dear Father, thank You for Your deep compassion and Your grace that never fails to let anyone return to relationship with You. Your mercy is undeserved and marvelous. Thank You! Amen.

DAY 201

Compassion at Work

Morning

Encourage anyone who feels left out, help all who are weak, and be patient with everyone.

1 THESSALONIANS 5:14 CEV

If I could speak all the languages of earth and of angels, but didn't love others, I would only be a noisy gong or a clanging cymbal.

1 CORINTHIANS 13:1 NLT

True compassion gets busy. Imagine a friend of yours is going through a tough time. Rather than avoid her company, you seek it out. Because you feel compassion, you listen and understand, encourage and comfort. That's compassion at work!

Loving God, help me to pursue people like You do, especially when I know they are hurting. Amen.

Evening

Bear one another's burdens, and so fulfill the law of Christ.

GALATIANS 6:2 ESV

"Do to others whatever you would like them to do to you."

MATTHEW 7:12 NLT

When you take time to make someone's way easier, assist a person less able than yourself, and remember those who are suffering, you are responding to the compassion God shows you. With your kindness in action, you are doing nothing less than demonstrating God's love for all the world.

Heavenly Father, You are so good! May Your compassion and comfort be my example and inspiration. Amen.

DAY 202

Godly Confidence

Morning

If you think you
are standing strong,
be careful not to fall.
1 CORINTHIANS 10:12 NLT

"Let the one who boasts
boast in the Lord."
2 CORINTHIANS 10:17 NIV

Your confidence, if not planted firmly in God's grace and the Holy Spirit's power to nurture and cultivate it, rests on shaky ground. Make sure your confidence is planted not in yourself or other people or any earthly structure, but rather in the Lord.

Almighty God, I want my confidence to be in nothing and no one but You! You are the source of all good things in my life. Amen.

Evening

The LORD is on my side;
I will not fear. What
can man do to me?
PSALM 118:6 ESV

In the fear of the LORD one has
strong confidence, and his
children will have a refuge.
PROVERBS 14:26 ESV

With your self-confidence built on God's love for you, you are free to show every kindness to others, even those who aren't kind to you. When He is the source of your self-confidence, you can meet others with tenderness and grace.

Almighty God, it is an honor to know You, serve You, and have You on my side. I'm so thankful for Jesus' saving grace that lets me call You my Father and do all things with confidence in You! Amen.

DAY 203

Godly Contentment

Morning

*I say it is better to
be content with what
little you have. Otherwise,
you will always be struggling
for more, and that is like
chasing the wind.*
ECCLESIASTES 4:6 NCV

*Be content with what you have,
for he has said, "I will never
leave you nor forsake you."*
HEBREWS 13:5 ESV

The struggle to get more things leaves little heart space for spiritual possessions like selflessness, compassion, kindness, peace, and joy. All those God-given gifts come your way when you say, "Enough." That one word empties your heart to receive the untold riches of true contentment.

*Dear God, help me to say, "Enough."
You supply all my needs and
offer true contentment. You alone
are enough for me. Amen.*

Evening

*I have learned to
be content whatever
the circumstances.*
PHILIPPIANS 4:11 NIV

*Godliness with contentment
is great gain, for we brought
nothing into the world, and
we cannot take anything
out of the world.*
1 TIMOTHY 6:6–7 ESV

Is contentment always possible? With your faith placed firmly in God, the answer is yes. Even if your circumstances are less than ideal right now, you know the Lord stands beside you to strengthen and encourage you. You can rely on Him.

Father God, no matter what my ever-changing circumstances, You never change. You are the provision and the peace and the contentment my heart longs for. Thank You! Amen.

DAY 204

Disappearing Dragons

Morning

The Lord is my light
and my salvation—
so why should I be afraid?
Psalm 27:1 NLT

I sought the Lord, and he
answered me and delivered
me from all my fears.
Psalm 34:4 ESV

Job loss, financial hardship, and broken relationships are only a few fire-breathing beasts with the power to send shivers down anyone's spine. As a caring parent rushes in to calm a frightened child, God moves to calm your heart.

Almighty God, please take my fears from me. I have no business dwelling on them when You, my Father, are the King of kings and Lord of lords and You care so much about me! Amen.

Evening

They will have no fear
of bad news; their hearts are
steadfast, trusting in the Lord.
Their hearts are secure, they will
have no fear; in the end they will
look in triumph on their foes.
Psalm 112:7–8 NIV

"I have said these things to
you, that in me you may have
peace. In the world you will
have tribulation. But take heart;
I have overcome the world."
John 16:33 ESV

God's words soothe you, His love embraces you, and His presence assures you that He is still in control. The light of His love scatters the shadows, and you no longer fear. As your courage grows, your worries disappear.

Heavenly Father, thank You for Your presence in my life and for Your soothing holy Word that has the power to banish every fear from my mind. Amen.

DAY 205

On the Right Path

Morning

Give a kind and respectful answer and keep your conscience clear. This way you will make people ashamed for saying bad things about your good conduct as a follower of Christ.

1 PETER 3:16 CEV

"Enter by the narrow gate. For the gate is wide and the way is easy that leads to destruction, and those who enter by it are many. For the gate is narrow and the way is hard that leads to life, and those who find it are few."

MATTHEW 7:13–14 ESV

When you choose to walk carefully on God's path instead of skipping along the most popular one, you're sure to hear some criticism.

Dear Lord, following You on earth was never meant to be easy. Despite the scoffers, help me to live for You and point others to You. Amen.

Evening

A soft answer turns away wrath, but a harsh word stirs up anger. The tongue of the wise commends knowledge, but the mouths of fools pour out folly.

PROVERBS 15:1–2 ESV

Bearing with one another and, if one has a complaint against another, forgiving each other; as the Lord has forgiven you, so you also must forgive.

COLOSSIANS 3:13 ESV

God's path requires us to set aside harsh words and make only loving, respectful responses to critical remarks. The knowledge that you are going forward as God's will would have you shields you from the shadows of shame, anger, and discouragement along the way.

Dear God, please give me tough skin to handle criticism for following You. Help me respond to it in a way that shows Your deep love and grace for all people. Amen.

DAY 206

Little Things Matter

Morning

"Whoever can be trusted with very little can also be trusted with much."
LUKE 16:10 NIV

Don't be hateful to people, just because they are hateful to you. Rather, be good to each other and to everyone else.
1 THESSALONIANS 5:15 CEV

Most days are filled not with larger-than-life opportunities to show kindness but rather with little chances to scatter goodness. With each friendly smile, welcoming word, and helping hand, you are proving yourself a devoted follower of God.

Dear God, You give me so many opportunities every day to share Your love. Help me to realize how important even small acts of kindness are. Amen.

Evening

Love is patient and kind.
1 CORINTHIANS 13:4 ESV

Worry weighs a person down; an encouraging word cheers a person up.
PROVERBS 12:25 NLT

Your small kindnesses become known to all, and your thoughtful ways illustrate how to walk with God each day, consistently and faithfully. Yes, all those little kindnesses you have done and continue to do matter tremendously; later you may discover that they've been the most important things of all.

Dear God, help my testimony for You to be filled with consistent kindness in both big and small ways. Amen.

DAY 207

First in His Eyes

Morning

"Anyone who wants to be first must be the very last, and the servant of all."
MARK 9:35 NIV

Humble yourselves before the Lord, and he will lift you up.
JAMES 4:10 NIV

Most people like being first—first in line, first to know. But being first often means pushing others out of the way, insisting on pride of place, and even ignoring the just claim of someone else. For the serious "first place" wannabe, kindness isn't an option! But Jesus tells us how to become first in His eyes: Desire to be last.

Dear Father, please squelch the selfish desires in me that make me want to put myself before others. Please humble me and help me to put others first. Amen.

Evening

Finally, all of you, be like-minded, be sympathetic, love one another, be compassionate and humble. Do not repay evil with evil or insult with insult.
1 PETER 3:8–9 NIV

Be humble and consider others more important than yourselves.
PHILIPPIANS 2:3 CEV

Promote others ahead of yourself. Help them succeed in their plans and objectives. While humbly speaking of yourself, sing the praises of others. Wherever something needs to be done, be the first to do it.

Father God, please give me a heart that delights in serving others, not in being served. I want to be more like You! Amen.

DAY 208
Solid Ground

Morning

Anyone who doubts
is like an ocean wave
tossed around in a storm.
JAMES 1:6 CEV

Jesus immediately reached out
his hand and took hold of him,
saying to him, "O you of little
faith, why did you doubt?"
MATTHEW 14:31 ESV

In practical as well as spiritual matters, doubt puts you on shaky soil! It undermines growth, progress, and satisfaction. If you doubt God's presence in your life, anxiety and fear keep you from living freely and joyfully. If you doubt yourself, lack of confidence makes you afraid to embrace the things that bring fulfillment to your life.

Dear Father, please forgive
me for my doubt, and bolster
my belief in You. Amen.

Evening

Jesus said to them, "If you
have faith and don't doubt,
I promise you can do what I
did to this tree. And you will be
able to do even more. You can
tell this mountain to get up and
jump into the sea, and it will."
MATTHEW 21:21 CEV

"Anyone who listens to my
teaching and follows it is
wise, like a person who builds
a house on solid rock."
MATTHEW 7:24 NLT

Do you doubt God? Yourself? Today, take all your doubts to Him in prayer, trusting in His kindness and compassion. Let Him put you back on solid ground.

Almighty God, I have no good reason
to doubt You when evidence of You
and Your love is all around me. Help
me to build my life solidly and firmly
on the truth of Your Word. Amen.

DAY 209

Overwhelming Emotions

Morning

Whoever has no rule over his own spirit is like a city broken down, without walls.
PROVERBS 25:28 NKJV

A fool gives full vent to his spirit, but a wise man quietly holds it back.
PROVERBS 29:11 ESV

God knows the power of human emotion, and He knows where feelings can carry you. Have you been there? Come, let Him embrace you in His forgiveness, comfort, and kindness. His overwhelming emotion toward you is love.

Dear Father, too often I let emotions overwhelm me, and I act out in ways I regret. Please forgive me and help me control my emotions in healthy ways. Amen.

Evening

Rejoice with those who rejoice, weep with those who weep.
ROMANS 12:15 ESV

I praise you, for I am fearfully and wonderfully made.
PSALM 139:14 ESV

Used as God intended, emotions sweeten and strengthen bonds of family, friendship, marriage, and community. How long has it been since you thanked God for His kindness to you in the stirrings of your emotions? Indeed, you are fearfully and wonderfully made!

Dear Father, when I keep my emotions in check in ways that honor You, they are so fulfilling, a true blessing! Thank You! Amen.

DAY 210

Kindness Personified

Morning

Though the Lord is supreme, he takes care of those who are humble.

Psalm 138:6 NCV

"The virgin will conceive and give birth to a son, and they will call him Immanuel" (which means "God with us").

Matthew 1:23 NIV

"God's in His heaven," the poet Robert Browning exclaimed, "all's right with the world!" Certainly God is in His heaven, but He's also right here on earth and right here with you. Rather than holding Himself far above the creatures He created, He moves among all people, understanding their concerns and caring about their troubles.

Dear Lord, may I never forget how close You are. You are the almighty God who is sovereign over all; You are the loving Savior, Jesus Christ; and You are the Holy Spirit ever present in my life. I praise You! Amen.

Evening

Jesus understands every weakness of ours, because he was tempted in every way that we are. But he did not sin!

Hebrews 4:15 CEV

So whenever we are in need, we should come bravely before the throne of our merciful God. There we will be treated with undeserved grace, and we will find help.

Hebrews 4:16 CEV

God empathizes. He sent His Son, Jesus, to show just how much He identifies with your sorrows, your burdens, and your cares. That's empathy carried to heavenly heights! That's kindness personified.

Loving Savior, that You empathize with my every weakness, burden, and sorrow makes me weep with gratitude. Thank You for Your boundless compassion and care. Amen.

DAY 211

Take Time to Encourage

Morning

Strengthen those
who have tired hands,
and encourage those who
have weak knees.
Isaiah 35:3 NLT

Encourage and help each other,
just as you are already doing.
1 Thessalonians 5:11 CEV

A simple word of encouragement or act of kindness can live in memory for years and even a lifetime. Perhaps your "Wonderful job!" is the confidence booster someone is longing to hear. It's possible your thumbs-up is all it will take for someone to know that others notice, understand, and care.

Dear Father, remind me continually how powerful simple words of encouragement are to others and how easily I can share them. What a blessing it is to lift others up with kind words and deeds. Amen.

Evening

"Do all that is in your heart,
for the Lord is with you."
2 Samuel 7:3 NKJV

Whatever is true, whatever
is noble, whatever is right,
whatever is pure, whatever
is lovely, whatever is
admirable—if anything is
excellent or praiseworthy—
think about such things.
Philippians 4:8 NIV

Every day, why not encourage yourself? Take a few moments to fill your thoughts with gentle words of assurance and affirmation. Reflect on God's many kindnesses toward you in the past, and visualize the good plans He has for you right now.

Dear Lord, help me to drop the discouraging talk in my head and fill my mind instead with encouraging thoughts based on all the good things You are and are doing. Amen.

DAY 212

A Good Example

Morning

These things happened
as a warning to us,
so that we would not crave
evil things as they did.
1 CORINTHIANS 10:6 NLT

Be an example to all believers
in what you say, in the way
you live, in your love, your
faith, and your purity.
1 TIMOTHY 4:12 NLT

A bad example serves as a warning to the wise. When you examine your own behavior, measure it against God's wise counsel, which is designed to keep you safe. The good example you set doing kind and thoughtful things is a blessing to those who would follow you.

Dear Lord, help me to set a good example that will attract others to knowing You as Savior too. Amen.

Evening

Always set a good
example for others.
TITUS 2:7 CEV

Dear brothers and sisters,
pattern your lives after
mine, and learn from those
who follow our example.
PHILIPPIANS 3:17 NLT

Whenever you're out among people, your words and conduct are on display. If others like what they see, they will listen when you say that your example is Jesus Christ, because your actions back up your words. By setting a godly example, you open the ears of others to the voice of God's kindness and love.

Dear Father, I want others to see a true reflection of You in everything I do! Amen.

DAY 213

Family in Christ

Morning

"Anyone who does God's will is my brother and sister and mother."

MARK 3:35 NLT

See what kind of love the Father has given to us, that we should be called children of God; and so we are.

1 JOHN 3:1 ESV

Where humanity draws boundaries between nations and highlights differences between people, God gathers together into one family all those who believe in Him. Whether your earthly family numbers few or many, your spiritual family includes all who know Jesus as their Lord and Savior.

Father God, what a gift it is to be Your child and to be part of Your family! I thank You and praise You! Amen.

Evening

To all who believed him and accepted him, he gave the right to become children of God.

JOHN 1:12 NLT

Whenever we have the opportunity, we should do good to everyone—especially to those in the family of faith.

GALATIANS 6:10 NLT

You are a sister in Christ with all believers of the past, present, and future! As the Lord has extended His great kindness to you, let your heart pour out kindness on all, especially those who belong to your family of faith.

Heavenly Father, in times of loneliness, remind me of the vast and loving family of faith You have called me into. I so look forward to eternity with You and our big happy family reunion. Amen.

DAY 214

Family Unity

Morning

Whoever troubles his own household will inherit the wind.

PROVERBS 11:29 ESV

But those who won't care for their relatives, especially those in their own household, have denied the true faith. Such people are worse than unbelievers.

1 TIMOTHY 5:8 NLT

When disharmony, struggle, and conflict enter a home, family life becomes unbearable. If bitterness or discontent has a place at the table, there is no peace in the house, even for people who live alone. It's time to open the door wide and invite God inside.

Heavenly Father, family relationships can be difficult at times, but You are greater than any conflict. Please help us defeat the enemy who wants to tear families apart. Amen.

Evening

Love bears all things, believes all things, hopes all things, endures all things.

1 CORINTHIANS 13:7 ESV

Above all, keep loving one another earnestly, since love covers a multitude of sins.

1 PETER 4:8 ESV

Selfishness slips away with the knowledge that God will provide for everyone's needs, and dissension disappears when all matters are submitted to His will. Peace comes to your home as respect produces unity, kindness rules behavior, and love infuses relationships.

Dear Father, help my family to submit to Your will in our relationships and activities. You are our provider, our strength, and our one true source of forgiveness and love. Amen.

DAY 215

Faithful Finances

Morning

Don't worry and ask yourselves, "Will we have anything to eat? Will we have anything to drink? Will we have any clothes to wear?"
MATTHEW 6:31 CEV

Keep your life free from love of money, and be content with what you have.
HEBREWS 13:5 ESV

Money enables you to provide for your well-being and the well-being of others. Trouble occurs, however, if money becomes your sole focus. Treat money as the blessing that God intends, and money will treat you kindly too.

Dear Lord, help me to honor You in every way possible with my finances. Amen.

Evening

Command them to do good, to be rich in good deeds, and to be generous and willing to share.
1 TIMOTHY 6:18 NIV

"Bring all the tithes into the storehouse so there will be enough food in my Temple. If you do," says the LORD of Heaven's Armies, "I will open the windows of heaven for you. I will pour out a blessing so great you won't have enough room to take it in! Try it! Put me to the test!"
MALACHI 3:10 NLT

No matter how much or how little you have in your bank account, God invites you to share it with others. He knows that a healthy and wholesome relationship with money depends on it. Share in proportion to the blessings God has given you, and your financial problems will dwindle.

Dear Lord, please give me a healthy relationship with money. I want to be a good steward who is not obsessed with gaining wealth and who is always ready to share. Amen.

DAY 216

God's Forgiveness

Morning

As far as the east is from the west, so far has He removed our transgressions from us.

PSALM 103:12 NKJV

If we confess our sins, he is faithful and just to forgive us our sins and to cleanse us from all unrighteousness.

1 JOHN 1:9 ESV

Perhaps something burdens your heart today. God pleads with you to let go of that burden and anything else weighing on your heart. The death and resurrection of His Son, Jesus Christ, has removed your guilt, and all your sins are completely forgiven. Yes, even that one.

Heavenly Father, please forgive me of my sin, and give me confidence that You completely remove it from me as far as the east is from the west. What sweet relief there is in Your grace! Thank You! Amen.

Evening

"But if you do not forgive others their trespasses, neither will your Father forgive your trespasses."

MATTHEW 6:15 ESV

Be kind and loving to each other, and forgive each other just as God forgave you in Christ.

EPHESIANS 4:32 NCV

You show great kindness to the person you forgive from the heart. And in forgiving, you're also showing great kindness to yourself. God has forgiven you completely and without reservation. Forgive with the same measure of benevolence, and you will receive forgiveness in return.

Dear Lord, I can't truly forgive others in my own power. I need Your grace to fill me completely so that I can extend it to others. Amen.

DAY 217

A Forever Friend

Morning

"You are my friends if you do what I command you."
JOHN 15:14 ESV

"I have called you friends, for everything that I learned from my Father I have made known to you."
JOHN 15:15 NIV

God may have blessed you with a few close friends. Not only do they know you well, but sometimes they seem to know you better than you know yourself! Even more of a blessing, however, is the friend you have in Jesus.

Dear Jesus, You truly are the best friend anyone could ever have. I'm so thankful for my relationship with You! Amen.

Evening

And the Scripture was fulfilled that says, "Abraham believed God, and it was counted to him as righteousness"—and he was called a friend of God.
JAMES 2:23 ESV

A man of many companions may come to ruin, but there is a friend who sticks closer than a brother.
PROVERBS 18:24 ESV

No matter who may come or go in your life, Jesus' presence remains. He invites you to talk to Him in prayer. He extends His comfort and counsel to you in scripture. His friendship is something you can depend on forever.

Dear Lord, Your constant presence in my life is such an encouragement and comfort. Thank You for being a friend who never leaves or forsakes me. Amen.

DAY 218

Clear Goals

Morning

You should say, "If the Lord wants, we will live and do this or that."
JAMES 4:15 NCV

I will instruct you and teach you in the way you should go; I will counsel you with my eye upon you.
PSALM 32:8 ESV

It's exciting to have goals for the future. Having a clear destination gives your life's journey direction and purpose. But sometimes you run up against a detour or even a roadblock, and you're left bewildered, wondering what to do next. Ask God!

Dear Father, once again I've neglected to ask You for direction. Please forgive me and help me get back on the right path. I want to do Your will for my life. Amen.

Evening

We can make our plans, but the LORD determines our steps.
PROVERBS 16:9 NLT

If you do what the LORD wants, he will make certain each step you take is sure. The LORD will hold your hand, and if you stumble, you still won't fall.
PSALM 37:23–24 CEV

Perhaps God wants to point out another path for you to take before you reach your goal, or maybe He has a new and better destination in mind for you. Or it could be He simply wants you to take it a little slower. Yes, work toward your goals, but leave the future entirely in God's hands.

Heavenly Father, I trust You. Please guide me in every area of my life. Amen.

DAY 219

Replacing Worry with Trust

Morning

"Do not worry about tomorrow, for tomorrow will worry about its own things."

MATTHEW 6:34 NKJV

I give you peace, the kind of peace only I can give. It isn't like the peace this world can give. So don't be worried or afraid.

JOHN 14:27 CEV

"If you see ten troubles coming down the road," Calvin Coolidge remarked, "you can be sure that nine will run into the ditch before they reach you." And for the one trouble that might reach you, worrying about it beforehand won't help at all! God gives you each day minute by minute, hour by hour.

Loving God, please quiet my worries and fear, and fill me with the supernatural peace only You can give. Amen.

Evening

"And which of you by being anxious can add a single hour to his span of life?"

LUKE 12:25 ESV

When the cares of my heart are many, your consolations cheer my soul.

PSALM 94:19 ESV

Why waste a moment of your day fretting over what God, in His wisdom, is withholding until tomorrow? In His loving-kindness, He frees you to live fully and to love deeply in the present hour. Trust Him to do the same with each new tomorrow.

Father, please forgive me for all the time I waste fretting over things I have no business worrying about! Please free me from anxiety as I trust You moment by moment. Amen.

DAY 220

Strength in Gentleness

Morning

"Bless those who curse you, pray for those who mistreat you."
LUKE 6:28 NIV

"Bless those who persecute you; bless and do not curse them."
ROMANS 12:14 ESV

What does it take to respond gently to a spiteful comment, hurtful insult, belligerent challenge, or hostile remark? Certainly not human weakness but heavenly strength. Only a strong commitment to God's divine command to bless others restrains the natural impulse to meet hurt with hatred.

Oh Father, what a challenge it is to want to bless those who mistreat me! It's utterly impossible on my own, but never impossible with Your help. Please give me Your powerful loving grace toward my enemies. Amen.

Evening

A gentle answer deflects anger, but harsh words make tempers flare.
PROVERBS 15:1 NLT

You have given me the shield of your salvation, and your right hand supported me, and your gentleness made me great.
PSALM 18:35 ESV

It takes strength of character tested and honed in real-life situations to return gentleness for harshness, kindness for cruelty. In the face of offense, no response makes you stronger than gentleness.

Dear Lord, I want to do Your will regarding those who mistreat me. Please strengthen my character with Your powerful gentleness, and help me to handle conflict with others in a way that pleases You. Amen.

DAY 221

You Never Know

Morning

Always be gentle with others.
PHILIPPIANS 4:5 CEV

"Take my yoke upon you, and learn from me, for I am gentle and lowly in heart, and you will find rest for your souls."
MATTHEW 11:29 ESV

You never know what others are going through. Though you may see nothing but the faces of ordinary men and women on the outside, inside are hearts burdened with intractable problems, terrible disappointments, devastating regrets, and overwhelming grief.

Loving Father, I can't see the hearts and minds of those around me, but You can. Please give me wisdom as I care for and encourage those around me. Amen.

Evening

He will tend his flock like a shepherd; he will gather the lambs in his arms; he will carry them in his bosom, and gently lead those that are with young.
ISAIAH 40:11 ESV

What does the LORD require of you? To act justly and to love mercy and to walk humbly with your God.
MICAH 6:8 NIV

It could be the warmth of your smile that lifts a heart today, or the kindness of your thoughtful gesture that shines a ray of brightness into someone's gloom. God may use your friendly words or your willingness to listen to give hope, faith, and courage to a despairing heart.

Heavenly Father, Your loving example of being a gentle shepherd is comforting, encouraging, and inspiring. Please teach me to be more like You. Amen.

DAY 222

When You Give

Morning

Whoever sows sparingly
will also reap sparingly, and
whoever sows bountifully
will also reap bountifully.
2 CORINTHIANS 9:6 ESV

You must each decide in
your heart how much to give.
And don't give reluctantly
or in response to pressure.
"For God loves a person
who gives cheerfully."
2 CORINTHIANS 9:7 NLT

The more you give, the more you get in return. When you give your work your best effort, you get more satisfaction out of your day. When you give your full attention to those around you, you get better relationships.

Dear Father, please help me to be
a cheerful giver of all resources,
abilities, and spiritual gifts
You have given me. Amen.

Evening

If you give to others,
you will be given a full amount
in return. It will be packed
down, shaken together, and
spilling over into your lap.
The way you treat others is
the way you will be treated.
LUKE 6:38 CEV

"Freely you have
received; freely give."
MATTHEW 10:8 NIV

When you give kindness, compassion, and understanding to others, you most often get the same in return. When you give a portion of each day to meditation, prayer, and Bible reading, you get the best of all—a strong, vibrant, and growing friendship with God.

Dear Father, please forgive me
when I'm feeling stingy. Teach
me to give freely, understanding
that You always give back
so much more. Amen.

DAY 223

Echo of Kindness

Morning

"Whatever you wish that others would do to you, do also to them."
MATTHEW 7:12 ESV

" 'Love the Lord your God with all your heart and with all your soul and with all your mind and with all your strength.' The second is this: 'Love your neighbor as yourself.' There is no commandment greater than these."
MARK 12:30–31 NIV

The Golden Rule sums up Jesus' teaching about relationships. He treated the people around Him with compassion and understanding, and in so doing, He set the example for anyone who would follow in His way.

Loving Father, please transform my mind and teach me to treat others the way I want to be treated. Amen.

Evening

"And as you wish that others would do to you, do so to them."
LUKE 6:31 ESV

"This is my commandment, that you love one another as I have loved you."
JOHN 15:12 ESV

If you desire warmth, friendliness, and consideration, don't wait for those things; show them. You will be surprised how often you get in return the blessing you extend to others. Like an echo, kindness comes back to you.

Dear Lord, it's easier to react to kindness than to be proactive about showing it. Please help me to take initiative and share Your love freely and boldly. Amen.

DAY 224

The Golden Rule

Morning

He is kind even to people
who are ungrateful.
LUKE 6:35 NCV

"If your enemies are hungry,
give them something to eat.
And if they are thirsty, give
them something to drink.
This will be the same as piling
burning coals on their heads."
Don't let evil defeat you,
but defeat evil with good.
ROMANS 12:20–21 CEV

What about the times you make every effort to be friendly but you're rebuffed? It happens! Even Jesus in His earthly ministry experienced the sting of rejection. Yet the Golden Rule still applies.

Lord Jesus, You know the sting of rejection so much more than I do. Yet Your love for people never fails. I am so grateful for Your example, and I praise You! Amen.

Evening

"But love your enemies,
and do good, and lend,
expecting nothing in return,
and your reward will be great."
LUKE 6:35 ESV

"If you love only those who
love you, what reward
is there for that?"
MATTHEW 5:46 NLT

Even when others don't respond to you with kindness, God still invites you and enables you to live up to His Golden Rule. Look at it this way—you haven't always responded to His generous overtures, but He in no way gave up His kind thoughts toward you. God, in His never-changing love, shows you how to obey the Golden Rule.

Loving Father, thank You for never giving up on me, even when I treat You poorly and neglect my relationship with You. Please forgive me and help me to extend Your kind of amazing grace to others. Amen.

DAY 225

Happy People

Morning

For the happy heart,
life is a continual feast.
PROVERBS 15:15 NLT

Happy is the person
who trusts the LORD.
PSALM 40:4 NCV

Happy people lift your spirits, make you smile, and leave you feeling good all day long. While they may have been born with a sunny disposition, it's more likely that at some point they simply opted for happiness. It starts with a conscious choice to count blessings and cultivate gratitude, and then it seems there's no end of things to be happy about.

Dear Father, I find such joy in knowing You as Savior and seeing how You work in my life. Thank You for the countless blessings You give! Amen.

Evening

Why am I discouraged?
Why is my heart so sad?
I will put my hope in God!
I will praise him again—
my Savior and my God!
PSALM 43:5 NLT

I delight to do your
will, O my God.
PSALM 40:8 ESV

When you catch yourself frowning at life, choose better for yourself and everyone around you. Offer God a "Thank You!" for the blessings all around you, and see how quickly you can have a happy day!

Dear Father, it's easy to get discouraged, but I'm grateful You are always present to lift my spirit. Please put my focus on You and Your incredible blessings in my life. True joy is all because of You! Amen.

DAY 226

Good Health

Morning

You formed my inward parts; You covered me in my mother's womb.
PSALM 139:13 NKJV

Do you not know that your body is a temple of the Holy Spirit within you, whom you have from God? You are not your own, for you were bought with a price. So glorify God in your body.
1 CORINTHIANS 6:19–20 ESV

The chief reason you want to avoid anything that would endanger your health is this one: Your body is a gift from God. Cherish the gift He has given you by treating your body kindly. Take care of your health.

Dear Father, please inspire me to want to take better care of this body You've created for me so that I can honor You and do Your will. Amen.

Evening

"Your eye is the lamp of your body. When your eyes are healthy, your whole body also is full of light."
LUKE 11:34 NIV

"Physical training is good, but training for godliness is much better, promising benefits in this life and in the life to come."
1 TIMOTHY 4:8 NLT

Even more important than your physical health is your spiritual health. Actively and effectively nurture your spiritual health. Read and meditate on God's Word, nourish God-pleasing thoughts, and practice kindness and compassion toward others. Do everything you can, and then He will take care of the rest.

Father, help me never to make my physical health a higher priority than my spiritual health. Amen.

DAY 227

Always Helping

Morning

"But the Helper,
the Holy Spirit, whom the
Father will send in my name,
he will teach you all things and
bring to your remembrance
all that I have said to you."
JOHN 14:26 ESV

God is faithful, and he will
not let you be tempted beyond
your ability, but with the
temptation he will also provide
the way of escape, that you
may be able to endure it.
1 CORINTHIANS 10:13 ESV

God tenderly invites you to come to Him when temptations are luring you away from God's path. Ask Him to help you stand firm against sin. No matter how many times the same temptation may pull at your heart and soul, God's help to resist is only a prayer away.

Dear Father, Your help is the power I need to overcome any temptation or problem in my life. May I come to You moment by moment for Your help in all things. Amen.

Evening

"Call on me in the day
of trouble; I will deliver you,
and you will honor me."
PSALM 50:15 NIV

God is our refuge and strength,
an ever-present help in trouble.
PSALM 46:1 NIV

God in His great kindness sends help in many ways, and you wouldn't want to miss His answer because you were looking for your own solution. Instead, keep your eyes open for the direction you may not have considered and the opening you didn't previously see.

Dear God, thank You for allowing me to bring every need I have to You with confidence that You will help me find a solution. Amen.

DAY 228

Expect the Best

Morning

"I know the plans I have for you," declares the LORD, "plans to prosper you and not to harm you, plans to give you hope and a future."
JEREMIAH 29:11 NIV

Surely there is a future, and your hope will not be cut off.
PROVERBS 23:18 ESV

Of God's many kindnesses to you, the gift of hope strengthens you today and allows you to face tomorrow with confidence and optimism. Your God-given hope, unlike wishful thinking, is based on what He has done for you already. He has brought you to this day and blessed you greatly up to this point.

Dear Lord, You are the one true hope of the world. Knowing You as my Savior gives me strength and confidence and peace as I look toward the future. Thank You! Amen.

Evening

And we know that God causes everything to work together for the good of those who love God and are called according to his purpose for them.
ROMANS 8:28 NLT

"My thoughts are nothing like your thoughts," says the LORD. "And my ways are far beyond anything you could imagine."
ISAIAH 55:8 NLT

Though you may wonder how God could possibly use some of the things that have happened to you for your good, He has in the past and He will in the future. Place your hope firmly in Him and expect the best—you'll get it!

Father, while I don't always understand Your ways, I trust You are working all things for good. I will continue to put my hope in You, no matter what. Amen.

DAY 229

Heart-Deep Humility

Morning

Toward the scorners he is scornful, but to the humble he gives favor.
PROVERBS 3:34 ESV

Do nothing from selfish ambition or conceit, but in humility count others more significant than yourselves.
PHILIPPIANS 2:3 ESV

Your aptitude for kindness depends on your attitude toward others. If, for example, a person looks down on others, she's unlikely to treat them with patience, tolerance, and compassion. But with a God-given humble heart, your capacity for kindness is limitless.

Dear Father, help me never to view myself too highly. I am a sinner saved by Your grace. I want my heart to be so filled with Your grace that it spills onto others. Amen.

Evening

Clothe yourselves, all of you, with humility toward one another, for "God opposes the proud but gives grace to the humble."
1 PETER 5:5 ESV

"It is the one who is least among you all who is the greatest."
LUKE 9:48 NIV

Jesus, in His earthly ministry, paid special attention to those who were little valued at the time—widows, children, the poor, people with skin diseases, and those with physical handicaps. His example teaches all who follow Him that God looks not at outward appearances or attainments, but at the heart.

Dear Jesus, help me to view people like You do and to love the "least" of those around me. I want to be like You! Amen.

DAY 230

Incomparable You

Morning

Thank you for making me so wonderfully complex! Your workmanship is marvelous—how well I know it.

PSALM 139:14 NLT

God has given different gifts to each of us.

1 CORINTHIANS 7:7 CEV

You've heard it said, "Don't compare apples to oranges." Though apples and oranges differ in appearance, texture, and sweetness, both taste good. It's possible you enjoy them equally! So when you compare yourself to others, guess what you're doing. Comparing apples to oranges.

Dear Lord, please forgive me for all the ways I compare myself to others. You created me uniquely, and my only comparison of myself should be with the example You have set for me and the truth in Your Word. Amen.

Evening

For we are his workmanship, created in Christ Jesus for good works, which God prepared beforehand, that we should walk in them.

EPHESIANS 2:10 ESV

As each has received a gift, use it to serve one another, as good stewards of God's varied grace.

1 PETER 4:10 ESV

Your gifts, talents, and abilities are different from those of other people, and at the same time, you're inferior to no one. Yes, let the positive attributes and notable accomplishments of others inspire and motivate you to do your best, but do not compare. Do yourself a kindness and cherish the God-given, incomparable you!

Dear God, thank You for creating me and giving me unique gifts. Please develop them in me, and give me wisdom to know how best to use them for Your honor and glory. Amen.

DAY 231

Singular Kindness

Morning

"Are not five sparrows sold for two pennies? And not one of them is forgotten before God."
LUKE 12:6 ESV

"The very hairs on your head are all numbered. So don't be afraid; you are more valuable to God than a whole flock of sparrows."
MATTHEW 10:30–31 NLT

Say you're in a hot-air balloon hovering high over a packed football stadium. From that distance, you see no individual faces but only a mass of people crowded around a patch of turf. How differently God sees you! To Him, you are not one of a huge population but an individual created and loved by Him.

Almighty God, I am in awe that You see me, know me, and care about me as a unique individual. I thank You and praise You! Amen.

Evening

For the LORD loves justice, and he will never abandon the godly. He will keep them safe forever.
PSALM 37:28 NLT

Yet Jerusalem says, "The LORD has deserted us; the Lord has forgotten us." "Never! Can a mother forget her nursing child? Can she feel no love for the child she has borne? But even if that were possible, I would not forget you!"
ISAIAH 49:14–15 NLT

There's no way God could ever forget about you or skip over you, any more than you would willfully ignore, forget, or neglect the people you love. To you, they are individuals whom you regard with singular kindness, just the way God regards you.

Father God, thank You for Your singular kindness to me. I am so grateful You know me so well and will never forget or forsake me. Amen.

DAY 232

Beware of Shortcuts

Morning

What will you gain,
if you own the whole world
but destroy yourself?
MARK 8:36 CEV

Do not those who plot evil go astray? But those who plan what is good find love and faithfulness.
PROVERBS 14:22 NIV

In life as in driving, shortcuts can take you where you don't want to go. Promises of easy money and effortless achievement most likely have an "if only" attached, and this "if only" is something that compromises your integrity. There's a price to pay, and it could be your honesty, reputation, principles, and self-respect.

Heavenly Father, please give me wisdom and help me not to fall into the temptation of taking "easy" shortcuts that don't keep me on the path You have for me. Amen.

Evening

Your word is a lamp to guide my feet and a light for my path. I've promised it once, and I'll promise it again: I will obey your righteous regulations.
PSALM 119:105–106 NLT

Show me the right path, O LORD; point out the road for me to follow. Lead me by your truth and teach me, for you are the God who saves me.
PSALM 25:4–5 NLT

The next time you're tempted to take a shortcut, do yourself a kindness. Consult the one who made the map. Ask God where the road leads before you take it.

Dear Lord, I want to follow You and You alone, no matter the road or where it takes me. Amen.

DAY 233

Lasting Joy

Morning

The fruit of the Spirit
is love, joy, peace.
GALATIANS 5:22 NKJV

Though you have not seen him,
you love him; and even though
you do not see him now, you
believe in him and are filled with
an inexpressible and glorious
joy, for you are receiving the
end result of your faith,
the salvation of your souls.
1 PETER 1:8–9 NIV

God-given joy is heart deep, and it doesn't depend on anything except God's presence in your life. You trust in His goodness, rely on His kindness, and rest in His love. What could ever take away your joy?

Dear God, the joy You give, no matter the circumstances, is endless and amazing—a constant source of strength in my life. I cannot imagine my life without You! Amen.

Evening

For our present troubles
are small and won't last very
long. Yet they produce for us
a glory that vastly outweighs
them and will last forever!
2 CORINTHIANS 4:17 NLT

So we don't look at the troubles
we can see now; rather, we fix
our gaze on things that cannot be
seen. For the things we see now
will soon be gone, but the things
we cannot see will last forever.
2 CORINTHIANS 4:18 NLT

When you're undergoing any hardship, lean on God's strength and be joyful because He knows, understands, and cares. Joy and times of trouble definitely go together when God is part of the picture.

Dear Father, even when trouble comes my way, let Your joy shine brightly in my thoughts and attitudes. I know this life is only temporary and a perfect eternity is waiting for me! Amen.

DAY 234

A Lasting Leader

Morning

"My sheep listen to
my voice; I know them,
and they follow me."
JOHN 10:27 NIV

Then Jesus told his disciples,
"If anyone would come after me,
let him deny himself and take
up his cross and follow me."
MATTHEW 16:24 ESV

"Take me to your leader," the extraterrestrial says to the astonished human who discovers the UFO in his backyard. But consider this: What if your shadow gave you the same directive? Would you lead her to a political figure, a public speaker, a relative, a friend, your own thoughts and ideas, or God?

Dear Lord, You are my shepherd
and leader. Let all who know
me know I follow You! Amen.

Evening

For to this you have
been called, because Christ
also suffered for you, leaving
you an example, so that you
might follow in his steps.
1 PETER 2:21 ESV

Make me to know your ways,
O LORD; teach me your paths.
Lead me in your truth and
teach me, for you are the
God of my salvation; for you
I wait all the day long.
PSALM 25:4–5 ESV

If your leader is anything or anyone less than God, your leader is fallible, frail, and temporary. Such leaders lead for a time, but their power and influence eventually diminish. Take those in your life—including yourself—to the lasting leader—God alone.

Dear Lord, I'm so grateful to be
under Your leadership. Help me to
bring others alongside me on this
journey of following You too. Amen.

DAY 235

Love to Learn

Morning

If you have good sense, instruction will help you to have even better sense. And if you live right, education will help you to know even more.

PROVERBS 9:9 CEV

An intelligent heart acquires knowledge, and the ear of the wise seeks knowledge.

PROVERBS 18:15 ESV

God's Spirit promotes lifelong learning. That's how He nurtures compassion, kindness, tenderness, understanding, and love in you. The Spirit's fruit just keeps growing as long as you're willing to keep learning.

Dear Father, help me never to tire of learning and developing, especially in my spiritual wisdom. Amen.

Evening

Anyone who wanders away from this teaching has no relationship with God. But anyone who remains in the teaching of Christ has a relationship with both the Father and the Son.

2 JOHN 9 NLT

Whoever heeds instruction is on the path to life, but he who rejects reproof leads others astray.

PROVERBS 10:17 ESV

Pray that God will put you in contact with someone who knows God's Word, will speak His truth in love to you, and will challenge you to grow and increase in wisdom. Look for someone who teaches not only in words but by example. Search until you find such a teacher, because your spiritual learning is for a lifetime—and beyond.

Dear Lord, please bring teachers and leaders into my life who love and follow You and who will instruct me in Your Word. Amen.

DAY 236

A Sacred Trust

Morning

*Give honor to marriage,
and remain faithful to one
another in marriage.*
HEBREWS 13:4 NLT

*He who finds a wife finds
a good thing and obtains
favor from the LORD.*
PROVERBS 18:22 ESV

Whether you are married or single, you have a responsibility concerning marriage. Your marriage and the marriages of others have been brought into existence through the solemn promises spoken by husband and wife. Marriage is a sacred trust.

Dear Father, thank You for the gift of marriage. May I never take it lightly. Amen.

Evening

*Let marriage be held in
honor among all, and let the
marriage bed be undefiled,
for God will judge the sexually
immoral and adulterous.*
HEBREWS 13:4 ESV

*Husbands, love your wives,
as Christ loved the church
and gave himself up for her.*
EPHESIANS 5:25 ESV

You honor marriage when you do everything you can to support and encourage all married people to love, cherish, and remain faithful to each other. Speaking kindly about your husband and refusing to disrespect anyone's spouse are two ways you can fulfill your responsibility concerning marriage.

Dear Father, help me to honor and promote marriage as You intend it. Amen.

DAY 237

Remember Yesterday

Morning

Watch yourselves closely so that you do not forget the things your eyes have seen or let them fade from your heart as long as you live.

DEUTERONOMY 4:9 NIV

Bless the LORD, O my soul, and forget not all his benefits.

PSALM 103:2 ESV

At times you may feel as if you're at a spiritual standstill. You can't see where God is working in your life, and you haven't experienced His presence in a while. Why not do what His people have done throughout history? Remember how He has helped you in the past.

Dear Lord, when I'm struggling in my circumstances and can't quite see where You are or how You're working, please remind me how You've carried me through so many challenges in the past. Amen.

Evening

"Be careful not to forget the LORD, who rescued you from slavery in the land of Egypt."

DEUTERONOMY 6:12 NLT

I remember your name in the night, O LORD, and keep your law.

PSALM 119:55 ESV

The unexpected opportunities, narrow escapes, remarkable insights, out-of-nowhere courage, and boldness when you needed it—God will do all those things for you again! Rest in the comfort of knowing you remain in His loving care.

Dear Lord, I have no need to worry when I know You are caring for me. You have been so good to me in the past, and I'm certain You always will be! Amen.

DAY 238

The Right Time

Morning

LORD, how long must I ask for help and you ignore me?
HABAKKUK 1:2 NCV

Dear friends, don't forget that for the Lord one day is the same as 1,000 years, and 1,000 years is the same as one day. The Lord isn't slow about keeping his promises, as some people think he is. In fact, God is patient, because he wants everyone to turn from sin and no one to be lost.
2 PETER 3:8–9 CEV

Perhaps you're used to getting answers, information, and products you want quickly if not instantly. But God doesn't work that way. Though technology and other innovations have considerably sped up many functions, God continues to set the pace of events.

Dear Lord, please forgive me for expecting You to act immediately in all circumstances. I submit to Your schedule because I know it's always best. Amen.

Evening

But if we hope for what we do not see, we wait for it with patience.
ROMANS 8:25 ESV

Be still before the LORD and wait patiently for him.
PSALM 37:7 ESV

The change or development you yearn to see happen, the goal you can't wait to reach, is on God's schedule. To you it might seem a long time in coming, but be patient. God alone knows the right time.

Dear Lord, it's so easy to want You to work according to my schedule, but that's not right. Your timing is always perfect. Please give me patience to wait on You as I trust in You. Amen.

DAY 239

A Model of Power

Morning

*For He spoke,
and it was done;
He commanded,
and it stood fast.*
PSALM 33:9 NKJV

*That your faith might not
rest in the wisdom of men
but in the power of God.*
1 CORINTHIANS 2:5 ESV

Wherever you hold power over others—family, workplace, church, community—you can use it to worsen or improve their condition, to enrich yourself, or to enhance the lives of those under your authority. Look to God for your model!

*Almighty God, please fill me
with Your power to do good, to
share Your love, and to spread
Your hope and truth. Amen.*

Evening

*Being strengthened with
all power, according to his
glorious might, for all endurance
and patience with joy.*
COLOSSIANS 1:11 ESV

*Finally, be strong in the Lord
and in the strength of his might.*
EPHESIANS 6:10 ESV

By His power God created a world of infinite beauty, formed life in His divine image, and continues to treat His people with limitless kindness and compassion. That's how to handle power that never corrupts but rather enables His love to reach out, lift up, and do good. That's the power He has given you.

*Almighty God, I'm so thankful
for Your incredible power that is
incorruptible. I praise You! Amen.*

DAY 240

Hear the Praises

Morning

They loved praise
from people more than
praise from God.
JOHN 12:43 NCV

And it is my prayer that your love may abound more and more, with knowledge and all discernment, so that you may approve what is excellent, and so be pure and blameless for the day of Christ.
PHILIPPIANS 1:9–10 ESV

Praise makes you feel good. More important than the praise itself, though, is who is doing the praising. If your kudos are coming from those who disregard God's ways, that's a signal you could be straying from His path.

Dear Lord, help me to be wise about where my praise comes from. Please give me caution and discernment. Amen.

Evening

Do your work willingly, as though you were serving the Lord himself, and not just your earthly master. In fact, the Lord Christ is the one you are really serving, and you know he will reward you.
COLOSSIANS 3:23–24 CEV

Show yourself in all respects to be a model of good works, and in your teaching show integrity, dignity.
TITUS 2:7 ESV

If you're hearing choruses of "Good job!" and "Well done!" and "Thanks for your kindness!" from people who know and love God, then give thanks. You are an inspiration to everyone around you.

Dear Lord, while it's nice to receive a pat on the back once in a while, more importantly I want to work toward the goal of hearing You say one day, "Well done, good and faithful servant."

DAY 241

First Things First

Morning

"You shall have no other gods before me."
EXODUS 20:3 ESV

"You shall love the LORD your God with all your heart and with all your soul and with all your might."
DEUTERONOMY 6:5 ESV

Setting aside daily time with God is often put off until "later" or "tomorrow," even though it's the most important and the most meaningful thing anyone can do. If this has been happening in your life, do yourself the ultimate kindness: Put time with God first on your to-do list, and you'll be surprised how well the day proceeds!

Dear Lord, please forgive me when I put other people and things ahead of You. I want You first and foremost in my life. Amen.

Evening

Pursue righteousness and a godly life, along with faith, love, perseverance, and gentleness.
1 TIMOTHY 6:11 NLT

"Seek first God's kingdom and what God wants. Then all your other needs will be met as well."
MATTHEW 6:33 NCV

If someone's number one priority is God and His will for her life, she'll devote her mental, emotional, physical, and material resources to applying God's teachings to real-life situations. Instead of focusing her eyes on herself, she'll look for ways to serve others with God's love, kindness, and compassion.

Dear Lord, help me wisely prioritize all the good things You've given me— with my relationship with You at the very top of the list. Amen.

DAY 242

Useful Problems

Morning

We also have joy with our troubles, because we know that these troubles produce patience. And patience produces character, and character produces hope.

ROMANS 5:3–4 NCV

While you are in the world, you will have to suffer. But cheer up! I have defeated the world.

JOHN 16:33 CEV

Though problems aren't welcome, they show up anyway. Big or small, however, problems can bring out the best in you if you meet them not with fear but with calm confidence in your God-given abilities and resources.

Dear Father, help me to see that there is value in problems—when I depend on You to guide me through them and learn lessons I wouldn't have learned otherwise. Amen.

Evening

"Behold, I am sending you out as sheep in the midst of wolves, so be wise as serpents and innocent as doves."

MATTHEW 10:16 ESV

He comforts us when we are in trouble, so that we can share this same comfort with others in trouble.

2 CORINTHIANS 1:4 CEV

Ask God to give you the confidence you need to reach godly and practical solutions to all your problems. And what better kindness could you show than to help others solve theirs?

Heavenly Father, You have helped me so much through so many problems and provided just the right resources and relationships I needed. Please use me to help others as well. Amen.

DAY 243

Not a Problem!

Morning

The Lord is good,
a stronghold in the
day of trouble.
NAHUM 1:7 NKJV

This poor man cried, and the
Lord heard him and saved
him out of all his troubles.
PSALM 34:6 ESV

God has never promised a problem-free life, but He has promised His help with any and all problems. No matter how the problem came about or how many times it has cropped up in your life, you can rely on His strength and wisdom to help you deal with it.

Almighty God, I'm so grateful for Your strength and grace to help me through every kind of problem. Please carry me through with victory! Amen.

Evening

I am in deep distress,
but I love your teachings.
Your rules are always fair.
Help me to understand
them and live.
PSALM 119:143–144 CEV

Let us then with confidence draw
near to the throne of grace, that
we may receive mercy and find
grace to help in time of need.
HEBREWS 4:16 ESV

If a problem concerns you, it concerns God. Let God express His kindness toward you by allowing Him to hear whatever weighs on your mind, fully trusting that He listens, cares, and will help you find the right solution for you and those you love.

Heavenly Father, thank You for hearing me and caring about every concern and challenge I face. Please guide me. Amen.

DAY 244

Protect and Be Protected

Morning

Live under the protection of God Most High and stay in the shadow of God All-Powerful.
PSALM 91:1 CEV

He will cover you with his feathers. He will shelter you with his wings. His faithful promises are your armor and protection.
PSALM 91:4 NLT

Kindness compels you to protect those weaker than yourself. The time you take to ensure the safety of children, calm a fearful friend, or rescue an animal in distress is your kindness at work. Yet what you're doing is only a shadow of the protection that God, in His love, provides for you.

Dear Father, thank You for Your perfect protection. May I do my best to care for and protect others in need around me because of Your great example. Amen.

Evening

We are hard pressed on every side, but not crushed; perplexed, but not in despair; persecuted, but not abandoned; struck down, but not destroyed.
2 CORINTHIANS 4:8–9 NIV

The Lord is faithful, and he will strengthen you and protect you from the evil one.
2 THESSALONIANS 3:3 NIV

God watches over your soul so you are able to withstand temptation and resist those things that would take you away from Him. He keeps you safe, gives you His guidelines, and rescues you when you're in trouble. You are protected now and always!

Dear Lord, no matter how hard life gets, I am never out of Your care, never in a place where You are unable to rescue me. Thank You for seeing me and protecting me at all times. Amen.

DAY 245

God-Given Purpose

Morning

In Christ we were chosen to be God's people, because from the very beginning God had decided this in keeping with his plan.

EPHESIANS 1:11 NCV

The LORD will fulfill his purpose for me; your steadfast love, O LORD, endures forever.

PSALM 138:8 ESV

The events of your life are part of God's purpose for you. Though you may wonder why something happened or fail to see how it possibly could have played a part in the plan of a kind and loving God, He knows. Even if you can't understand His purpose for you right now, take heart, because He does.

Father God, I trust You even when I don't understand You. I know You are working out the greatest good. Amen.

Evening

Whether you eat or drink, or whatever you do, do all to the glory of God.

1 CORINTHIANS 10:31 NKJV

For we are his workmanship, created in Christ Jesus for good works, which God prepared beforehand, that we should walk in them.

EPHESIANS 2:10 ESV

When you think about your life's purpose, perhaps your thoughts go directly to a particular calling or momentous mission. More often than not, however, God puts things on a smaller but no less important scale. He blesses you with day-to-day responsibilities that He intends for you to do with acceptance, gratitude, and joy.

Dear God, please keep showing me Your purpose for me day by day, moment by moment. Please make Your plans and good works You've intended for me the only goals I want to achieve. Amen.

DAY 246

No Regrets

Morning

Godly sorrow brings repentance that leads to salvation and leaves no regret.
2 CORINTHIANS 7:10 NIV

If we confess our sins, he is faithful and just to forgive us our sins and to cleanse us from all unrighteousness.
1 JOHN 1:9 ESV

If you have more than a few candles on your birthday cake, you're likely to harbor a measure of regret. You remember the time you could have helped but didn't or the time you said something better left unsaid. For all those times, your compassionate God accepts your heartfelt repentance and comforts you with His complete forgiveness.

Father, I find such relief and freedom when I come to You in repentance. I praise You for Your great mercy! Amen.

Evening

Have mercy on me, O God, because of your unfailing love. Because of your great compassion, blot out the stain of my sins. Wash me clean from my guilt. Purify me from my sin.
PSALM 51:1–2 NLT

Forgetting what lies behind and straining forward to what lies ahead.
PHILIPPIANS 3:13 ESV

In kindness, God removes the burden of regret, strengthening your capacity to understand and willingness to forgive those who wrong you. No regrets! Only wisdom, maturity, and peace of mind.

Loving Savior, as You remove burdens from me through forgiveness, help me to do likewise and forgive those who offend me. Amen.

DAY 247

Right Relationships

Morning

Since we have been made right with God by our faith, we have peace with God. This happened through our Lord Jesus Christ.

ROMANS 5:1 NCV

May you always be filled with the fruit of your salvation—the righteous character produced in your life by Jesus Christ—for this will bring much glory and praise to God.

PHILIPPIANS 1:11 NLT

Jesus Christ made it possible for all who believe to enjoy a living and vibrant relationship with God, a relationship open to you today. The kindness you show others and the selfless things you do for them will reflect the most important relationship in your life—the one with God that Jesus has made possible for you.

Almighty God, I am in awe that I can come before You in right relationship, and it's all because of the righteousness offered through Your Son, Jesus. How grateful I am! Amen.

Evening

Don't fool yourselves. Bad friends will destroy you.

1 CORINTHIANS 15:33 CEV

Whoever walks with the wise becomes wise, but the companion of fools will suffer harm.

PROVERBS 13:20 ESV

Your relationships matter to you and to God. As much as possible, surround yourself with people who will encourage your godly values, walk with you in your spiritual journey, and support you in your desire to grow in kindness, tenderness, and love.

Dear Lord, help me to choose friends wisely and develop relationships with others that please You. Amen.

DAY 248

Soul Restoration

Morning

He restores my soul; He leads me in the paths of righteousness for His name's sake.

Psalm 23:3 NKJV

You who have made me see many troubles and calamities will revive me again; from the depths of the earth you will bring me up again. You will increase my greatness and comfort me again.

Psalm 71:20–21 ESV

From the depths of despair, it's hard to believe that God will—or would want to—pick up the pieces of your broken heart. Yet He does! No place you land is so low that God cannot reach down to lift, restore, and renew your soul when you cry out to Him for help.

Loving God, remind me there is nowhere I can go that is too far for Your hand of grace to reach me and pull me back to You. But please help me never to let go of Your hand. Amen.

Evening

Restore to me the joy of your salvation, and uphold me with a willing spirit.

Psalm 51:12 ESV

Create in me a pure heart, O God, and renew a steadfast spirit within me.

Psalm 51:10 NIV

If you are able to confess your transgression, God is more than able to forgive you, comfort you, and return you to a peaceful and productive relationship with Him.

Dear Lord, I confess my sin to You. I long for the cleansing only You can provide. Thank You, dear Savior! Amen.

DAY 249

Rest at Ease

Morning

"Come to Me, all you who labor and are heavy laden, and I will give you rest."
MATTHEW 11:28 NKJV

God gives rest to his loved ones.
PSALM 127:2 NLT

God puts His compassion in motion by inviting you to bring your tired heart and mind to Him in prayer. Let yourself relax in the comfort of His love for you. Allow Him to lift your burdens from you; experience the freedom of knowing that He is there for you. Rest at ease in Him!

Dear Father, I get so weary at times. In those moments, please lift my burdens as I come to You for truly peaceful rest. Amen.

Evening

We ought always to thank God for you, brothers and sisters, and rightly so, because your faith is growing more and more, and the love all of you have for one another is increasing.
2 THESSALONIANS 1:3 NIV

I thank my God every time I remember you.
PHILIPPIANS 1:3 NIV

A genuinely kind person offers rest for tired spirits and burdened hearts in a way no one else can. Give thanks for the kind people you know. And be blessed for all the times your kind ways have offered others soul-deep rest.

Dear Father, please help me to be someone others feel safe coming to for encouragement, peace, and rest. Amen.

DAY 250

A Righteous Life

Morning

If you suffer for doing right, you are blessed.
1 PETER 3:14 NCV

"Blessed are you when people insult you, persecute you and falsely say all kinds of evil against you because of me. Rejoice and be glad, because great is your reward in heaven, for in the same way they persecuted the prophets who were before you."
MATTHEW 5:11–12 NIV

When you live a righteous life, you draw people's attention. You stand out because you don't go along with the crowd or agree with popular opinion or approve what God has condemned. Your principled words and actions make people think, and some will turn against you, even mocking you or insulting your intelligence.

Dear Lord, no matter who might mock me, I want to keep living for You. There is no better way to live than according to Your holy Word! Amen.

Evening

Many are the afflictions of the righteous, but the LORD delivers him out of them all.
PSALM 34:19 ESV

The sufferings of this present time are not worth comparing with the glory that is to be revealed to us.
ROMANS 8:18 ESV

Your commitment to God and His principles gives you strength, power, and a willingness to respond with unfailing kindness to those who scorn you, further establishing you in a life of God-blessed righteousness.

Almighty God, no trouble is too great for You to handle. No situation I'm in surprises or scares You. Your power is matchless! Amen.

DAY 251

God Is Salvation

Morning

"The Son of Man came to look for and to save people who are lost."

LUKE 19:10 CEV

You can be sure that whoever brings the sinner back from wandering will save that person from death and bring about the forgiveness of many sins.

JAMES 5:20 NLT

When someone you love turns away from God's path and spurns His love, you're sick at heart. It's like watching a person head into an overgrown forest without a map, compass, or provisions. But here's another picture: God Himself scouring that same forest looking for your loved one.

Loving Father, You know my heartache over my loved one who has turned away from You, but more importantly, You know their heartache. I pray they will allow You to draw them back to You. Amen.

Evening

"If a man has a hundred sheep and one of them gets lost, what will he do? Won't he leave the ninety-nine others in the wilderness and go to search for the one that is lost until he finds it?"

LUKE 15:4 NLT

"In the same way, there is more joy in heaven over one lost sinner who repents and returns to God than over ninety-nine others who are righteous and haven't strayed away!"

LUKE 15:7 NLT

When God hears a cry for help, He comes running. He will delve into the deepest cavern or climb the steepest precipice to rescue one soul.

Dear Father, You never give up on anyone. Your love and mercy and power to save are endless and unconditional. I pray for my loved one to reach out to You for rescue. Amen.

DAY 252

Always Secure

Morning

Those who trust in the
Lord are like Mount Zion,
which cannot be moved,
but abides forever.
PSALM 125:1 ESV

Jesus Christ is the same
yesterday and today and forever.
HEBREWS 13:8 ESV

In a world of uncertainty, security seems like a relic of a bygone era. But because God never changes, you can always feel secure in His presence, His protection, and His kindness toward you. In addition, you can provide others with the gift of security.

Dear Father, thank You for the sweet stability You bring to my life! Amen.

Evening

I know the Lord is always
with me. I will not be shaken,
for he is right beside me.
PSALM 16:8 NLT

Whoever walks in integrity
walks securely, but he who
makes his ways crooked
will be found out.
PROVERBS 10:9 ESV

Your faithfulness in loving, serving, and being there lets others know they can depend on you. They can trust you, secure in the knowledge that you have their best interests at heart and will stand by them in time of need. Security isn't gone but is alive and well in every God-filled heart.

Dear God, with You as my example, help me to be a dependable friend to others. I want to be trustworthy and full of integrity. Amen.

DAY 253

A Higher Power

Morning

I want to do what is good, but I don't. I don't want to do what is wrong, but I do it anyway.
ROMANS 7:19 NLT

Better to be patient than powerful; better to have self-control than to conquer a city.
PROVERBS 16:32 NLT

Someone with a short fuse quickly loses control over thoughts and feelings, words and actions. Someone who won't control personal wants and desires quickly descends into a life of selfishness and greed. But though human emotions can run high, God's power is even higher—divinely so!

Dear Lord, I'm way too quick to become angry sometimes. I need Your power to help me control my emotions. Amen.

Evening

For those who live according to the flesh set their minds on the things of the flesh, but those who live according to the Spirit set their minds on the things of the Spirit.
ROMANS 8:5 ESV

Walk by the Spirit, and you will not gratify the desires of the flesh.
GALATIANS 5:16 ESV

Pray for God to bless you with His power to control your emotions and reactions so nothing stands between you and the ability to respond kindly to others, treat them with gentleness and respect, and enjoy serenity and peace of mind.

Dear God, help me to live and walk in Your way! May my actions and reactions be controlled by Your Holy Spirit who dwells in me. Amen.

DAY 254

The Heart Counts

Morning

Now we serve God in a new way with the Spirit, and not in the old way with written rules.
ROMANS 7:6 NCV

Work willingly at whatever you do, as though you were working for the Lord rather than for people.
COLOSSIANS 3:23 NLT

Imagine your server hands you the menu, takes your order, brings out your food, and gives you your check. Yet in all this time, she hasn't smiled once or done anything beyond the minimum requirements of her job. Clearly, her heart isn't in it. This is not the kind of service God desires from you.

Dear Lord, serving You is an honor, and I want my attitude while working for You to show my gratitude. Amen.

Evening

Each one must do just as he has decided in his heart, not reluctantly or under compulsion, for God loves a cheerful giver.
2 CORINTHIANS 9:7 NASB

Do everything without complaining and arguing, so that no one can criticize you. Live clean, innocent lives as children of God, shining like bright lights in a world full of crooked and perverse people.
PHILIPPIANS 2:14–15 NLT

One kindness done with joy and enthusiasm ranks higher than several performed with indifference or out of obligation. With God, it's not simply what you do but how you do it that counts.

Dear Lord, may I constantly feel the deep joy of giving to others, so much so that I never want to stop. Amen.

DAY 255

Simply Spiritual

Morning

"All you need to say is simply 'Yes' or 'No'; anything beyond this comes from the evil one."
MATTHEW 5:37 NIV

A devout life does bring wealth, but it's the rich simplicity of being yourself before God.
1 TIMOTHY 6:6 MSG

Many people have found that giving up high-maintenance possessions and time-consuming pursuits simplifies their lives considerably. Now their days are freer and their activities more manageable. In the spiritual life too, simplicity proves to be a great benefit.

Father, help me not to make my Christian life more complicated than it needs to be. Simply walking with You day by day, following Your Word and trusting Your guidance, is the very best way to live. Amen.

Evening

The teaching of your word gives light, so even the simple can understand.
PSALM 119:130 NLT

For our boast is this, the testimony of our conscience, that we behaved in the world with simplicity and godly sincerity, not by earthly wisdom but by the grace of God, and supremely so toward you.
2 CORINTHIANS 1:12 ESV

Simple faith, simple trust, simple kindness, and simple love are all it takes to have a strong, vibrant, and purposeful spiritual life that you, by God's grace, can manage and enjoy every day.

Dear Father, I simply want to do my best to love and follow You in all I do. Please help me. Amen.

DAY 256

Sweet Slumber

Morning

Those who work
hard sleep in peace.
ECCLESIASTES 5:12 NCV

I lie down and sleep;
I wake again, because
the LORD sustains me.
PSALM 3:5 NIV

Find a workable way to get the sleep you need at least most nights. It matters to you because you'll feel better, to others because you'll serve them more joyfully, and to God because He delights to give you rest.

Dear Lord, forgive me for the way I run myself ragged at times. Help me to be disciplined in getting the rest I need so that I can better serve You. Amen.

Evening

He who keeps Israel will
neither slumber nor sleep.
PSALM 121:4 ESV

When you lie down, you will
not be afraid; when you lie
down, your sleep will be
sweet. . .for the LORD will be at
your side and will keep your
foot from being snared.
PROVERBS 3:24–26 NIV

God's love for you would never allow Him to turn away from you for one moment, much less shut His eyes and doze off. During even the darkest night, His watchful eyes protect you. Sleep in peace, because He knows, He cares, and He will help.

Dear Lord, I can rest securely because of Your unfailing protection and care. Thank You so much. Amen.

DAY 257

Strong Words

Morning

When you talk, you should always be kind and pleasant so you will be able to answer everyone in the way you should.
COLOSSIANS 4:6 NCV

Let my words and my thoughts be pleasing to you, LORD.
PSALM 19:14 CEV

Truly strong language consists of words that inspire, empower, and encourage; words that create understanding, show compassion, and build community; words that possess precise meaning and informative value. When you speak, use strong language—the kind with real strength!

Father, please regularly remind me of the great power in words—to encourage or discourage, to heal or harm, to spread Your love or hinder it. Amen.

Evening

"Out of the abundance of the heart the mouth speaks."
MATTHEW 12:34 ESV

"I tell you, on the day of judgment people will give account for every careless word they speak, for by your words you will be justified, and by your words you will be condemned."
MATTHEW 12:36–37 ESV

To speak kind words to others, fill your heart with positive feelings, compassionate views, tender thoughts, and a gracious attitude toward everyone. That way, should you ever blurt something out, you won't have to worry—it will be a bonus kindness!

Father, please fill my heart so full of love and grace that I can't help but spill out encouraging words for others. Amen.

DAY 258

Sure and Steady Growth

Morning

We will not be influenced by every new teaching we hear from people who are trying to fool us.

EPHESIANS 4:14 NCV

Anyone who wanders away from this teaching has no relationship with God. But anyone who remains in the teaching of Christ has a relationship with both the Father and the Son.

2 JOHN 9 NLT

Fads in music, food, and fashion sweep the country, and suddenly it seems as if everyone is caught up in them. In faith matters also, fads pull many away from God-centered beliefs and biblically sound teachings with the promise of instant insights or quick rewards. Don't waste your time!

Dear Lord, in a world so full of new ideas, help me to discern real truth and disregard anything that does not align with Your Word. Amen.

Evening

But grow in the grace and knowledge of our Lord and Savior Jesus Christ. To him be the glory both now and to the day of eternity. Amen.

2 PETER 3:18 ESV

I pray that your love will overflow more and more, and that you will keep on growing in knowledge and understanding.

PHILIPPIANS 1:9 NLT

For sure and steady spiritual growth, feed your faith with God's unchanging and nourishing Word. Let His Spirit deepen your understanding of all things spiritual at His pace and lead you along the way He has laid out ahead of you.

Dear Lord, daily deepen my wisdom and understanding of You. Thank You for never changing and for allowing me to know and follow You! Amen.

DAY 259

Daily Bread

Morning

"People do not live by bread alone; rather, we live by every word that comes from the mouth of the Lord."

DEUTERONOMY 8:3 NLT

Jesus replied, "I am the bread of life. Whoever comes to me will never be hungry again. Whoever believes in me will never be thirsty."

JOHN 6:35 NLT

If you were to buy a rosebush and plant it in good soil but never water it, the bush would not thrive for long. While you provided soil, you didn't provide water; the plant needs both. You too need two things to thrive: food for your body and food for your soul.

Dear Lord, I cannot thrive without a relationship with You. Please draw me ever closer. Amen.

Evening

"Yes, I am the bread of life! Your ancestors ate manna in the wilderness, but they all died. Anyone who eats the bread from heaven, however, will never die."

JOHN 6:48–50 NLT

"Man shall not live by bread alone, but by every word that comes from the mouth of God."

MATTHEW 4:4 ESV

Even if every physical need were met, you would still sense a lack in your life without your spiritual questions answered and your spiritual longings satisfied. Look to God to provide your daily bread—the physical kind and the spiritual kind.

Dear Lord, I can never be satisfied apart from You. Thank You for being all I need. Amen.

DAY 260

God Our Helper

Morning

The Lord is my strength and song, and He has become my salvation.
Psalm 118:14 NKJV

No temptation has overtaken you that is not common to man. God is faithful, and he will not let you be tempted beyond your ability, but with the temptation he will also provide the way of escape, that you may be able to endure it.
1 Corinthians 10:13 ESV

DIYers take notice: Building a life of godly kindness isn't a do-it-yourself project! No one, without Spirit-planted power, has the strength of heart and mind to consistently resist the pull of selfishness and impatience.

Almighty God, I can't possibly do life without Your power, and I'm so thankful I don't have to. You are here and You are helping me. I praise You! Amen.

Evening

For God is working in you, giving you the desire and the power to do what pleases him.
Philippians 2:13 NLT

The Lord is my strength and shield. I trust him with all my heart. He helps me, and my heart is filled with joy. I burst out in songs of thanksgiving.
Psalm 28:7 NLT

God promises to help you as you build more kindness, more gentleness, and more love into your thoughts and actions. He gives you the spiritual strength to do the God-pleasing things you desire.

Dear Lord, please lead me in Your will and give me the power to do the good things You have planned for me. Amen.

DAY 261

God's Powerful Love

Morning

Where sin was powerful,
God's gift of undeserved grace
was even more powerful.
ROMANS 5:20 CEV

Just as Christ was raised
from the dead by the glorious
power of the Father, now we
also may live new lives.
ROMANS 6:4 NLT

The pull of temptation is strong—extremely strong! And the weight of guilt is powerful enough to crush even the most resilient spirit. God's love for you, however, is much stronger and more powerful than any force of darkness.

Dear Lord, with Your saving grace and power, I can live a new life free from the burden of sin. What sweet relief I find in that truth! Amen.

Evening

[God] is able to do far more
abundantly than all that we
ask or think, according to
the power at work within us.
EPHESIANS 3:20 ESV

For the kingdom of God does not
consist in talk but in power.
1 CORINTHIANS 4:20 ESV

God's kind heart and compassionate feelings toward you compel Him to brace you against temptation, forgive you whenever you stumble, and shine the light of His wisdom and guidance ahead of you. You need never walk in the shadows or suffer under the weight of despair. Because of His kindness to you, you possess true strength and power.

Almighty God, by Your power, may I resist temptation and live a life that points others to You. Amen.

DAY 262

Strength in Weakness

Morning

"The spirit is willing,
but the flesh is weak."
MATTHEW 26:41 NIV

Many are the afflictions of
the righteous, but the Lord
delivers him out of them all.
PSALM 34:19 ESV

Even your most fervent desire to think, act, and speak with kindness will fail from time to time. But take heart and be glad! The fact that you recognize your weakness shows that the eyes of your soul have 20/20 vision. Your sorrowful thoughts reveal that you're listening to God's Spirit when He whispers words of caution or censure.

Father, please let my
weaknesses cause me to lean
harder on You. Amen.

Evening

Likewise the Spirit helps
us in our weakness.
ROMANS 8:26 ESV

I take pleasure in my
weaknesses, and in the insults,
hardships, persecutions,
and troubles that I suffer
for Christ. For when I am
weak, then I am strong.
2 CORINTHIANS 12:10 NLT

Your weaknesses are working to bring you closer to God and His will for you as you go to Him for forgiveness, accept the comfort of His grace, and thank Him once again for His many great kindnesses to you.

Dear Lord, I thank You for my
weaknesses. They show me
how strong You are! Amen.

DAY 263

One-Stop Shop

Morning

In Christ lives all the fullness of God in a human body. So you also are complete through your union with Christ.
COLOSSIANS 2:9–10 NLT

"The thief comes only to steal and kill and destroy. I came that they may have life and have it abundantly."
JOHN 10:10 ESV

You might say that God runs a one-stop shop. In His presence, you find everything you need for spiritual health and wholeness. But unlike a store where you pick out what you want, God equips you with exactly what you need, in exactly the right amount, and at exactly the right time.

Dear Lord, please stop me quickly when I'm looking for fulfillment outside of You. Amen.

Evening

You know you learn to endure by having your faith tested. But you must learn to endure everything, so you will be completely mature and not lacking in anything.
JAMES 1:3–4 CEV

And he is before all things, and in him all things hold together.
COLOSSIANS 1:17 ESV

All you have to do is open your arms wide and accept the abundance God has for you. And another difference in His one-stop shop: You don't pay a cent for what you get. He gives it all to you for free out of His heart of never-ending kindness!

Dear Lord, it's crazy to think of the amount of money we spend looking for satisfaction, when the true satisfaction only You can provide is free and abundant. Thank You for Your amazing gifts! Amen.

DAY 264

Evidence of Wisdom

Morning

If any of you lacks wisdom, you should ask God, who gives generously to all without finding fault, and it will be given to you.

JAMES 1:5 NIV

Listen to advice and accept instruction, that you may gain wisdom in the future.

PROVERBS 19:20 ESV

If you don't consider yourself wise, you're wiser than you think! Only those who realize that they don't know everything have an incentive to ask questions, acquire knowledge, evaluate answers, and gain insight. Spiritual wisdom, like practical understanding, comes with time, experience, and faithful reflection.

Dear Lord, I never want to stop seeking You and learning from Your great wisdom. Amen.

Evening

Wisdom makes life pleasant and leads us safely along. Wisdom is a life-giving tree, the source of happiness for all who hold on to her.

PROVERBS 3:17–18 CEV

And this I pray, that your love may abound still more and more in knowledge and all discernment.

PHILIPPIANS 1:9 NKJV

As you search scripture and listen to the Spirit of God speaking within you, wisdom fills your heart and permeates your thoughts, words, and actions. The gentle words you speak and kind things you do make your God-sent wisdom evident to all who know you.

Dear Lord, as others observe me, may they see Your wisdom filling my attitudes and actions. Amen.

DAY 265

Your Life's Work

Morning

Those who work hard make a profit.
PROVERBS 14:23 NCV

"Do not work for the food that perishes, but for the food that endures to eternal life, which the Son of Man will give to you."
JOHN 6:27 ESV

While "life's work" sounds like a momentous spiritual concept, you are doing your life's work in the small, practical things you do every day. Your work—whether inside or outside the home—gives you the chance to take what God's Spirit teaches you and apply it to real-life situations.

Dear Lord, help me to honor You in even the smallest tasks of my day, knowing that all of them have the potential to add up to a life lived well for Your glory. Amen.

Evening

Pay careful attention to your own work, for then you will get the satisfaction of a job well done, and you won't need to compare yourself to anyone else. For we are each responsible for our own conduct.
GALATIANS 6:4–5 NLT

Let all that you do be done in love.
1 CORINTHIANS 16:14 ESV

You can practice being patient when you're stressed out—responding kindly when your temper is short or going out of your way to help someone even though you're busy enough already. When you do these things, you're doing your life's work wherever your work takes you!

Dear Lord, I invite You into every part of my life's work. Thank You for wanting to be present with me! I'm so grateful for Your help and care. Amen.

DAY 266

Good Work's Reward

Morning

The Lord Christ is the one you are really serving, and you know he will reward you.
COLOSSIANS 3:24 CEV

But someone will say, "You have faith and I have works." Show me your faith apart from your works, and I will show you my faith by my works.
JAMES 2:18 ESV

God invites you to meet Him in private prayer and meditative study, but that's only half of what it means to spend time with Him. The other half involves other people, because He is present in their lives, needs, and godly desires too.

Dear Father, as I spend time with You, please ignite my desire to serve others. Amen.

Evening

Don't use your freedom to satisfy your sinful nature. Instead, use your freedom to serve one another in love.
GALATIANS 5:13 NLT

"If I then, your Lord and Teacher, have washed your feet, you also ought to wash one another's feet."
JOHN 13:14 ESV

When you extend your kindness to others, you are extending it to God. When you make it your work to pray for others and care about them, to comfort them in their sorrows and encourage them in their aspirations, you're doing the work of God. His work rewards with fulfillment, pleasure, and peace of heart and mind.

Dear Lord, Your life here on earth set an amazing example of loving service. I want to be more like You. Amen.

DAY 267

Single-Minded Worship

Morning

Oh come, let us worship and bow down; let us kneel before the LORD, our Maker!

PSALM 95:6 ESV

"Worship the Lord your God, and serve him only."

MATTHEW 4:10 NIV

It's hard to focus on too many things at once! Multitaskers learn this lesson when their attention fragments so much that they can do nothing well. Multitasking doesn't work in your spiritual life either, because God insists on your full attention when you worship Him.

Almighty God, You and You alone are worthy of all my worship and praise! Amen.

Evening

Jesus answered him, "It is written, 'You shall worship the Lord your God, and him only shall you serve.'"

LUKE 4:8 ESV

Let us offer to God acceptable worship, with reverence and awe.

HEBREWS 12:28 ESV

Your single-minded concentration allows you to more fully appreciate the spiritual blessings God showers on you during worship and also prepares you to focus on realistic ways you can translate His kindness to you into kindness to others. And here's a special kindness no multitasker can ever manage—giving full and undivided attention to someone else!

Dear Lord, please forgive me when I allow the focus of my worship to wander from You. Please redirect my attention to Your majesty and love. Amen.

DAY 268

Life-Giving Worship

Morning

"God is Spirit, so those who worship him must worship in spirit and in truth."
JOHN 4:24 NLT

Give your bodies to God because of all he has done for you. Let them be a living and holy sacrifice—the kind he will find acceptable. This is truly the way to worship him.
ROMANS 12:1 NLT

Worship is lifeless unless accompanied by practical action. God's Spirit enlivens your worship by helping you love others so you can meet them with understanding and compassion, the same way God meets you.

Heavenly Father, I give all of myself to You in service and in worship. Amen.

Evening

Let the message of Christ dwell among you richly as you teach and admonish one another with all wisdom through psalms, hymns, and songs from the Spirit, singing to God with gratitude in your hearts.
COLOSSIANS 3:16 NIV

And whatever you do, whether in word or deed, do it all in the name of the Lord Jesus, giving thanks to God the Father through him.
COLOSSIANS 3:17 NIV

You stamp your worship with value in God's sight by taking the time to do small kindnesses and bringing the blessings of love, laughter, and comfort to the lives of others. That's lively—and life-giving—worship!

Dear Lord, help me to love and serve and give to others in Your name, that You alone may receive the glory. Amen.

DAY 269

Christ-Balance

Morning

"You'll be built solid,
grounded in righteousness,
far from any trouble—
nothing to fear!"
ISAIAH 54:12 MSG

People with integrity walk
safely, but those who follow
crooked paths will be exposed.
PROVERBS 10:9 NLT

Just when we think we have it all together, life has a tendency to come crashing down around our ears. But even in the midst of life's most chaotic moments, God gives us grace; He keeps us balanced in His love.

Dear Lord, no matter what is crumbling around me, help me never to fall apart. Hold me together with Your great love and strength. Amen.

Evening

People with their minds
set on you, you keep
completely whole, steady
on their feet, because they
keep at it and don't quit.
ISAIAH 26:3 MSG

Therefore. . .stand firm.
Let nothing move you.
1 CORINTHIANS 15:58 NIV

When our life's equilibrium is shaken, we feel anxious, out of control. But if we rely on Christ, He will pick us up, dust us off, and give us the grace to find our balance in Him.

Loving Father, when I fall, You are always there to pick me up and stand me on solid ground again. I don't know what I'd ever do without You! Amen.

DAY 270

The Powerful Word

Morning

Your word is a lamp
to guide my feet and
a light for my path.
PSALM 119:105 NLT

I inherited your book on living;
it's mine forever—what a gift!
And how happy it makes me!
PSALM 119:111 MSG

We sometimes take scripture for granted. These ancient words, though, continue to shine with light, just as they did centuries ago. In them, God's grace is revealed to us. In them, we gain new insight into ourselves and our lives.

Dear Lord, help me never to take Your Word for granted. It truly is my help and guide in all things. I'm so thankful for the way You speak to me through it. Amen.

Evening

For the word of God is
alive and powerful. It is
sharper than the sharpest
two-edged sword, cutting
between soul and spirit,
between joint and marrow.
It exposes our innermost
thoughts and desires.
HEBREWS 4:12 NLT

"Is not my word like fire, declares
the LORD, and like a hammer
that breaks the rock in pieces?"
JEREMIAH 23:29 ESV

God's words are living things that work their way into our hearts and minds, revealing the fears and hopes we've kept hidden away, sometimes even from ourselves. Like a doctor's scalpel that cuts in order to heal, God's Word slices through our carefully created facades and exposes our deepest truths.

Almighty God, Your Word is powerful, relevant, and timeless. It convicts me and challenges me. It is truly alive! I praise You! Amen.

DAY 271

Small Things

Morning

[Jesus said,] "The greatest among you should be like the youngest."
LUKE 22:26 NIV

Don't you see that children are GOD's best gift?
PSALM 127:3 MSG

In some ways, we need to look to children as our role models. We get so used to functioning in the adult world, loaded down with responsibilities, that we forget the child's knack for living in the present moment, for taking delight in small things, for loving unconditionally.

Dear Lord, please humble me and let me learn from little ones who love others and show gratitude so well. Amen.

Evening

"Unless you change and become like little children, you will never enter the kingdom of heaven."
MATTHEW 18:3 NIV

Like newborn babies, crave pure spiritual milk, so that by it you may grow up in your salvation, now that you have tasted that the Lord is good.
1 PETER 2:2–3 NIV

Jesus asks us to let go of our grown-up dignity and allow ourselves to enter into His presence as children. When we do, we encounter His grace anew.

Heavenly Father, help me to trust and adore You just like a child loves her daddy. You are my Abba, and I love You! Amen.

DAY 272

A Thousand Generations

Morning

From everlasting to
everlasting the Lord's love
is with those who fear him,
and his righteousness with
their children's children.
Psalm 103:17 NIV

But when Jesus saw it, he was
indignant and said to them,
"Let the children come to me;
do not hinder them, for to such
belongs the kingdom of God."
Mark 10:14 ESV

We can rely on God's love for the children in our lives. As we send those children out into the world so terribly vulnerable, we can know with absolute certainty that God's grace goes with them.

Heavenly Father, please remind me that You love my children even more than I do. I know they are safe in Your protection and care. Please guide me with wisdom as I care for them too. Amen.

Evening

"But I lavish unfailing love
for a thousand generations
on those who love me and
obey my commands."
Exodus 20:6 NLT

Know therefore that the Lord
your God is God; he is the faithful
God, keeping his covenant of
love to a thousand generations
of those who love him and
keep his commandments.
Deuteronomy 7:9 NIV

Just as God's love reached us through our parents and the other adults who shaped our lives, God will also spread His love through us to the generations to come.

Dear Father, thank You for Your everlasting provision and love from generation to generation! Amen.

DAY 273

A Look at Creation

Morning

The heavens declare the glory of God; the skies proclaim the work of his hands.
PSALM 19:1 NIV

For by him all things were created, in heaven and on earth, visible and invisible.
COLOSSIANS 1:16 ESV

Look up, and be reminded of how wonderful God truly is. The same God who created the sun and the atmosphere, the stars and the galaxies, the same God who day by day creates a new sunrise and a new sunset, that same God loves you and creates beauty in your life each day!

Almighty God, You are above and beyond the best words I could use to describe You! I praise You! Amen.

Evening

"Worthy are you, our Lord and God, to receive glory and honor and power, for you created all things, and by your will they existed and were created."
REVELATION 4:11 ESV

[Jesus said,] "Instead of looking at the fashions, walk out into the fields and look at the wildflowers."
MATTHEW 6:28 MSG

You don't have to spend hours to realize how beautifully God made the world. A single flower, if you really look at it, could be enough to fill you with awe. Sometimes we only need something very simple to remind us of God's grace.

Almighty God, may I never lose the wonder of looking at nature in total awe of Your magnificent creation. Amen.

DAY 274

Good Direction

Morning

I pondered the direction of my life, and I turned to follow your laws.
PSALM 119:59 NLT

The mouth of the righteous utters wisdom, and his tongue speaks justice. The law of his God is in his heart; his steps do not slip.
PSALM 37:30–31 ESV

Sometimes we can't help but feel confused and uncertain. That's when we need to turn to God's law, His rule for living. Love is His law, the foundation that always holds firm. When we cling to God's love, we find direction.

Dear Lord, please remind me every day that everything I need for direction is found in Your holy Word. Amen.

Evening

He leads me in paths of righteousness for his name's sake.
PSALM 23:3 ESV

Without good direction, people lose their way; the more wise counsel you follow, the better your chances.
PROVERBS 11:14 MSG

Often, God makes use of other people when He wants to guide you. His grace flows to you through others' experiences and wisdom. Keep your ears open for His voice speaking to you through the good advice of those you trust.

Dear Lord, please humble me and help me to listen well to those who have wisdom and good advice. Amen.

DAY 275

Closer to God

Morning

"When the Spirit of truth comes, he will guide you into all truth. He will not speak on his own but will tell you what he has heard."
JOHN 16:13 NLT

Come near to God and he will come near to you.
JAMES 4:8 NIV

God's Spirit is truth. In Him there are no lies. You can trust Him absolutely to lead you ever closer to God. This is how you recognize true grace: It will always bring you nearer to the one who loves you most.

Dear Lord, Your Holy Spirit is true and good and always guiding me. Please draw me nearer to You. Amen.

Evening

May the Lord direct your hearts into God's love and Christ's perseverance.
2 THESSALONIANS 3:5 NIV

Blessed are those you choose and bring near to live in your courts! We are filled with the good things of your house, of your holy temple.
PSALM 65:4 NIV

Allow God to lead you each day. His grace will lead you deeper and deeper into the love of God—a love that heals your wounds and works through you to touch those around you.

Dear Lord, as You lead me in Your love, please show me how to share that love with others. Amen.

DAY 276

Disciples of Jesus

Morning

[Jesus said,] "Whoever serves me must follow me; and where I am, my servant also will be. My Father will honor the one who serves me."
JOHN 12:26 NIV

Then Jesus told his disciples, "If anyone would come after me, let him deny himself and take up his cross and follow me."
MATTHEW 16:24 ESV

A disciple is someone who follows. That is the discipline we practice: We follow Jesus. Wherever He is, we go. In His presence we find the daily grace we need to live.

Dear Jesus, there is no better leader than You, no one I'd rather follow than You! Amen.

Evening

As obedient children, do not conform to the evil desires you had when you lived in ignorance. But just as he who called you is holy, so be holy in all you do; for it is written: "Be holy, because I am holy."
1 PETER 1:14–16 NIV

Don't sin by letting anger control you. Think about it overnight and remain silent.
PSALM 4:4 NLT

As Christ's disciples, we are called to live like Him. The challenge of that calling is often greatest in life's small, daily frustrations. But as we practice saying no to anger, controlling it rather than allowing it to control us, God's grace helps us develop new skills, even ones we never thought possible!

Dear Jesus, as I follow You, please develop my character to be more like Yours. Amen.

DAY 277

The Value of Discipline

Morning

My child, do not reject the LORD's discipline, and don't get angry when he corrects you. The LORD corrects those he loves, just as parents correct the child they delight in.
PROVERBS 3:11–12 NCV

Blessed is the one you discipline, LORD, the one you teach from your law.
PSALM 94:12 NIV

God doesn't send us to time-out or take us over His knee and spank us. Instead, His discipline comes to us through the circumstances of life. By saying yes to whatever we face, no matter how difficult and frustrating it may be, we allow God's grace to permeate each moment of our day.

Dear Lord, help me to say yes to any hard thing I face today, because I have confidence that You will help me through it. Amen.

Evening

But since we belong to the day, let us be sober, putting on faith and love as a breastplate, and the hope of salvation as a helmet.
1 THESSALONIANS 5:8 NIV

For the moment all discipline seems painful rather than pleasant, but later it yields the peaceful fruit of righteousness to those who have been trained by it.
HEBREWS 12:11 ESV

We sometimes think of discipline as a negative thing. But really the word has more to do with the grace we receive from instruction and learning, from following a master. Like an athlete who follows her coach's leading, we are called to follow our Master.

Dear Lord, help me not to balk at discipline. May I accept it, value it, and learn from it. Amen.

DAY 278

Reaching Out

Morning

I pray that God, who gives hope, will bless you with complete happiness and peace because of your faith. And may the power of the Holy Spirit fill you with hope.

ROMANS 15:13 CEV

Your words have supported those who were falling; you encouraged those with shaky knees.

JOB 4:4 NLT

God knows how weak and shaky we feel some days. He understands how prone humans are to discouragement. His grace is always there, like a hand held out to us, simply waiting for us to reach out and grasp it.

Loving Father, I'm so thankful You're always reaching out to me, ready to hold and help me no matter my circumstances. Amen.

Evening

Whoever has the gift of encouraging others should encourage.

ROMANS 12:8 NCV

You obey the law of Christ when you offer each other a helping hand.

GALATIANS 6:2 CEV

When God encourages us, His own heart reaches out to us and His strength becomes ours. As we rely on His grace, we are empowered in turn to reach out to those around us, lending them our hearts and strength.

Dear Lord, please increase my outreach to others. I want to share the love You so freely give me. Amen.

DAY 279

Reciprocation

Morning

When we get together,
I want to encourage you in
your faith, but I also want to
be encouraged by yours.
ROMANS 1:12 NLT

Treat others just as you
want to be treated.
LUKE 6:31 CEV

Encouragement is always reciprocal. When we encourage others, we ourselves are encouraged. We are connected to each other, like parts of a body. Whatever we do that is good for another is good for us as well.

Dear Lord, help me to recognize what joy there is in the circle of encouragement. As I encourage others, so am I greatly encouraged! Amen.

Evening

"But you, take courage!
Do not let your hands
be weak, for your work
shall be rewarded."
2 CHRONICLES 15:7 ESV

"Give, and you will receive.
Your gift will return to you in
full—pressed down, shaken
together to make room for
more, running over, and poured
into your lap. The amount
you give will determine the
amount you get back."
LUKE 6:38 NLT

In the world's economy, we pay a price in order to receive something we want; in other words, we give up something to get something. But in God's economy, we always get back what we give up.

Dear Lord, please remind me that I can never outgive You. Your blessings overflow when I am willing to be generous with them. Amen.

DAY 280

Sticking Together

Morning

Families stick together
in all kinds of trouble.
PROVERBS 17:17 MSG

Pay close attention, friend, to
what your father tells you; never
forget what you learned at
your mother's knee. Wear their
counsel like a winning crown,
like rings on your fingers.
PROVERBS 1:8–9 MSG

When it comes right down to it, your family members are the ones who show you God's grace even when life is hard. They're the ones who stick by you no matter what (even when they make you crazy!).

Heavenly Father, no matter how
stressful things can get at times,
I am so thankful for my family.
What a blessing to have people who
love me and stick by me. Amen.

Evening

God sets the lonely in families.
PSALM 68:6 NIV

It is truly wonderful
when the people of God
live together in peace.
PSALM 133:1 CEV

God knows that we need others. That's why He gives us families. Families don't need to be related by blood though. They might be the people you work with, or the people you go to church with, or the group of friends you've known since grade school. Whoever they are, they're the people who make God's grace real to you every day.

Dear Lord, thank You so much for
those people who have become
like family to me, dear friends and
loved ones who encourage and
help me along life's way. Amen.

DAY 281

Family Ties

Morning

Jesus, who makes people holy, and those who are made holy are from the same family. So he is not ashamed to call them his brothers and sisters.
HEBREWS 2:11 NCV

But to all who believed him and accepted him, he gave the right to become children of God. They are reborn—not with a physical birth resulting from human passion or plan, but a birth that comes from God.
JOHN 1:12–13 NLT

You and Jesus are family! Jesus, the one who made you whole and clean in God's sight, is your brother. Family ties connect you to Him and to all those with whom He is connected.

Dear Lord, becoming a part of Your family is the best thing that has ever happened to me. Thank You! Amen.

Evening

In Christ's family there can be no division into Jew and non-Jew, slave and free, male and female. Among us you are all equal.
GALATIANS 3:28 MSG

And above all these put on love, which binds everything together in perfect harmony.
COLOSSIANS 3:14 ESV

By grace Jesus has removed all barriers between God and ourselves. God asks that as members of His family we also knock down all the walls we've built between ourselves and others.

Dear Lord, help me to build unity with other members of Your family, not create division. Help us to love each other as You love us. Amen.

DAY 282

Hungry

Morning

"Give us today
our daily bread."
MATTHEW 6:11 NIV

"Every moving thing that lives shall be food for you. And as I gave you the green plants, I give you everything."
GENESIS 9:3 ESV

We need food each day. Healthy fruits and vegetables, whole grains, and lean protein for our bodies—and times of prayer and quiet for our souls. Like a loving mother, God delights in nourishing His children.

Heavenly Father, thank You for nourishing me both physically and spiritually. Amen.

Evening

You serve me a six-course dinner right in front of my enemies. You revive my drooping head; my cup brims with blessing.
PSALM 23:5 MSG

Jesus said to them, "I am the bread of life; whoever comes to me shall not hunger, and whoever believes in me shall never thirst."
JOHN 6:35 ESV

Do you ever go too long without eating and then your body demands food? We often do the same thing to our spirits, depriving them of the spiritual nourishment they need—and then we wonder why life seems so overwhelming and bleak. But dinner is on the table, and God is waiting to revive us with platefuls of grace and cups brimming with blessings.

Dear Father, please forgive me when I starve my spirit of the nourishment You offer so freely. Please fill me up as only You can. Amen.

DAY 283

Merciful Forgiveness

Morning

For the honor of your name, O LORD, forgive my many, many sins.

PSALM 25:11 NLT

Let them come back to GOD, who is merciful, come back to our God, who is lavish with forgiveness.

ISAIAH 55:7 MSG

Like all gifts of grace, forgiveness by its very definition is something that can never be earned. Forgiveness is what God gives us when we deserve nothing but punishment.

Loving Father, I praise You for Your merciful forgiveness. Time and time again I need it. Thank You! Amen.

Evening

GOD is sheer mercy and grace; not easily angered, he's rich in love. He doesn't endlessly nag and scold, nor hold grudges forever. He doesn't treat us as our sins deserve, nor pay us back in full for our wrongs.

PSALM 103:8–10 MSG

How great is the goodness you have stored up for those who fear you.

PSALM 31:19 NLT

God forgives us not because we merit it but because of His own honor. Over and over, we will turn away from God, but over and over, He will bring us back. That's who He is!

Dear God, Your awesome goodness is what allows me to return to You after I've done wrong. There simply aren't enough words to express my gratitude. Amen.

DAY 284

Constant Companion

Morning

Our Lord, you are the friend of your worshipers, and you make an agreement with all of us.

PSALM 25:14 CEV

"I no longer call you servants, because a servant does not know his master's business. Instead, I have called you friends, for everything that I learned from my Father I have made known to you."

JOHN 15:15 NIV

God is our friend. He is our companion through life's journey; He is the one who always understands us; and no matter what we do, He always accepts us and loves us.

Dear Lord, there is no better friend than You. I'm so blessed to have You as my constant companion. Amen.

Evening

My friends scorn me, but I pour out my tears to God.

JOB 16:20 NLT

A man of many companions may come to ruin, but there is a friend who sticks closer than a brother.

PROVERBS 18:24 ESV

Sometimes even the best friends can let you down. Human beings aren't perfect. But God's grace will never fail you. When even your closest friends don't understand you, take your hurt to Him.

Dear Lord, thank You for caring about any and every need I have and never letting me down. What a wonderful friend I have in You! Amen.

DAY 285

What You Crave

Morning

Take delight in the LORD,
and he will give you
your heart's desires.
PSALM 37:4 NLT

When I awake, I will see you
face to face and be satisfied.
PSALM 17:15 NLT

God is the one who placed your heart's desires deep inside you. As you turn to Him, knowing that He alone is the source of all true delight, He will grant you what your heart most truly craves.

Dear Lord, You are my hope and delight and one true source of satisfaction. Forgive me when I forget that, and draw me back to You. Amen.

Evening

Satisfy us in the
morning with your unfailing
love, that we may sing for joy
and be glad all our days.
PSALM 90:14 NIV

And the LORD will guide you
continually and satisfy your
desire in scorched places.
ISAIAH 58:11 ESV

God wants to fulfill you. He wants you to feel satisfied with life so that you will catch yourself humming under your breath all day long. Even when life is hard, He is waiting to comfort you with His unfailing love so that gladness will fill your heart once more.

Dear God, please fill my heart with a song that praises You no matter what my circumstances. You satisfy like nothing else. Amen.

DAY 286

A Safe Future

Morning

"For I know the plans
I have for you," says the Lord.
"They are plans for good
and not for disaster, to give
you a future and a hope."
Jeremiah 29:11 NLT

"I have told you all this so that
you may have peace in me.
Here on earth you will have
many trials and sorrows.
But take heart, because I
have overcome the world."
John 16:33 NLT

Don't worry about the future. No matter how frightening it may look to you sometimes, God is waiting there for you. He has plans for you, wonderful plans that will lead you deeper and deeper into His grace and love.

Dear Father, Your plans for me are good, and I believe You are working through every circumstance in my life, both good and bad, to make me more like You—until one day I am with You forever! Amen.

Evening

My life is in your hands.
Save me from my enemies and
from those who are chasing me.
Psalm 31:15 NCV

The Lord is my strength and
my shield; in him my heart
trusts, and I am helped.
Psalm 28:7 ESV

Do you ever feel like trouble is chasing you? No matter how fast you run or how you try to hide, it comes after you relentlessly. Maybe you need to stop running and stop hiding and instead let yourself drop into God's hands, knowing He holds your future.

Dear Lord, life can be so full of things to fear; help me to trust You more. You are my source of courage and protection. Keep me safe according to Your will. Amen.

DAY 287

Wonderful Things Ahead

Morning

Everything God made is waiting with excitement for God to show his children's glory completely.
ROMANS 8:19 NCV

But our citizenship is in heaven, and from it we await a Savior, the Lord Jesus Christ.
PHILIPPIANS 3:20–21 ESV

God doesn't want us to be ostriches, hiding our heads in the sand, refusing to acknowledge what's going on in the world. But He also wants us to believe that the future is full of wonderful things He has planned. The whole world is holding its breath, waiting for God's wonderful grace to reveal itself.

Dear Lord, help me to fight the discouragement that rises in me when I hear of awful current events. You are coming back, and You will prevail with love and justice. I cannot wait! Amen.

Evening

She is clothed with strength and dignity, and she laughs without fear of the future.
PROVERBS 31:25 NLT

And the one sitting on the throne said, "Look, I am making everything new!"
REVELATION 21:5 NLT

God wants to clothe us with His strength, His dignity. He wants us to be whole and competent, full of His grace. When we are, we can look at the future and laugh, knowing that God will take care of the details as we trust Him to be the foundation of our lives.

Dear God, I look forward to the future with great hope and joy because of Your promises! Thank You! Amen.

DAY 288

Longing for Home

Morning

And he said to him,
"Truly, I say to you,
today you will be with
me in paradise."
LUKE 23:43 ESV

"No eye has seen, no ear
has heard, and no mind has
imagined what God has prepared
for those who love him."
1 CORINTHIANS 2:9 NLT

None of us knows exactly what lies on the other side of death's dark door. But we do know this: Death will take us home. Jesus promised us that. He wouldn't have said it just to make us feel better; Jesus wasn't one for telling polite lies!

Dear Jesus, I trust that the heavenly home You are preparing will far exceed my imagination. I never need to fear death because it will bring me straight to You! Amen.

Evening

"There is plenty of room
for you in my Father's home.
If that weren't so, would I have
told you that I'm on my way to
get a room ready for you?"
JOHN 14:2 MSG

For we know that if the tent
that is our earthly home is
destroyed, we have a building
from God, a house not made with
hands, eternal in the heavens.
2 CORINTHIANS 5:1 ESV

We can trust that right now Jesus is getting our home in heaven ready for us, filling it with His grace. When we enter the door, we will find it is exactly right for us, the place for which we have always longed.

Dear Father, when I'm feeling out of place here on earth, remind me that's the way it should be. I'm just a stranger here, and my real home is in heaven. I'm so eager to be with You forever. Amen.

DAY 289

Cheerful Hospitality

Morning

When God's people are in need, be ready to help them. Always be eager to practice hospitality.

ROMANS 12:13 NLT

Do not neglect to show hospitality to strangers, for thereby some have entertained angels unawares.

HEBREWS 13:2 ESV

God opens Himself to you, offering you everything He has, and calls you to do the same for others. Just as He has made you welcome, make others welcome in your life. Be eager for opportunities to practice the grace of hospitality.

Dear Lord, You are warm and welcoming to anyone who calls on You. Help me to follow Your example. Amen.

Evening

Be quick to give a meal to the hungry, a bed to the homeless—cheerfully.

1 PETER 4:9 MSG

Contribute to the needs of the saints and seek to show hospitality.

ROMANS 12:13 ESV

Because our homes are our private places, sometimes it's hard to open them to others. But God calls us to offer our hospitality, and He will give us grace to do it joyfully.

Dear Lord, help me to be open and generous with my home. Please show me the needs of others and how I can help them. Amen.

DAY 290

Simple Hospitality

Morning

"Then those 'sheep' are going to say, 'Master, what are you talking about? When did we ever see you hungry and feed you, thirsty and give you a drink? And when did we ever see you sick or in prison and come to you?' Then the King will say, 'I'm telling the solemn truth: Whenever you did one of these things to someone overlooked or ignored, that was me—you did it to me.' "

MATTHEW 25:37–40 MSG

We're given the opportunity to offer hospitality to Jesus each time we're faced with another person in need. His grace reaches out through us when we minister to those who feel misunderstood or overlooked.

Dear Lord, I need to remember that anything I do for others is a service done for You. Help me to be cheerful and loving as I serve. Amen.

Evening

If your enemy is hungry, feed him. If he is thirsty, give him a drink.

PROVERBS 25:21 NCV

"When you give a dinner or a banquet, do not invite your friends or your brothers or your relatives or rich neighbors, lest they also invite you in return and you be repaid. But when you give a feast, invite the poor, the crippled, the lame, the blind, and you will be blessed, because they cannot repay you. For you will be repaid at the resurrection of the just."

LUKE 14:12–14 ESV

God calls us to reach out in practical, tangible ways to everyone. Seek His grace to do this in some way each and every day.

Dear Lord, my hospitality shouldn't always feel easy and comfortable. Please nudge me out of my comfort zone and into better relationships with friends and neighbors. Amen.

DAY 291

Thinking Habits

Morning

And now, dear brothers and sisters, one final thing. Fix your thoughts on what is true, and honorable, and right, and pure, and lovely, and admirable. Think about things that are excellent and worthy of praise.
PHILIPPIANS 4:8 NLT

Those who are dominated by the sinful nature think about sinful things, but those who are controlled by the Holy Spirit think about things that please the Spirit.
ROMANS 8:5 NLT

Our brains are gifts from God, intended to serve us well, special gifts of grace we often take for granted. In return, we need to offer our minds back to God.

Dear Lord, please take over my thoughts and fix them on You! Amen.

Evening

Letting your sinful nature control your mind leads to death. But letting the Spirit control your mind leads to life and peace.
ROMANS 8:6 NLT

We take captive every thought to make it obedient to Christ.
2 CORINTHIANS 10:5 NIV

Practice thinking positive thoughts. Focus on what is true rather than on lies; pay attention to beautiful things and stop staring at the ugly things in life. Discipline your mind to take on God's habits of thinking.

Dear Lord, I want to give Your Holy Spirit complete control of my mind because I know His leadership leads to life and peace. Truth is found in You alone. Amen.

DAY 292

Beyond Intelligence

Morning

The fastest runner does not always win the race, the strongest soldier does not always win the battle, the wisest does not always have food, the smartest does not always become wealthy, and the talented one does not always receive praise. Time and chance happen to everyone.

ECCLESIASTES 9:11 NCV

"For my thoughts are not your thoughts, neither are your ways my ways, declares the LORD."

ISAIAH 55:8 ESV

How smart do you think you are? Do you assume you'll be able to think your way through life's problems? Many of us do—but God reminds us that some things are beyond the scope of our intelligence.

Dear Lord, there are just some things I will never understand this side of heaven because Your thoughts and ways are much higher than mine. You have a perfect perspective on all things, and I don't. But I choose to trust You no matter what. Amen.

Evening

"As the heavens are higher than the earth, so are my ways higher than your ways and my thoughts than your thoughts."

ISAIAH 55:9 ESV

You keep him in perfect peace whose mind is stayed on you, because he trusts in you.

ISAIAH 26:3 ESV

Some days life simply doesn't make sense. But even then, grace is there with us in the chaos. When we can find no rational answers to life's dilemmas, we have no choice but to rely absolutely on God.

Dear Lord, I choose to keep my mind on You no matter what chaos is going on around me. I always find peace when I trust in Your plans. Amen.

DAY 293

Joy and Harmony

Morning

"The joy of the Lord is your strength."
NEHEMIAH 8:10 NIV

You make known to me the path of life; you will fill me with joy in your presence, with eternal pleasures at your right hand.
PSALM 16:11 NIV

Our God is a God of joy. He is not a God of sighing and gloom. Open yourself to His joy. It is a gift of grace He longs to give you. He knows it will make you strong.

Dear God, being Your child is the best reason to be filled with joy. Please strengthen me constantly with the awesome joy of calling You Abba! Amen.

Evening

The hope of the righteous will be gladness, but the expectation of the wicked will perish.
PROVERBS 10:28 NKJV

Therefore, since we have been justified by faith, we have peace with God through our Lord Jesus Christ.
ROMANS 5:1 ESV

When we try to live our lives apart from God, we put ourselves in a place where we can no longer see His grace. Joy flows from being in harmony with God.

Dear God, I'm so thankful that because of Jesus, I can be in complete harmony with You! Amen.

DAY 294

Married Love

Morning

Let love be genuine.
ROMANS 12:9 ESV

Above all, clothe yourselves with love, which binds us all together in perfect harmony.
COLOSSIANS 3:14 NLT

Marriage is the place where you are most vulnerable with another person. Your spouse is the person who sees you naked, clothed only in love. But love is the best clothing. When as married partners we strip off all our defensiveness and selfishness, then nothing comes between us but love.

Dear Lord, please protect my marriage. Help my spouse and me to be completely honest and vulnerable with each other and always clothed in love. Amen.

Evening

Keep your eyes open, hold tight to your convictions, give it all you've got, be resolute, and love without stopping.
1 CORINTHIANS 16:13–14 MSG

Love bears all things, believes all things, hopes all things, endures all things.
1 CORINTHIANS 13:7 ESV

Romantic love will come and go throughout a marriage. The kind of love that gets you through dark nights, angry fights, and long, busy days—that love is the resolute kind, the stubborn love that never gives up.

Dear Lord, help my husband and me to have unconditional love for each other, with You as our example, and let us grow deeper in it day by day. Amen.

DAY 295

Sow Generously

Morning

The earth is the LORD's,
and everything in it.
PSALM 24:1 NLT

Honor the LORD with your
wealth and with the firstfruits
of all your produce.
PROVERBS 3:9 ESV

Giving 10 percent of your income specifically to God's work is a good discipline. But sometimes we forget that everything is God's. Through grace, He shares all of creation with us. When we look at it that way, our 10 percent tithe seems a little stingy!

Heavenly Father, forgive me when
I get caught up in what's mine.
Remind me that everything comes
from You. Help me to give of my
blessings generously. Amen.

Evening

Give me neither poverty
nor riches! Give me just
enough to satisfy my needs.
PROVERBS 30:8 NLT

Whoever sows generously
will also reap generously.
2 CORINTHIANS 9:6 NIV

God gives us what we need, and He knows exactly what and how much that is. Whatever He has given you financially, He knows that is what you need right now. Trust His grace. He will satisfy your needs.

Dear Lord, please remind me
that I never need to worry about
money. You will continually provide
exactly what I need. Amen.

DAY 296

Accepted

Morning

The LORD has heard my cry for mercy; the LORD accepts my prayer.

PSALM 6:9 NIV

For he chose us in him before the creation of the world to be holy and blameless in his sight. In love he predestined us for adoption to sonship through Jesus Christ, in accordance with his pleasure and will.

EPHESIANS 1:4–5 NIV

People talk about "accepting" God into their lives. But it's God's acceptance of us that makes this possible. Because Jesus gave His life to pay the price for all the wrongs we've ever done, our perfect God can accept us wholeheartedly, even though we're far from perfect people.

Dear Lord, I am the worst of all sinners, yet You accept me and forgive me. I praise You! Amen.

Evening

And pray in the Spirit on all occasions with all kinds of prayers and requests.

EPHESIANS 6:18 NIV

Likewise the Spirit helps us in our weakness. For we do not know what to pray for as we ought, but the Spirit himself intercedes for us with groanings too deep for words.

ROMANS 8:26 ESV

God not only accepts us, but He also accepts our imperfect prayers. We don't have to worry about saying just the right words. The "perfect" prayer is simply sharing what's on our hearts.

Dear Father, thank You that I can talk to You just as I would a friend. You listen and hear all of my imperfect prayers. Amen.

DAY 297

God's Coworker

Morning

Unless the Lord builds the house, the builders labor in vain.
PSALM 127:1 NIV

You have given me your shield of victory. Your right hand supports me; your help has made me great.
PSALM 18:35 NLT

We were designed to do great things hand in hand with a very great God. So why not invite God to be your helper in every endeavor you undertake today? Call on Him throughout the day, anytime you need wisdom, peace, or perseverance.

Dear Lord, I invite You into every task I take on, both big and small. When I'm working for You and with You, I know I will see great success! Amen.

Evening

Therefore, if anyone cleanses himself from what is dishonorable, he will be a vessel for honorable use, set apart as holy, useful to the master of the house, ready for every good work.
2 TIMOTHY 2:21 ESV

May the favor of the Lord our God rest on us; establish the work of our hands for us—yes, establish the work of our hands.
PSALM 90:17 NIV

Allow God to infuse you with creativity, humility, and compassion, regardless of the size of the task at hand. Your hard work, guided by prayer and undergirded by the Spirit of a mighty God, can accomplish amazing things.

Dear Lord, please equip me for the good works You want me to do. Amen.

DAY 298

Made Well

Morning

I praise you because I am fearfully and wonderfully made.

PSALM 139:14 NIV

So God created man in his own image, in the image of God he created him; male and female he created them.

GENESIS 1:27 ESV

You are a living, breathing reason for praise. God formed only one of you, unique in appearance, intricate in design, priceless beyond measure. You were fashioned with both love and forethought.

Almighty God, thank You for creating me! Thank You for seeing my heart that is not perfect but longs to please You! Amen.

Evening

With your very own hands you formed me; now breathe your wisdom over me so I can understand you.

PSALM 119:73 MSG

But now, O LORD, you are our Father; we are the clay, and you are our potter; we are all the work of your hand.

ISAIAH 64:8 ESV

Use the mirror as a springboard for praise. Ask God, "What do You see when You look at me?" Listen quietly as God's truth helps retool your self-image.

Dear Lord, help me to see myself as You see me. Please give me confidence not in my outward appearance but in the character You are building in me. Amen.

DAY 299

Forever Faith

Morning

I will exalt you, my God the King; I will praise your name for ever and ever. Every day I will praise you and extol your name for ever and ever.

PSALM 145:1–2 NIV

Your righteousness is righteous forever, and your law is true.

PSALM 119:142 ESV

Conventional wisdom tells us nothing lasts forever. Thankfully, just because a saying is often quoted doesn't make it true. The time-tested wisdom of the Bible assures us that God always has been and always will be.

Almighty God, You alone are constant and eternal. I find such stability and peace in knowing and following You! Amen.

Evening

The LORD will work out his plans for my life— for your faithful love, O LORD, endures forever.

PSALM 138:8 NLT

The LORD will watch over your coming and going both now and forevermore.

PSALM 121:8 NIV

Because of Jesus, *forever* is a word that can apply to us as well. When we follow Jesus here on earth, we follow Him straight to heaven. We have the assurance of knowing our true life span is "forevermore."

Dear Lord, I'm so thankful that faith in You is not just a fleeting idea but a permanent promise of forever life with You! Amen.

DAY 300

God's Good Heart

Morning

I would have lost heart,
unless I had believed that I
would see the goodness of the
Lord in the land of the living.
PSALM 27:13 NKJV

I myself am satisfied about
you, my brothers, that you
yourselves are full of goodness,
filled with all knowledge and
able to instruct one another.
ROMANS 15:14 ESV

Knowing a friend's heart toward you can help you relax and be yourself. With a friend like this, you can honestly share your deepest secrets, feelings, and failures without fear of ridicule or reprisal.

Dear Lord, thank You for
friends who truly care for me.
What a gift they are! Amen.

Evening

Oh, how abundant is your
goodness, which you have
stored up for those who fear
you and worked for those who
take refuge in you, in the sight
of the children of mankind!
PSALM 31:19 ESV

Oh, taste and see that
the Lord is good!
PSALM 34:8 ESV

The Psalms remind us over and over again that God's heart toward us is good. Believing in God's innate goodness means we can entrust every detail of our lives to Him without hesitation.

Dear Lord, thank You for the
goodness You always extend to me.
I don't deserve it because of my
sin, but because of Your grace You
lavish me with it! Amazing! Amen.

DAY 301

Satisfied by God's Word

Morning

Everything in the Scriptures is God's Word. All of it is useful for teaching and helping people and for correcting them and showing them how to live.

2 TIMOTHY 3:16 CEV

You thrill to God's Word, you chew on Scripture day and night.

PSALM 1:2 MSG

Imagine God's words as your favorite meal, each bite a delicacy to be savored. You relish the unique blend of ingredients, the flavor and texture. When the meal is complete, you're nourished and satisfied.

Dear God, Your Word nourishes my soul like nothing else. Help me to crave it every day. Amen.

Evening

"It is written, 'Man shall not live by bread alone, but by every word that comes from the mouth of God.'"

MATTHEW 4:4 ESV

[They] have tasted the goodness of the word of God.

HEBREWS 6:5 NLT

Scripture is a well-balanced meal for your heart and soul, a meal that can continue long after your Bible is back on the shelf. Ponder what you've read. Meditate on God's promises. Chew on the timeless truths that add zest to your life.

Dear Lord, help me to make a daily habit of coming to Your Word to be spiritually fed. Please bring Your truth and promises constantly to my mind so that I might apply them to my circumstances. Amen.

DAY 302

A Love Letter

Morning

Every word you give me is a miracle word—how could I help but obey? Break open your words, let the light shine out, let ordinary people see the meaning.

PSALM 119:129 MSG

For the word of God is alive and active. Sharper than any double-edged sword, it penetrates even to dividing soul and spirit, joints and marrow; it judges the thoughts and attitudes of the heart.

HEBREWS 4:12 NIV

The Bible isn't a novel to be read for entertainment, a textbook to be skimmed for knowledge, a manual for living, or a collection of inspirational sayings. The Bible is a love letter.

Almighty God, Your love for Your people is evident all throughout Your Word. I am so grateful to be Your child. Amen.

Evening

Jesus replied, "But even more blessed are all who hear the word of God and put it into practice."

LUKE 11:28 NLT

And we also thank God constantly for this, that when you received the word of God, which you heard from us, you accepted it not as the word of men but as what it really is, the word of God, which is at work in you believers.

1 THESSALONIANS 2:13 ESV

The Bible is the story of God's love for His children from the beginning of the world until the end and beyond. It's a book that takes time to know well, but God promises His own Spirit will help us understand what we read. All we need to do is ask.

Dear Lord, please grow me in my understanding of Your Word. Amen.

DAY 303

Bearing Burdens

Morning

Cast your burden on the Lord, and He shall sustain you; He shall never permit the righteous to be moved.

PSALM 55:22 NKJV

Humble yourselves, therefore, under the mighty hand of God so that at the proper time he may exalt you, casting all your anxieties on him, because he cares for you.

1 PETER 5:6–7 ESV

Casting our burdens on God is as easy as speaking to Him in prayer. It's calling for help when we need it, admitting our sin when we've fallen, and letting our tears speak for our hearts when words fail us.

Dear Lord, it's ridiculous how often I try to carry my burdens alone when You tell me to give them to You. What relief there is in asking for Your help and knowing You will sustain me. Amen.

Evening

Praise be to the Lord, to God our Savior, who daily bears our burdens.

PSALM 68:19 NIV

The Lord upholds all who are falling and raises up all who are bowed down.

PSALM 145:14 ESV

The mental and emotional burdens we bear are too heavy to carry alone. The good news is that strength, peace, comfort, and hope are only a prayer away. We're never alone in our pain or struggle. God is always near, right beside us, ready to help carry what's weighing us down.

Dear Father, I'm so weary of this burden and I need Your loving arms to lift it from me. Thank You! Amen.

DAY 304

Change

Morning

I trust in you, Lord;
I say, "You are my God."
My times are in your hands.
Psalm 31:14–15 NIV

"For I the Lord do not change."
Malachi 3:6 ESV

Change can be exciting. It can also be uncomfortable, unwanted, and at times even terrifying. If you're facing change and find yourself feeling anxious or confused, turn to the God of order and peace.

Dear Lord, even though my circumstances change regularly, You never do. I'm so grateful for the stability and strength You lend to my life. Amen.

Evening

"For the mountains may move and the hills disappear, but even then my faithful love for you will remain. My covenant of blessing will never be broken."
Isaiah 54:10 NLT

"Do not be afraid or discouraged, for the Lord will personally go ahead of you. He will be with you; he will neither fail you nor abandon you."
Deuteronomy 31:8 NLT

God holds every twist and turn of your life in His hands. Try looking at change through God's eyes, as an opportunity for growth and an invitation to trust Him with your deepest hopes and fears.

Dear Lord, help me not to fear change but to see it as an opportunity to learn from You and lean on You. Amen.

DAY 305

Character Makeover

Morning

Test my thoughts and
find out what I am like.
PSALM 26:2 CEV

You have searched me,
LORD, and you know me.
PSALM 139:1 NIV

Some women spend a great amount of time trying to look beautiful on the outside while paying little attention to what's on the inside. God's words and His Spirit can help reveal the true you, from the inside out.

Dear Father, only You truly know my heart, and I want it to be beautiful to You. Please cleanse me and cultivate me to be more like You! Amen.

Evening

Charm is deceptive,
and beauty is fleeting;
but a woman who fears the
LORD is to be praised.
PROVERBS 31:30 NIV

Let your adorning be the
hidden person of the heart with
the imperishable beauty of a
gentle and quiet spirit, which
in God's sight is very precious.
1 PETER 3:4 ESV

Ask God where your character needs some touching up—or perhaps a total makeover. See if your thoughts, your words, and your actions line up with the woman you'd like to see smiling back at you in the mirror each morning.

Dear Lord, show me my sin and help me to flee from it. Forgive me and make me whole and beautiful in Your eyes. Amen.

DAY 306

More Than Motherly Love

Morning

Children are a heritage
from the Lord, offspring
a reward from him.
PSALM 127:3 NIV

Then our sons in their youth will
be like well-nurtured plants,
and our daughters will be like
pillars carved to adorn a palace.
PSALM 144:12 NIV

Like adults, children have spiritual needs as well as physical and emotional ones. That's why praying for your children every day is more than just a good idea. It's a reminder that your children need more than motherly love. They also need their heavenly Father's involvement in their lives.

Dear Lord, help me to care for
my children well and especially
to do everything I can to
lead them to You. Amen.

Evening

"Let the little children come
to me, and do not hinder
them, for the kingdom of God
belongs to such as these."
LUKE 18:16 NIV

"Truly I tell you, anyone
who will not receive the
kingdom of God like a little
child will never enter it."
LUKE 18:17 NIV

Jesus talked about how our faith should resemble a child's. To understand why, consider this: Children believe what they hear, say what they think, and love unconditionally. What a wonderful way to relate to God.

Dear Father, help me to be more
childlike in my relationship with
You. I want to trust You completely,
communicate with You freely, and
love You wholeheartedly. Amen.

DAY 307

Wise Choices

Morning

My choice is you, God,
first and only. And now I
find I'm your choice!
PSALM 16:5 MSG

For we must all appear before the judgment seat of Christ, so that each of us may receive what is due us for the things done while in the body, whether good or bad.
2 CORINTHIANS 5:10 NIV

When we decide to follow Jesus, it affects every choice we make from that moment forward. The more we involve God in our decision process, the wiser our choices will be.

Dear Lord, please remind me of Your presence with every choice I make. I want to consult with You on everything because You are wise and good! Amen.

Evening

"Choose this day
whom you will serve."
JOSHUA 24:15 ESV

Guide my steps by your word,
so I will not be overcome by evil.
PSALM 119:133 NLT

When it comes to the road of life, the Bible is a map that helps guide you every step of the way. The more you read it, the better prepared you are to make good choices. When facing a fork in the road of life, stop to consider which direction God's Word would have you go.

Dear Lord, help me not to make hasty decisions. I want to take time to prayerfully consider my options and measure them according to Your Word. Please show me Your will in all things. Amen.

DAY 308

The Best Source of Comfort

Morning

God's a safe-house for the battered, a sanctuary during bad times. The moment you arrive, you relax; you're never sorry you knocked.

Psalm 9:9–10 MSG

My comfort in my suffering is this: Your promise preserves my life.

Psalm 119:50 NIV

When women are in need of comfort, they seem to instinctively turn to a spouse or close friend. There's nothing wrong with seeking a human shoulder to cry on when you need it. Just remember that the Bible refers to Jesus as both our bridegroom and our friend.

Loving Father, thank You for loved ones who comfort me when I'm in need, and thank You that You are my greatest source of comfort. You are always present, and Your Word is powerful to console me. Amen.

Evening

Even when I walk through the darkest valley, I will not be afraid, for you are close beside me. Your rod and your staff protect and comfort me.

Psalm 23:4 NLT

Let your steadfast love comfort me.

Psalm 119:76 ESV

The comfort God provides runs deeper than anything people can offer. God sees your problems as part of a larger, eternal picture and can offer perspective as well as solace.

Loving Father, You truly give peace that passes all understanding. No person or earthly pursuit can provide that. I praise You for the great comfort found only in You. Amen.

DAY 309

Broken Hearts

Morning

The Lord is near to those who have a broken heart, and saves such as have a contrite spirit.

Psalm 34:18 NKJV

Jesus wept.

John 11:35 NIV

Putting your faith in Jesus doesn't mean you'll never have a broken heart. Scripture tells us even Jesus wept. Jesus knew the future. He knew His heavenly Father was in control. He knew victory was certain. But He still grieved.

Dear Father, it helps so much to know You understand grief. I grieve with hope because of Your promises. Amen.

Evening

You have kept count of my tossings; put my tears in your bottle. Are they not in your book?

Psalm 56:8 ESV

He heals the brokenhearted and binds up their wounds.

Psalm 147:3 ESV

When your heart is broken, only God has the power to make it whole again. It won't happen overnight. But when you draw close to God, you draw close to the true source of peace, joy, and healing.

Dear Lord, You keep track of every tear I cry, and You care about each one. Please hold me close while I weep. Amen.

DAY 310

Like Wedding Vows

Morning

He always stands by his covenant— the commitment he made to a thousand generations.

PSALM 105:8 NLT

Who shall separate us from the love of Christ?

ROMANS 8:35 ESV

God has made a commitment to you similar to a wedding vow. He promises to love and cherish you through sickness and health, prosperity or poverty, good times and bad. But with God, this commitment doesn't just last until "death do you part."

Dear Lord, Your commitment to me inspires me to commit my life wholly to You. I am in awe of Your unconditional love for me! Amen.

Evening

Neither death nor life, nor angels nor rulers, nor things present nor things to come, nor powers, nor height nor depth, nor anything else in all creation, will be able to separate us from the love of God in Christ Jesus our Lord.

ROMANS 8:38–39 ESV

Because of the LORD's great love we are not consumed, for his compassions never fail.

LAMENTATIONS 3:22 NIV

Even in death and beyond, God is with you. There's nothing you can do that will make Him turn His face from you. His commitment to love and forgive you stands steadfast, come what may.

Loving Father, without Your steadfast love, my life would be in ruins. I praise You and thank You that nothing can ever destroy Your love for me. Amen.

DAY 311

Someone to Trust

Morning

But you, Lord, are a compassionate and gracious God, slow to anger, abounding in love and faithfulness.
PSALM 86:15 NIV

As a father has compassion on his children, so the LORD has compassion on those who fear him.
PSALM 103:13 NIV

Without love and compassion, an all-powerful God would be something to fear instead of Someone to trust. That's one reason Jesus came to earth: to help us see the compassionate side of the Almighty.

Dear God, You are holy and just and also full of compassion. I'm thankful that while I absolutely revere You, I have no need to be afraid of You. Amen.

Evening

When he went ashore he saw a great crowd, and he had compassion on them, because they were like sheep without a shepherd. And he began to teach them many things.
MARK 6:34 ESV

"The Son of Man did not come to be served, but to serve, and to give his life as a ransom for many."
MATTHEW 20:28 NIV

Throughout the Gospels we read how Jesus reached out to the hurting—the outcasts, the infirm, the poor or abandoned. He didn't turn His back on sinners but embraced them with open arms. His arms are still open. Will you run toward His embrace?

Loving Father, I need Your arms around me. Thank You for always welcoming me with open arms. Amen.

DAY 312

Well-Placed Confidence

Morning

Those who are righteous
will be long remembered.
They do not fear bad news;
they confidently trust the LORD
to care for them. They are
confident and fearless and can
face their foes triumphantly.
PSALM 112:6–8 NLT

For the LORD will be your
confidence and will keep your
foot from being caught.
PROVERBS 3:26 ESV

We live in uncertain times, economically, politically, and globally. Yet you can greet each new day with your head held high, confident and unafraid. Why? Because you have a God who cares deeply about you and the world around you.

Dear God, don't let me forget that I have every reason to be confident in You. Amen.

Evening

Don't be afraid. I am with
you. Don't tremble with fear.
I am your God. I will make you
strong, as I protect you with my
arm and give you victories.
ISAIAH 41:10 CEV

So we can confidently say, "The
Lord is my helper; I will not
fear; what can man do to me?"
HEBREWS 13:6 ESV

When your confidence is placed firmly in God instead of your own abilities, bank account, or "good karma," you need not fear the future. It's in God's powerful, capable, and compassionate hands.

Dear God, forgive me when I put my confidence in anything or anyone but You. Amen.

DAY 313

Our Good Shepherd

Morning

The Lord is my shepherd;
I shall not want.
PSALM 23:1 ESV

For you were straying
like sheep, but have now
returned to the Shepherd and
Overseer of your souls.
1 PETER 2:25 ESV

Sheep frighten easily, tend to follow the crowd, and have a limited ability to defend themselves. That's why sheep thrive best with a shepherd who guides, protects, and cares for their needs. Our good shepherd will do the same for us.

Dear Lord, oh how I need You as my shepherd! Thank You for lovingly guiding me and caring for me. Amen.

Evening

Now may the God of peace—
who brought up from the dead
our Lord Jesus, the great
Shepherd of the sheep, and
ratified an eternal covenant
with his blood—may he equip
you with all you need for doing
his will. May he produce in you,
through the power of Jesus
Christ, every good thing that
is pleasing to him. All glory to
him forever and ever! Amen.
HEBREWS 13:20–21 NLT

"For the Lamb in the midst of the
throne will be their shepherd,
and he will guide them to springs
of living water, and God will wipe
away every tear from their eyes."
REVELATION 7:17 ESV

Worry, fear, and discontent are products of a "sheepish" mentality. But the peace of true contentment can be ours when we follow God's lead.

Dear Lord, please banish fear and discontent from my mind as I grow to trust You more every day. Amen.

DAY 314

Women of Courage

Morning

When I called,
you answered me;
you greatly
emboldened me.
PSALM 138:3 NIV

The wicked flee when no one
pursues, but the righteous
are bold as a lion.
PROVERBS 28:1 ESV

Women are often characterized as timid creatures—fleeing from spiders, screaming over mice, cowering behind big, burly men when danger is near. But the Bible characterizes women of God as bold and courageous.

Dear Lord, help me not to hide behind fear but to boldly do Your will, share Your love, and proclaim Your gospel. Amen.

Evening

This man had a very
beautiful and lovely young
cousin, Hadassah, who
was also called Esther.
ESTHER 2:7 NLT

Deborah, the wife of Lappidoth,
was a prophet who was
judging Israel at that time.
JUDGES 4:4 NLT

Queen Esther risked her life to save God's children from genocide. Deborah led an army and judged the tribes of Israel. And in the book of Joshua, Rahab dared to hide Israelite spies to save her family. Today, God will supply the courage you need to accomplish whatever He's asked you to do.

Dear Lord, Your Word shares such amazing examples of courageous women! Please help me to learn from their lives lived for You! Amen.

DAY 315

Timely Courage

Morning

Wait on the Lord; be of good courage, and He shall strengthen your heart; wait, I say, on the Lord!

Psalm 27:14 NKJV

Be strong, and let your heart take courage, all you who wait for the Lord!

Psalm 31:24 ESV

Foolhardiness can look like courage at first glance. However, true courage counts the cost before it forges ahead. If you're faced with a risky decision, it's not only wise to think before you act—it's biblical.

Dear Lord, help me to analyze a situation well rather than jump to a decision too quickly. Amen.

Evening

For the evildoers shall be cut off, but those who wait for the Lord shall inherit the land.

Psalm 37:9 ESV

For God alone, O my soul, wait in silence, for my hope is from him.

Psalm 62:5 ESV

Ecclesiastes 3:1 (MSG) reminds us, "There's an opportune time to do things, a right time for everything on the earth." Waiting for that right time takes patience and courage. Don't simply pray for courage. Pray for the wisdom to discern that "opportune time."

Dear Lord, please give me the wisdom I need to know when to act and when to wait. Amen.

DAY 316

A Clean Slate

Morning

Clean the slate, God,
so we can start the day
fresh! Keep me from stupid
sins, from thinking I can
take over your work.
PSALM 19:13 MSG

How far has the LORD taken our
sins from us? Farther than the
distance from east to west!
PSALM 103:12 CEV

Yesterday is over. Today is a brand-new day. Any mistakes or bad choices you've made in the past are behind you. God doesn't hold those things against you. He has wiped your past clean with the power of forgiveness.

Dear God, please forgive me and help me to let go of my sin like You do. I can't describe how grateful I am that You don't hold grudges or hold my sins against me. Amen.

Evening

His compassions fail not.
They are new every morning;
great is Your faithfulness.
LAMENTATIONS 3:22–23 NKJV

But I wipe away your
sins because of who I am.
And so, I will forget the
wrongs you have done.
ISAIAH 43:25 CEV

The only thing left for you to do with the past is learn from it. Celebrate each new day by giving thanks to God for what He has done and actively anticipating what He's going to do with the clean slate of today.

Dear Lord, help me not to beat myself up over the past. I've asked You to forgive my sin, and I trust that You have. Please help me to learn from the past and move forward in confidence because of Your great mercy. Amen.

DAY 317

Staying Attached

Morning

In the morning, Lord,
you hear my voice; in the
morning I lay my requests before
you and wait expectantly.
PSALM 5:3 NIV

Stay joined to me, and I will stay joined to you. Just as a branch cannot produce fruit unless it stays joined to the vine, you cannot produce fruit unless you stay joined to me. I am the vine, and you are the branches. If you stay joined to me, and I stay joined to you, then you will produce lots of fruit. But you cannot do anything without me.
JOHN 15:4–5 CEV

Scheduling time to pray and read the Bible can feel like just another item on your to-do list. But getting to know God is not a project. It's a relationship.

Dear Lord, please remind me daily that You are the vine and I am a branch. I must stay connected to You to do anything good with my life. Amen.

Evening

"Greater love has no one than this, that someone lay down his life for his friends."
JOHN 15:13 ESV

"You are my friends if you do what I command you. No longer do I call you servants, for the servant does not know what his master is doing; but I have called you friends."
JOHN 15:14–15 ESV

Best friends don't spend time together just because they feel they should. They do it because they enjoy each other's company and long to know each other better. The more consistent you are in spending time with God each day, the closer you will feel to Him.

Dear Lord, I'm sorry I struggle with inconsistency in my quiet time. Help me to make spending time with You a regular part of my days. Amen.

DAY 318

Devoted to God

Morning

Protect me, for I am devoted to you. Save me, for I serve you and trust you. You are my God.

PSALM 86:2 NLT

I have been crucified with Christ. It is no longer I who live, but Christ who lives in me. And the life I now live in the flesh I live by faith in the Son of God, who loved me and gave himself for me.

GALATIANS 2:20 ESV

The heart of devotion isn't duty. It's love. The deeper your love, the deeper your devotion. What does being devoted to God look like? It's characterized by a "God first" instead of "me first" mentality.

Dear God, I want everything I do to be for You! Please help me quash my selfish desires and follow You with full devotion. Amen.

Evening

"In all things I have shown you that by working hard in this way we must help the weak and remember the words of the Lord Jesus, how he himself said, 'It is more blessed to give than to receive.'"

ACTS 20:35 ESV

While it's true that being devoted to God means you'll spend time with Him, it also means you'll give your time to others. Your love for God will spill over onto the lives of those around you. Your devotion to God is beneficial to everyone!

Dear Lord, living for You means living for others, because that's exactly the example You set for us. Everything about Your life was a loving sacrifice; help me to spend my life ministering to others too. Amen.

DAY 319

Answered Prayer

Morning

The humble will see their God at work and be glad. Let all who seek God's help be encouraged.

PSALM 69:32 NLT

And this is the confidence that we have toward him, that if we ask anything according to his will he hears us.

1 JOHN 5:14 ESV

There's encouragement in answered prayer. Sometimes God's answers look exactly like what we were hoping for. Other times they reveal that God's love, wisdom, and creativity far surpass ours.

Almighty God, help me to trust You no matter what the answer to my prayers. I know Your perspective is perfect. Amen.

Evening

And without faith it is impossible to please him, for whoever would draw near to God must believe that he exists and that he rewards those who seek him.

HEBREWS 11:6 ESV

Therefore, confess your sins to one another and pray for one another, that you may be healed. The prayer of a righteous person has great power as it is working.

JAMES 5:16 ESV

To be aware of God's answers to prayer, we have to keep our eyes and hearts open. Be on the alert for answers to prayer today. When you catch sight of one, thank God. Allow the assurance of God's everlasting care to encourage your soul.

Dear Lord, I face so many distractions in my walk with You. As I pray, please help me to discern Your will and Your answers. Amen.

DAY 320

Strong Endurance

Morning

Those who trust in the Lord are like Mount Zion, which cannot be shaken but endures forever.

PSALM 125:1 NIV

I can do everything through Christ, who gives me strength.

PHILIPPIANS 4:13 NLT

Alpine peaks endure sun and showers, heat and hail. They don't yield or bow to adverse conditions but continue to stand firm, being exactly what God created them to be—majestic mountains. God created you to be a strong, victorious woman.

Dear Lord, help me to be strong and victorious. I can endure anything as long as I am in Your care! Amen.

Evening

For you have need of endurance, so that when you have done the will of God you may receive what is promised.

HEBREWS 10:36 ESV

Let us run with endurance the race God has set before us.

HEBREWS 12:1 NLT

You were designed to endure the changing seasons of this life with God's help. Lean on Him when the winds of life begin to buffet you. God and His Word are solid ground that will never shift beneath your feet.

Almighty God, I praise You for the strength and stability You give to my life. Remind me moment by moment that nothing can shake me when I'm grounded in You! Amen.

DAY 321

Little by Little

Morning

Invigorate my soul so I can praise you well, use your decrees to put iron in my soul.
PSALM 119:175 MSG

"As for [the seed that fell] in the good soil, they are those who, hearing the word, hold it fast in an honest and good heart, and bear fruit with patience."
LUKE 8:15 ESV

A marathon runner doesn't start out running twenty-six miles. She has to start slow, remain consistent, and push herself a bit farther day by day. That's how endurance is built. The same is true in life.

Dear Lord, when life seems overwhelming, help me to take things day by day, sometimes just moment by moment, as I trust in You to walk with me and help me through any situation. Amen.

Evening

"Give us today our daily bread."
MATTHEW 6:11 NIV

"The one who stands firm to the end will be saved."
MATTHEW 10:22 NIV

If what lies ahead seems overwhelming, don't panic thinking you need to tackle everything at once. Ask God to help you do what you can today. Then celebrate the progress you've made, rest, and repeat. Endurance grows one day at a time.

Dear Lord, please show me Your will for today, and give me confidence that You and I can accomplish it together. Amen.

DAY 322

Our Ultimate Example

Morning

I will study your teachings and follow your footsteps.

PSALM 119:15 CEV

Imitate God, therefore, in everything you do, because you are his dear children. Live a life filled with love, following the example of Christ. He loved us and offered himself as a sacrifice for us, a pleasing aroma to God.

EPHESIANS 5:1–2 NLT

In the Bible we read about heroes like Abraham, Moses, and David. Though these men did admirable things, they were also flawed. They made mistakes and poor choices. Nevertheless, God used them in remarkable ways.

Dear God, remind me that I don't have to be perfect for You to accomplish good things through me. I just have to be willing to obey You and let You use me. Amen.

Evening

We know that we have come to know him if we keep his commands.

1 JOHN 2:3 NIV

If anyone obeys his word, love for God is truly made complete in them. This is how we know we are in him: Whoever claims to live in him must live as Jesus did.

1 JOHN 2:5–6 NIV

The only person in the Bible who lived a perfect life is Jesus. He is our ultimate example. If you're searching for the best way to live and love, Jesus' footsteps are the only ones wholly worth following.

Dear Lord, thank You for being a perfect leader! I will follow You wherever You want me to go! Amen.

DAY 323

Leading Well

Morning

My life is an example to many, because you have been my strength and protection.
Psalm 71:7 NLT

Dear brothers and sisters, pattern your lives after mine, and learn from those who follow our example.
Philippians 3:17 NLT

If people follow your example, where will it lead? Will they find themselves headed toward God or away from Him? As you allow God to change you from the inside out, your life will naturally point others in His direction.

Dear Lord, I want to lead others well, straight to You! Please change me and make me a good example and leader. Amen.

Evening

"In the same way, let your light shine before others, so that they may see your good works and give glory to your Father who is in heaven."
Matthew 5:16 ESV

And you yourself must be an example to them by doing good works of every kind. Let everything you do reflect the integrity and seriousness of your teaching.
Titus 2:7 NLT

Being an example worth following doesn't mean you're under pressure to be perfect. It's God's power shining through the lives of imperfect people that whispers most eloquently, "There's more going on here than meets the eye. God is at work."

Dear Lord, let my life be one that others can admire, not because of what I do but because of You shining through me. Amen.

DAY 324

Great Expectations

Morning

The eyes of all look expectantly to You, and You give them their food in due season.
PSALM 145:15 NKJV

The hopes of the godly result in happiness, but the expectations of the wicked come to nothing.
PROVERBS 10:28 NLT

Praying without expecting God to answer is kind of like wishing on a star. You don't believe it's going to make any difference, but you do it anyway—just in case there really is something behind all those fairy tales.

Dear Lord, please forgive me when I pray halfheartedly, not truly believing You will work. Let me pray with great faith in Your promises. Amen.

Evening

And we know that God causes everything to work together for the good of those who love God and are called according to his purpose for them.
ROMANS 8:28 NLT

Now all glory to God, who is able, through his mighty power at work within us, to accomplish infinitely more than we might ask or think.
EPHESIANS 3:20 NLT

When you pray, do so with great expectation. God is at work on behalf of a child He dearly loves—you! Just remember, God's answers may arrive in ways and at times you least expect.

Dear Father, I know You will answer my prayers in exactly the way that is best. You work all things together for good, and I trust You! Amen.

DAY 325

Why Adversity?

Morning

[Jesus said,] "In this world you will have trouble. But take heart! I have overcome the world."
JOHN 16:33 NIV

Be sober-minded; be watchful. Your adversary the devil prowls around like a roaring lion, seeking someone to devour.
1 PETER 5:8 ESV

We have all asked why there has to be adversity in the world. Only God knows the whole answer, but we can be sure of this: Adversity is to the soul what exercise is to the body.

Dear Lord, though it hurts and is hard, help me to see the value in adversity. Please train me through it, like an athlete trains her body. Amen.

Evening

Dear friends, don't be surprised at the fiery trials you are going through, as if something strange were happening to you.
1 PETER 4:12 NLT

And after you have suffered a little while, the God of all grace, who has called you to his eternal glory in Christ, will himself restore, confirm, strengthen, and establish you.
1 PETER 5:10 ESV

As we struggle against our circumstances and practice placing complete trust in our heavenly Father, we are working our spiritual muscles, growing in strength and confidence. We can thank God even for the hard times.

Dear Lord, I don't understand hard times, but I will choose to praise You and thank You for them and the work You are doing in them. Amen.

DAY 326
Painful Afflictions

Morning

Many are the afflictions of the righteous, but the LORD delivers him out of them all.
PSALM 34:19 NKJV

Together with Christ we are heirs of God's glory. But if we are to share his glory, we must also share his suffering.
ROMANS 8:17 NLT

We will all experience affliction of some kind at one time or another in this world. It is part of the human condition. But when we put our trust in God, we can know for certain that any and all afflictions are temporary.

Dear Lord, help me to remember that any pain or hardship I experience here on earth is temporary and nothing compared to the freedom and perfection I will experience in heaven forever. Please help me to endure well as a testimony to You! Amen.

Evening

Yet what we suffer now is nothing compared to the glory he will reveal to us later.
ROMANS 8:18 NLT

While we live in these earthly bodies, we groan and sigh, but it's not that we want to die and get rid of these bodies that clothe us. Rather, we want to put on our new bodies so that these dying bodies will be swallowed up by life. God himself has prepared us for this, and as a guarantee he has given us his Holy Spirit.
2 CORINTHIANS 5:4–5 NLT

Even if afflictions follow us throughout our lives, God has prepared for each of us a new body free from pain and suffering. One day we will be with Him and we will never hurt again. Praise God!

Dear Lord, help me to persevere with patience in this life and in this failing body until I receive the rewards in heaven that You have promised. Amen.

DAY 327

Angelic Encounters

Morning

Are not all angels ministering spirits sent to serve those who will inherit salvation?

HEBREWS 1:14 NIV

For he will command his angels concerning you to guard you in all your ways.

PSALM 91:11 ESV

Almost all children believe in angels, but it seems that when we get older, many of us relegate heavenly beings to imagination and folklore. The thing is, it just isn't so. The Bible is filled with angelic encounters and interventions.

Dear Lord, please lead me to the scriptures to learn more about Your angels, and help my faith to grow. Amen.

Evening

The angel of the LORD encamps around those who fear him, and delivers them.

PSALM 34:7 ESV

"See that you do not despise one of these little ones. For I tell you that in heaven their angels always see the face of my Father who is in heaven."

MATTHEW 18:10 ESV

We are told that angels serve God, in part, by looking after us. How precious we must be to our heavenly Father, and how grateful we should be that He would direct the angels on our behalf.

Dear Father, may all the accounts of angels caring for people remind me of how precious I am to You. I'm so grateful for Your loving protection! Amen.

DAY 328

What We Don't Deserve

Morning

The Lord *wants to show his mercy to you. He wants to rise and comfort you.*
Isaiah 30:18 NCV

Let us then with confidence draw near to the throne of grace, that we may receive mercy and find grace to help in time of need.
Hebrews 4:16 ESV

No one enjoys sadness and sorrow, yet we often bring them on ourselves. We make poor choices, dismissing the wisdom of others and even the discernment God places in our hearts.

Dear Lord, please forgive me when I bring trouble on myself. Please cover me with Your grace and draw me back to You in obedience. Amen.

Evening

He saved us, not because of works done by us in righteousness, but according to his own mercy, by the washing of regeneration and renewal of the Holy Spirit.
Titus 3:5 ESV

Remember your mercy, O Lord*, and your steadfast love, for they have been from of old.*
Psalm 25:6 ESV

When we go our own way and then it all falls apart and we come to our senses, we find in God what we don't deserve. Like a loving father, He reaches out to us and comforts our aching hearts. His great love and mercy surround us.

Loving Father, please wrap me in Your great mercy. I don't deserve it, but I am so grateful for it. Amen.

DAY 329

Keeping Commandments

Morning

Praise the Lord!
Blessed is the man
who fears the Lord,
who delights greatly in
His commandments.
Psalm 112:1 NKJV

Love means doing what
God has commanded us.
2 John 6 NLT

God's commandments are intended to keep us safe and well, and they also are designed to help us reach our maximum potential. The superficial things we might be asked to give up to honor Him can never compare to the rewards that result from obeying His instructions.

Dear Lord, I know Your commandments are intended not to hinder me but to help me live the best life possible! It is a blessing and honor to obey You! Amen.

Evening

"If you obey all the decrees
and commands I am giving
you today, all will be well with
you and your children."
Deuteronomy 4:40 NLT

With my whole heart I seek
you; let me not wander from
your commandments!
Psalm 119:10 ESV

God is a wise and loving Father who wants to see us become all we can be. His commandments are intended to help us get there.

Dear God, please forgive me when I ignore Your Word and do my own thing. Remind me of Your wisdom and love, and help me to treasure Your commandments. Amen.

DAY 330

Quiet Confrontation

Morning

Thus says the Lord God,
the Holy One of Israel:
"In returning and rest
you shall be saved; in
quietness and confidence
shall be your strength."
ISAIAH 30:15 NKJV

"The Lord will fight for you, and
you have only to be silent."
EXODUS 14:14 ESV

When things go wrong in our lives, we often become upset and agitated. This is a normal human response. Thankfully, God has given us an alternative. He asks that we quiet our minds, refusing to give in to the rush of troubling thoughts and images.

Dear Lord, please quiet my troubled mind and spirit. Remind me that You are the almighty God, and You will fight for me, protect me, and provide for me. Amen.

Evening

"Be still, and know that
I am God! I will be honored by
every nation. I will be honored
throughout the world."
PSALM 46:10 NLT

You will keep in perfect peace
all who trust in you, all whose
thoughts are fixed on you!
ISAIAH 26:3 NLT

God says to focus on Him—putting our complete confidence in Him. When we do, we are lifted out of the waters churning around us and into God's capable hands.

Dear Lord, help me to fix my eyes, my mind, my heart, my soul— all of me!—on You and Your power and love. Amen.

DAY 331

Bitterness

Morning

Don't let anyone become bitter and cause trouble for the rest of you.
HEBREWS 12:15 CEV

Get rid of all bitterness, rage, anger, harsh words, and slander, as well as all types of evil behavior.
EPHESIANS 4:31 NLT

Drop a speck of dirt into a glass of clean water, and the water is no longer fit to drink. Dirt and purity cannot coexist, and neither can bitterness and peace of mind.

Dear Lord, the bitterness I've been carrying around drains me and causes me such strife. Help me to let it go. Amen.

Evening

Watch out that no poisonous root of bitterness grows up to trouble you, corrupting many.
HEBREWS 12:15 NLT

But if you harbor bitter envy and selfish ambition in your hearts, do not boast about it or deny the truth. Such "wisdom" does not come down from heaven but is earthly, unspiritual, demonic.
JAMES 3:14–15 NIV

God invites us to come to Him with whatever makes us feel the least bit bitter, whether it's memories from long ago or circumstances in our lives right now. He longs to replace bitterness with blessings, resentment with rest, and anger with acceptance.

Dear Lord, please replace my bitterness with blessings, my resentment with rest, and my anger with acceptance. I don't want to let them consume me any longer. Amen.

DAY 332

Constructive Criticism

Morning

Whoever heeds life-giving correction will be at home among the wise. Those who disregard discipline despise themselves, but the one who heeds correction gains understanding.

PROVERBS 15:31–32 NIV

Whoever loves discipline loves knowledge, but he who hates reproof is stupid.

PROVERBS 12:1 ESV

When someone criticizes us, it's only natural for us to feel hurt and upset. But what did we actually hear––a mean-spirited opinion or an uncomfortable fact? To find out usually requires soul-searching, prayer, and perhaps consultation with a trustworthy friend or family member.

Dear Lord, help me to discern what is constructive criticism and good correction versus what is just careless or cruel chatter. Amen.

Evening

Listen, friends, to some fatherly advice; sit up and take notice so you'll know how to live. I'm giving you good counsel; don't let it go in one ear and out the other.

PROVERBS 4:1–2 MSG

Refuse good advice and watch your plans fail; take good counsel and watch them succeed.

PROVERBS 15:22 MSG

Once we understand the spirit behind the criticism, peace is ours. We can dismiss the remark or thank the person who cares about us enough to bring an important issue to our attention.

Dear Lord, please keep me humble to accept constructive criticism, and give me wisdom to apply it. Amen.

DAY 333

Deeper and Deeper

Morning

"Blessed is the man who trusts in the Lord, whose trust is the Lord. He is like a tree planted by water, that sends out its roots by the stream, and does not fear when heat comes, for its leaves remain green, and is not anxious in the year of drought, for it does not cease to bear fruit."

JEREMIAH 17:7–8 ESV

We walk our spiritual walk day after day, sometimes unsure of our progress. Nevertheless, our "faith roots" are going down. We can't see beneath the soil where God tends our faith, but the longer we continue to walk in His ways, the deeper His hold on us.

Dear Lord, I can't always see the progress You are making in me, but I trust that as I walk with You day by day, You are changing me to be more like You. Amen.

Evening

Oh, the joys of those who do not follow the advice of the wicked, or stand around with sinners, or join in with mockers. But they delight in the law of the Lord, meditating on it day and night. They are like trees planted along the riverbank, bearing fruit each season. Their leaves never wither, and they prosper in all they do.

PSALM 1:1–3 NLT

We came to God with nothing to use as a bargaining chip, just acceptance of His love. And that is all it takes to keep walking and growing deeper and deeper.

Dear Lord, I want to meditate on Your Word day and night. Please change me with it and develop me with it. Let my roots grow down deep in a strong foundation of faith. Amen.

DAY 334

Danger Signals

Morning

I beg you to avoid the evil things your bodies want to do that fight against your soul.
1 PETER 2:11 NCV

Stay alert! Watch out for your great enemy, the devil. He prowls around like a roaring lion, looking for someone to devour.
1 PETER 5:8 NLT

Like a flashing red light on the roadway, danger signals from God warn us of peril ahead. His warning signal may come as a troubled conscience, a nagging suspicion that our conduct needs correction, or a particular verse from the Bible that speaks to us at a gut-deep level.

Dear Lord, help me to be alert to the danger of temptation. Help me to flee from it! Amen.

Evening

Guard your heart above all else, for it determines the course of your life.
PROVERBS 4:23 NLT

Run from anything that stimulates youthful lusts. Instead, pursue righteous living, faithfulness, love, and peace. Enjoy the companionship of those who call on the Lord with pure hearts.
2 TIMOTHY 2:22 NLT

We avoid calamity by heeding God's signal immediately! He will restore our peace of mind and heart as we stop, pray, and listen, then follow His detour around the hazard.

Dear Lord, I don't want to spend any time entertaining thoughts that tempt me to sin. Help me to banish them from my mind immediately by focusing on the truth of Your Word. Amen.

DAY 335

Relax. . .

Morning

"Teach me, and I will be quiet. Show me where I have been wrong."
Job 6:24 NCV

Let my soul be at rest again, for the Lord has been good to me.
Psalm 116:7 NLT

Do you ever feel as though you simply can't sit still? Take a breath. Open your heart to God. Allow Him to quiet your frantic mind. Ask Him to show you how you can begin again, this time walking to the quiet pace of His grace.

Dear God, how do I slow down? Please show me. Help me take deep breaths and quiet my heart and soul and mind before You. Amen.

Evening

But I am calm and quiet, like a baby with its mother. I am at peace, like a baby with its mother.
Psalm 131:2 NCV

The Lord keeps you from all harm and watches over your life. The Lord keeps watch over you as you come and go, both now and forever.
Psalm 121:7–8 NLT

Like a baby lies completely limp in her mother's arms, let yourself relax in God's arms, wrapped in His grace. Life will go on around you, with all its noise and turmoil. Meanwhile, you are completely safe, totally secure, without a worry in the world. Lie back and enjoy the quiet!

Dear Lord, I choose to stop right now and just relax in Your promises and truth. May I close my eyes and feel Your loving embrace around me. Amen.

DAY 336

Riches That Last

Morning

"Yes, a person is a fool to store up earthly wealth but not have a rich relationship with God."
LUKE 12:21 NLT

Keep your life free from love of money, and be content with what you have, for he has said, "I will never leave you nor forsake you."
HEBREWS 13:5 ESV

Why would we want money in the bank and a house full of stuff if we lived in a world that was empty of grace? Only in God do we find riches that will last forever.

Dear Lord, help me to stay free from the love of money. I want to love my relationship with You most of all, trusting You to provide what I need when I need it. Amen.

Evening

Honor the LORD *with your wealth and with the best part of everything you produce.*
PROVERBS 3:9 NLT

I have riches and honor, as well as enduring wealth and justice. My gifts are better than gold, even the purest gold, my wages better than sterling silver!
PROVERBS 8:18–19 NLT

Your health, your abilities, your friends, your family, your physical strength, and your creative energy—all of these are parts of your true wealth. Grace brought all of these riches into your life, and when you use them to honor God, grace is multiplied still more.

Dear Lord, help me never to lose sight of what true wealth is. You have blessed me beyond measure just by making me Your child. Amen.

DAY 337

Into His Presence

Morning

But you want complete honesty, so teach me true wisdom.

PSALM 51:6 CEV

Every way of a man is right in his own eyes, but the LORD *weighs the heart.*

PROVERBS 21:2 ESV

Sometimes we are like Adam and Eve in the garden after they sinned; we are afraid to come naked into God's presence. We think we can hide ourselves from Him. But God cannot teach our hearts if we refuse to be open with Him.

Dear Lord, forgive me for the times I've tried to hide from You. I come before You now with all of my sin and fault and ask You to cleanse me and change me. Amen.

Evening

Search me, O God, and know my heart; test me and know my anxious thoughts. Point out anything in me that offends you, and lead me along the path of everlasting life.

PSALM 139:23–24 NLT

Prove me, O LORD, *and try me; test my heart and my mind.*

PSALM 26:2 ESV

We must take the risk of stepping into God's presence with complete honesty and vulnerability. When we do, His grace touches us at the deepest levels, and we are filled with His wisdom.

Dear Lord, please search me and know me and fill me with Your grace and wisdom. Amen.

DAY 338

The Lord's Work

Morning

Always give yourselves fully to the work of the Lord, because you know that your labor in the Lord is not in vain.
1 CORINTHIANS 15:58 NIV

Let us not become weary in doing good, for at the proper time we will reap a harvest if we do not give up.
GALATIANS 6:9 NIV

You may feel sometimes as though all your hard work comes to nothing. But if your work is the Lord's work, you can trust Him to bring it to fulfillment.

Dear Lord, I can't always see what good my work for You is doing, but I trust that You are using it. You fill me with such satisfaction when I am serving You! Amen.

Evening

"But you, be strong and do not lose courage, for there is a reward for your work."
2 CHRONICLES 15:7 NASB

Am I now trying to win the approval of human beings, or of God? Or am I trying to please people? If I were still trying to please people, I would not be a servant of Christ.
GALATIANS 1:10 NIV

Why do you work? For a paycheck? For respect? For a sense of self-worth? All of those are good reasons to work, but never forget that your work is part of a bigger picture. God wants to use your hands, your intelligence, and your efforts to build His kingdom, the place where grace dwells.

Dear Lord, I offer my talents, my time, my education, my hands, my feet—everything!—to do Your will. Please use me to help build Your kingdom! Amen.

DAY 339

In the Details

Morning

[Jesus said,] "Instead of looking at the fashions, walk out into the fields and look at the wildflowers."
MATTHEW 6:28 MSG

For his invisible attributes, namely, his eternal power and divine nature, have been clearly perceived, ever since the creation of the world, in the things that have been made. So they are without excuse.
ROMANS 1:20 ESV

Our God cares about details. You see it throughout His creation. Every species unique and every creature unique within its species. Human beings created in His image and yet each one of a kind. Flowers and trees awash with color and refinement. What beauty and splendor we see in the world around us!

Dear Lord, Your details are beautiful and amazing! What a gift Your creation is! Amen.

Evening

All things were made through him, and without him was not any thing made that was made.
JOHN 1:3 ESV

"Are not two sparrows sold for a penny? Yet not one of them will fall to the ground outside your Father's care. And even the very hairs of your head are all numbered. So don't be afraid; you are worth more than many sparrows."
MATTHEW 10:29–31 NIV

When you wonder if God is interested in the details of your life, consider the evidence in nature. He cares about everything—no matter how seemingly inconsequential.

Dear Lord, how awesome to know that You care so much about the details that even the hairs of my head are numbered by You. No one could ever love me like You do! Amen.

DAY 340

The Best of All Creation

Morning

*God's glory is on tour
in the skies, God-craft on
exhibit across the horizon.*
PSALM 19:1 MSG

*Look up into the heavens. Who
created all the stars? He brings
them out like an army, one after
another, calling each by its name.
Because of his great power
and incomparable strength,
not a single one is missing.*
ISAIAH 40:26 NLT

Look outside right now; better yet, go outside. Daytime or nighttime, it doesn't matter. Just look around you. Imagine for a moment the immensity of God's creation, the grandeur of it.

*Almighty God, Your creation
declares Your amazing glory!
I praise You! Amen.*

Evening

*In the image of God he
created them; male and
female he created them. Then
God blessed them and said,
"Be fruitful and multiply. Fill
the earth and govern it. Reign
over the fish in the sea, the birds
in the sky, and all the animals
that scurry along the ground."*
GENESIS 1:27–28 NLT

*"You, Lord, laid the foundation
of the earth in the beginning,
and the heavens are the
work of your hands."*
HEBREWS 1:10 ESV

God calls mankind His most splendid creation—all the rest was called into being only to benefit His human creation. God values you above all else. Look up at the sky and consider His great love.

*Almighty God, I am in awe of
how much You love and value
me. Thank You! Amen.*

DAY 341

The Nine

Morning

As he entered a village there, ten men with leprosy stood at a distance, crying out, "Jesus, Master, have mercy on us!" He looked at them and said, "Go show yourselves to the priests." And as they went, they were cleansed of their leprosy.

LUKE 17:12–14 NLT

Jesus asked, "Didn't I heal ten men? Where are the other nine?"

LUKE 17:17 NLT

In the New Testament, we read that ten lepers came to Jesus one morning asking to be healed. Jesus healed all ten of them—but only one came back to thank Him. Jesus looked around and asked where the other nine had gone.

Dear Lord, please forgive me when I forget to thank You. May I be constantly mindful of my blessings and regularly express my gratitude to You. Amen.

Evening

Give thanks in all circumstances; for this is the will of God in Christ Jesus for you.

1 THESSALONIANS 5:18 ESV

And give thanks for everything to God the Father in the name of our Lord Jesus Christ.

EPHESIANS 5:20 NLT

We should always remember to thank God for all the times He has rescued us, for all the gifts He has given us, for all the love and compassion and forgiveness He has bestowed on us.

Dear Lord, thank You for everything. Amen.

DAY 342

A Good Conscience

Morning

The goal of this command is love, which comes from a pure heart and a good conscience and a sincere faith.

1 TIMOTHY 1:5 NIV

And looking intently at the council, Paul said, "Brothers, I have lived my life before God in all good conscience up to this day."

ACTS 23:1 ESV

Not only do our consciences warn us about danger ahead, but they also help us rightly evaluate our spiritual and emotional well-being. When our consciences are clear, we have confidence that we are on the path to becoming the women God intends us to be.

Dear Lord, please make me keenly aware of my spiritual well-being so that I can keep a clear conscience before You. Amen.

Evening

For our guilty consciences have been sprinkled with Christ's blood to make us clean, and our bodies have been washed with pure water.

HEBREWS 10:22 NLT

Pray for us, for our conscience is clear and we want to live honorably in everything we do.

HEBREWS 13:18 NLT

When our consciences are stressed and gloomy, we are reminded that we must go to God and make things right. Without our consciences, we might miss the joy of receiving God's grace and forgiveness.

Dear Lord, thank You for my conscience that helps keep me in check. Help me to turn from sin quickly and make things right with You immediately. Amen.

DAY 343

Discernment

Morning

Preserve sound judgment and discretion; they will be life for you.
PROVERBS 3:21–22 NIV

Beloved, do not believe every spirit, but test the spirits to see whether they are from God, for many false prophets have gone out into the world.
1 JOHN 4:1 ESV

We live in a world where we can't trust our eyes and ears. Photographs and recordings can be altered. Everything is in a spin. . .smoke and mirrors. Never has there been a time when discernment was needed more.

Dear God, in a world so full of confusion and deception, please give me sharp discernment. Amen.

Evening

Let those who are wise understand these things. Let those with discernment listen carefully. The paths of the LORD *are true and right, and righteous people live by walking in them. But in those paths sinners stumble and fall.*
HOSEA 14:9 NLT

My child, don't lose sight of common sense and discernment. Hang on to them, for they will refresh your soul. They are like jewels on a necklace. They keep you safe on your way, and your feet will not stumble.
PROVERBS 3:21–23 NLT

True discernment, defined as "keenness of insight," comes from God. It's that little voice inside your head that says, "Wait. . .something's not right here." Listen for it. Trust it. Thank God for it. It's there to help us navigate murky waters.

Dear Lord, when I think of needing discernment, I think of how much I need quiet time with You and Your Word. Please help me to make it my top priority. Amen.

DAY 344

Moving Mountains

Morning

So faith comes from hearing,
and hearing through
the word of Christ.
ROMANS 10:17 ESV

And without faith it is impossible to please him, for whoever would draw near to God must believe that he exists and that he rewards those who seek him.
HEBREWS 11:6 ESV

Faith is a powerful thing. It can restore lives and bring families together. It can heal the sick and provide for our needs, even in extreme circumstances. With the eyes of faith, we can see beyond our pain and struggles.

Dear Lord, please increase my faith in You every day! Amen.

Evening

Now faith is the assurance of things hoped for, the conviction of things not seen.
HEBREWS 11:1 ESV

[Jesus] replied, "Truly I tell you, if you have faith as small as a mustard seed, you can say to this mountain, 'Move from here to there,' and it will move. Nothing will be impossible for you."
MATTHEW 17:20 NIV

Faith is powerful. Jesus told His disciples that a tiny bit of faith—the size of a mustard seed—could move a mountain. We can thank God that even the tiniest faith is powerful enough to conquer the biggest problem.

Dear Lord, faith is so powerful, and I don't give it enough credit. Help me to truly believe in who You are—the almighty Creator God of the universe! Amen.

DAY 345
Money

Morning

Whoever loves wealth is never satisfied with their income.
ECCLESIASTES 5:10 NIV

Keep your life free from love of money, and be content with what you have, for he has said, "I will never leave you nor forsake you."
HEBREWS 13:5 ESV

Some people think it's spiritual to say they don't care about money. But here on this earth, we have to care. The important thing is that we keep money in its proper place in our lives. It cannot take center stage.

Dear Lord, I never need to love money because You have promised never to leave me or forsake me. I trust that You will always provide for me. Amen.

Evening

As for the rich in this present age, charge them not to be haughty, nor to set their hopes on the uncertainty of riches, but on God, who richly provides us with everything to enjoy. They are to do good, to be rich in good works, to be generous and ready to share, thus storing up treasure for themselves as a good foundation for the future, so that they may take hold of that which is truly life.
1 TIMOTHY 6:17–19 ESV

We can't place our faith in money or expect money to rescue us in tough times. When we do, we put money in the place of God. Instead, we should always look to the heavenly Father for guidance in using our money. He will never lead us in the wrong direction.

Dear Lord, help me to know exactly how and where You'd like me to spend the money with which You've entrusted me. I want to use it to build Your kingdom for Your glory. Amen.

DAY 346

Justice

Morning

Many seek an audience with a ruler, but it is from the Lord *that one gets justice.*

PROVERBS 29:26 NIV

But let justice roll down like waters, and righteousness like an ever-flowing stream.

AMOS 5:24 ESV

A longing for justice is part of the God-seed placed inside us at creation. We sense it when we see a wrong done—especially when an innocent person is harmed. What we must remember, though, is that God's justice is perfect because He has all the facts. We fall short in that category.

Dear Lord, help me to remember that Your justice is perfect because Your perspective is perfect. Please use me however You wish to help deliver Your justice. Amen.

Evening

Beloved, never avenge yourselves, but leave it to the wrath of God, for it is written, "Vengeance is mine, I will repay, says the Lord."

ROMANS 12:19 ESV

For the Lord *is a God of justice; blessed are all those who wait for him.*

ISAIAH 30:18 ESV

When we perceive something to be unjust, it's important for us to go to God with our concerns before we act. The outcome is always best when we wait for God's instructions first.

Dear Lord, I often want to act too quickly. Please help me to wait on You in matters of justice. Amen.

DAY 347

Triumphing Over Injustice

Morning

What does the Lord require of you? To act justly and to love mercy and to walk humbly with your God.

MICAH 6:8 NIV

For I the Lord love justice.

ISAIAH 61:8 ESV

Justice is important to God. It's one of the three things He mentions when He tells us what He requires of His children. We are often helpless to right the wrongs we see every day, but we are empowered when it comes to living our own lives in a just manner.

Dear Lord, please give me the strength to do what You require of me—to act justly, love mercy, and walk humbly with You! Amen.

Evening

Turn away from evil and do good; so shall you dwell forever. For the Lord loves justice; he will not forsake his saints.

PSALM 37:27–28 ESV

He will judge the world with justice and rule the nations with fairness.

PSALM 9:8 NLT

Rather than becoming obsessed with injustice, we can overcome it by doing what our Savior calls us to do. We can give thanks to our wise God for showing us how to triumph in an often unjust world.

Dear Lord, there's no way I can keep track of all the awful injustices in this world. Please help me to just keep serving You and trust You to take care of them once and for all one day! Amen.

DAY 348
The Ways of God

Morning

All the ways of the L*ORD*
are loving and faithful
toward those who keep the
demands of his covenant.
PSALM 25:10 NIV

"My thoughts are not your
thoughts, neither are your ways
my ways," declares the L*ORD.*
ISAIAH 55:8 NIV

We've all looked back into our past and realized that at one time or another, something painful in our lives turned out to be fortuitous—bringing some unexpected blessing or even changing the entire course of our lives for the better.

Dear Father, thank You for taking the things that seem awful in my life and turning them into something good. Amen.

Evening

"I make known the end from
the beginning, from ancient
times, what is still to come.
I say, 'My purpose will stand,
and I will do all that I please.'"
ISAIAH 46:10 NIV

"You intended to harm me, but
God intended it for good to
accomplish what is now being
done, the saving of many lives."
GENESIS 50:20 NIV

We sheepishly recall lashing out in a difficult time, unaware of what God really had in store for us. Take heart. God won't allow suffering into our lives without some greater purpose. When we are hurting, we must thank God for seeing what we do not. We would be wise to trust His perspective—always.

Dear Father, please forgive me when I lash out at You over a difficult time. Remind me that You see what I cannot, You are working in ways I don't understand, and You are worthy of all my trust and praise even when I'm hurting. Amen.

DAY 349

God's Promises

Morning

The Lord always
keeps his promises;
he is gracious in all he does.
Psalm 145:13 NLT

My eyes stay open through the
watches of the night, that I may
meditate on your promises.
Psalm 119:148 NIV

At one time or another, we've all made promises we didn't keep, despite our good intentions. But God always keeps His promises—every one! Depending on how they are interpreted, between three thousand and five thousand promises are included in God's Word.

Almighty God, I am in awe of Your
promises and Your faithfulness!
I praise You for constantly
keeping Your Word! Amen.

Evening

Your promises have
been thoroughly tested,
and your servant loves them.
Psalm 119:140 NIV

For all of God's promises
have been fulfilled in Christ
with a resounding "Yes!"
2 Corinthians 1:20 NLT

God's promises represent the remarkable treasure we share when we walk in relationship with our generous and loving heavenly Father. Even when we aren't aware of it, God's promises clear the path before us. Our part is simply to say, "Thank You!"

Dear Father, my relationship
with You is truly my greatest
treasure. Thank You! Amen.

DAY 350

More Than We Deserve

Morning

Keep my commands in your heart, for they will prolong your life many years and bring you peace and prosperity.

PROVERBS 3:1–2 NIV

"Let the LORD be magnified, who has pleasure in the prosperity of His servant."

PSALM 35:27 NKJV

Very few earthly kings care about the prosperity of those who live within their kingdoms. Many kings live in opulence while giving little notice to the needs of their citizens. Not so in the kingdom of God.

Dear Lord, You make me prosper as I keep Your commands. What a joy and blessing it is to obey You! Amen.

Evening

"You shall remember the LORD your God, for it is he who gives you power to get wealth."

DEUTERONOMY 8:18 ESV

"Bring the full tithe into the storehouse, that there may be food in my house. And thereby put me to the test, says the LORD of hosts, if I will not open the windows of heaven for you and pour down for you a blessing until there is no more need."

MALACHI 3:10 ESV

God delights in blessing those who choose to live under His banner. Our welfare is of utmost concern to Him. And He isn't just concerned with meeting our physical needs. He showers us with blessings of every kind, more than we can count, so much more than we deserve.

Dear Lord, I am blessed beyond measure, and it's all because of You! Oh, how grateful I am to be Your child! Amen.

DAY 351

His Own Purpose

Morning

The one who cherishes understanding will soon prosper.
PROVERBS 19:8 NIV

The unfolding of your words gives light; it imparts understanding to the simple.
PSALM 119:130 ESV

As we live out our faith, there will be times when we understand what is going on around us. We really "get it." But there will be other times when we don't understand what's happening but must move forward anyway, trusting that God has His own purpose in mind.

Dear God, sometimes I just don't have a clue what Your plans or purposes are. Please help me in those times to keep on believing in Your goodness and ultimate victory. Amen.

Evening

"I am the Alpha and the Omega," says the Lord God, "who is, and who was, and who is to come, the Almighty."
REVELATION 1:8 NIV

Tune your ears to wisdom, and concentrate on understanding. Cry out for insight, and ask for understanding. Search for them as you would for silver; seek them like hidden treasures. Then you will understand what it means to fear the LORD, and you will gain knowledge of God.
PROVERBS 2:2–5 NLT

When we come to places of confusion or uncertainty, we must remember that God knows all things—the end from the beginning and everything in between—and we can take great comfort in that.

Dear God, You are the Alpha and Omega, the beginning and end. I trust You for all time. Amen.

DAY 352

Real Repentance

Morning

This is what the L*ORD says:*
"If you repent, I will restore you that you may serve me."
JEREMIAH 15:19 NIV

"Today I have given you the choice between life and death, between blessings and curses. Now I call on heaven and earth to witness the choice you make."
DEUTERONOMY 30:19–20 NLT

When God invested free will in the hearts of mankind, He took a big risk. He knew that, given the choice, some would reject Him. Yet He took that risk for our sake—for the sake of those who would choose to love Him in return.

Dear God, I thank You for free will. I choose You! Amen.

Evening

"Repent therefore, and turn back, that your sins may be blotted out."
ACTS 3:19 ESV

Whoever conceals his transgressions will not prosper, but he who confesses and forsakes them will obtain mercy.
PROVERBS 28:13 ESV

Repentance doesn't mean giving up our way. It means turning from the things that separate us from God so that we might live in constant fellowship with Him.

Dear Lord, please forgive me. I choose to turn from my sin and draw closer to You. Amen.

DAY 353

Just Say No

Morning

We each must carry our own load.
GALATIANS 6:5 CEV

But the Lord said to her, "My dear Martha, you are worried and upset over all these details! There is only one thing worth being concerned about. Mary has discovered it, and it will not be taken away from her."
LUKE 10:41–42 NLT

Because women carry so much day-to-day responsibility, it's easy for us to feel the weight of burdens that aren't even our own. Sometimes no is the absolute best answer to the extra activities that clamor for our commitment.

Dear Lord, please give me the wisdom I need to balance all the activities of life. Help me to know what You want me to do and when to say no. Amen.

Evening

Set your minds on things that are above, not on things that are on earth.
COLOSSIANS 3:2 ESV

So teach us to number our days that we may get a heart of wisdom.
PSALM 90:12 ESV

Taking on too much can distract us from our legitimate responsibilities, leaving us physically and emotionally drained. Moreover, we may slight others when we take on the tasks God meant for them to tackle. Ask God to help you say no when necessary.

Dear Lord, please forgive me when I've taken on too much and overwhelmed myself. Help me to seek after You first of all and let everything else fall into place. Amen.

DAY 354

God's Book

Morning

I have more insight than all my teachers, for I meditate on your statutes.

PSALM 119:99 NIV

"Heaven and earth will pass away, but my words will not pass away."

MARK 13:31 ESV

In our world there remains one great source of insight and revelation. It is the book God gave us—the Bible. Over the course of time, it has demonstrated its ability to provide wisdom, insight, and revelation concerning how best to live our lives.

Dear Lord, Your Word is timeless and always true. I am so grateful for the way it guides my life and leads me closer to You! Amen.

Evening

Your word is a lamp to my feet and a light to my path.

PSALM 119:105 ESV

The instructions of the LORD are perfect, reviving the soul. The decrees of the LORD are trustworthy, making wise the simple. The commandments of the LORD are right, bringing joy to the heart. The commands of the LORD are clear, giving insight for living.

PSALM 19:7–8 NLT

The Bible has often been described as a road map from God, to God, and about God. Much more than just words on a page, the Bible offers revelation that resonates with the Spirit of God.

Dear Lord, I desperately need the road map You've given in the Bible. Please lead me by it. Amen.

DAY 355

God's Words

Morning

[Jesus] opened their understanding, that they might comprehend the Scriptures.
LUKE 24:45 NKJV

All Scripture is God-breathed and is useful for teaching, rebuking, correcting and training in righteousness.
2 TIMOTHY 3:16 NIV

The Bible is not just another book. It's holy, because the words of the Bible weren't crafted by some clever wordsmith. Rather, they were given to men by revelation from God; therefore, they are holy words, God's words.

Dear Lord, may I never take the Bible for granted. May I honor it, treasure it, and live by it. Amen.

Evening

How can a young person stay on the path of purity? By living according to your word.
PSALM 119:9 NIV

Knowing this first of all, that no prophecy of Scripture comes from someone's own interpretation. For no prophecy was ever produced by the will of man, but men spoke from God as they were carried along by the Holy Spirit.
2 PETER 1:20–21 ESV

Some have tried to make light of the holy nature of the Bible, but its amazing symmetry, wisdom, and truth over the course of thousands of years cannot otherwise be explained. Thank God today for sending us His words.

Dear Lord, thank You for revealing Yourself to us all through Your living and holy Word! Amen.

DAY 356

Serving Others

Morning

There are different kinds of service, but the same Lord.
1 CORINTHIANS 12:5 NIV

"In all things I have shown you that by working hard in this way we must help the weak and remember the words of the Lord Jesus, how he himself said, 'It is more blessed to give than to receive.'"
ACTS 20:35 ESV

God's gift of service takes on many forms. There are those who serve by being sensitive to the needs of others, those who expound on God's Word, those who cover others with prayer. Some serve by providing financial assistance, others by giving their time in service to others.

Dear Lord, it is an honor to work for You! Please show me my gifts and where to serve others best. Amen.

Evening

And he sat down and called the twelve. And he said to them, "If anyone would be first, he must be last of all and servant of all."
MARK 9:35 ESV

The generous will prosper; those who refresh others will themselves be refreshed.
PROVERBS 11:25 NLT

God is pleased when we serve each other using the gifts He has placed in each of us. What a wonderful God to endow us with such generous and unique gifts.

Dear God, Your generosity and love are so inspiring. Nothing is more fulfilling than striving to be like You! Amen.

DAY 357

A Simple Message

Morning

The unfolding of your words gives light; it gives understanding to the simple.
PSALM 119:130 NIV

For I am not ashamed of the gospel, for it is the power of God for salvation to everyone who believes.
ROMANS 1:16 ESV

Jesus criticized the religious leaders of His day, saying that they had intentionally complicated faith in order to control the people. In fact, the message of faith is quite simple.

Dear Lord, Your gospel is simple and powerful. Please help me to live it and proclaim it. Amen.

Evening

And Peter said to them, "Repent and be baptized every one of you in the name of Jesus Christ for the forgiveness of your sins, and you will receive the gift of the Holy Spirit."
ACTS 2:38 ESV

For God so loved the world that he gave his one and only Son, that whoever believes in him shall not perish but have eternal life.
JOHN 3:16 NIV

God created us with the will to choose, and we chose to walk away. But through the sacrifice of His Son, Jesus, He bridged the gap between us, giving us a second opportunity to choose God. Some will accept His gift, and others will not. Nevertheless, He remains the God of second chances!

Dear Lord, thank You for second chances, all because of the gospel—the death and resurrection of Jesus to cover our sins and bring us into relationship with You! Amen.

DAY 358

Alone Time

Morning

It is good to wait quietly
for the salvation of the Lord.
LAMENTATIONS 3:26 NIV

"But when you pray, go into your room and shut the door and pray to your Father who is in secret. And your Father who sees in secret will reward you."
MATTHEW 6:6 ESV

Many people never learn to appreciate solitude. They feel uncomfortable with their own thoughts. But God desires for us to feel at home with ourselves, to be certain of the words we speak and the things we do.

Dear Lord, help me to regularly make time for solitude, with only You to listen to. Amen.

Evening

But now even more the report about him went abroad, and great crowds gathered to hear him and to be healed of their infirmities. But he would withdraw to desolate places and pray.
LUKE 5:15–16 ESV

And he said to them, "Come away by yourselves to a desolate place and rest a while."
MARK 6:31 ESV

God wants us to have confidence in what we believe and why, without needing the constant reinforcement of others. Give thanks to the heavenly Father today for moments of solitude when we need them most!

Dear Lord, thank You for quiet moments alone with You. Please use them to build my confidence in my relationship with You. Amen.

DAY 359

Tough Inside

Morning

Those who hope in the
Lord will renew their strength.
Isaiah 40:31 NIV

For God has not given us a
spirit of fear and timidity, but of
power, love, and self-discipline.
2 Timothy 1:7 NLT

Physical strength is good, but it's inner strength that really matters—that toughness that seeps out from our core and keeps us steady on our feet. That's the kind of toughness it takes to be a God follower.

Dear Lord, no amount of physical strength compares to the inner strength that only You can provide. Please fortify me with great faith in Your power! Amen.

Evening

But when you ask him,
be sure that your faith is in
God alone. Do not waver,
for a person with divided
loyalty is as unsettled as a
wave of the sea that is blown
and tossed by the wind.
James 1:6 NLT

We also pray that you will
be strengthened with all
his glorious power so you
will have all the endurance
and patience you need.
Colossians 1:11 NLT

Without rock-hard inner conviction, we would be tossed about, our faith challenged on every side. Thank God for the fortitude that comes when we know that He is on our side and always watching over us.

Dear Lord, please give me both a soft heart that loves and forgives like You do and a rock-hard conviction of the truth of Your Word. Amen.

DAY 360

Humble Yourself

Morning

All of you be subject one to another, and be clothed with humility.

1 PETER 5:5 KJV

Pride goes before destruction, a haughty spirit before a fall.

PROVERBS 16:18 NIV

The one thing pride does very well is alienate us from others. It causes us to think that we don't need anyone else in our lives. Its tendency to isolate is why pride so successfully dooms us to failure.

Dear Lord, please rid me of pride and let me accept help when I need it. Amen.

Evening

Humble yourselves, therefore, under God's mighty hand, that he may lift you up in due time.

1 PETER 5:6 NIV

The reward for humility and fear of the LORD is riches and honor and life.

PROVERBS 22:4 ESV

Humility has just the opposite effect of pride. It opens us up to new ideas and ways of doing things. Humility allows us to identify the resources of wisdom and experience God has given us.

Dear Lord, please make me humble, willing to learn from others and most importantly to learn from You and be changed by You. Amen.

DAY 361
Holiness

Morning

"There is no one
holy like the LORD."
1 SAMUEL 2:2 NIV

God did not call us to be
impure, but to live a holy life.
1 THESSALONIANS 4:7 NIV

The word *holy* sounds kind of old and religious, doesn't it? But its true meaning is always relevant. It means to be perfect in goodness. And that's what God is. . .perfect in His goodness to us.

Dear Lord, while I often don't understand how You are working in a situation, I believe wholeheartedly that You are good, and that is enough. Amen.

Evening

For the LORD is good and
his love endures forever;
his faithfulness continues
through all generations.
PSALM 100:5 NIV

As a father shows compassion
to his children, so the
LORD shows compassion
to those who fear him.
PSALM 103:13 ESV

God doesn't coddle or spoil us. He doesn't neglect or withhold from us. He isn't overcome by emotion. Nor is He rigid and stern, without feeling. He is the perfect Father—always there for us, always committed to our good.

Dear Father, You are truly the perfect Parent. With so many people in need of good fathers in their lives, please help me to share Your love and point others to You! Amen.

DAY 362

One True Love

Morning

God's love will continue forever.
PSALM 52:1 NCV

Walk in the way of love, just as Christ loved us.
EPHESIANS 5:2 NIV

We cling to those we love. We dig in deeply and confidently, even though we know that human love often fails. The brightest of romances often go sour. The love of friends sometimes does as well. The love of God is the only sure thing in this world.

Dear Lord, may I cling to You even more than I do my precious loved ones here on earth. You are my one true constant. Amen.

Evening

Whoever does not love does not know God, because God is love.
1 JOHN 4:8 NIV

If we love one another, God lives in us and his love is made complete in us.
1 JOHN 4:12 NIV

God's perfect love lasts forever. It is the one true and lasting love we can find, and it is His love alone that makes all other love possible. Thank your heavenly Father for His unconditional love today.

Dear Lord, truly we love because You first loved us. Without You and Your example, we wouldn't know love or have the capacity to love. I am in awe of Your love and so very grateful. Amen.

DAY 363

No Strings Attached

Morning

Whatever is good and perfect is a gift coming down to us from God our Father, who created all the lights in the heavens.

JAMES 1:17 NLT

[Jesus said,] "No one is good but One, that is, God."

MATTHEW 19:17 NKJV

Politicians never stop promising us good things, but what they deliver is most often something else altogether. That's not the case with our God. He keeps all His promises as only He can.

Dear God, so many things are promised by leaders here on earth, but apart from Your will, no good thing will be accomplished. May I never forget that all good things ultimately come from You. Amen.

Evening

How great is your goodness that you have stored up for those who fear you.

PSALM 31:19 NCV

For by grace you have been saved through faith. And this is not your own doing; it is the gift of God, not a result of works, so that no one may boast.

EPHESIANS 2:8–9 ESV

When God brings good into our lives, there are no strings attached. He isn't bargaining for our vote. He does it because He loves us completely. We can trust in His goodness always.

Dear God, thank You that You don't attach strings to Your gifts. You are full of blessing and love because of Your good and loving character. Amen.

DAY 364

Pure Waters

Morning

The generous soul will be made rich, and he who waters will also be watered himself.
PROVERBS 11:25 NKJV

[Jesus said,] "Live generously and graciously toward others, the way God lives toward you."
MATTHEW 5:48 MSG

All freshwater lakes have outlets. Without them, the water would become stagnant and brackish. The same is true in our lives. If we only receive and fail to give, we will become subject to greed. We will no longer be content with what we have; instead, it will take more and more to satisfy us.

Dear Lord, help me never to become stagnant. As I receive so much from You, may I constantly be pouring it out to bless others. Amen.

Evening

One gives freely, yet grows all the richer; another withholds what he should give, and only suffers want.
PROVERBS 11:24 ESV

Whoever is kind to the poor lends to the LORD, and he will reward them for what they have done.
PROVERBS 19:17 NIV

When we are generous with others, our lives remain in balance, our inner waters pure. We don't become slaves to what God has given but rather masters of His goodness.

Dear Father, I absolutely want to be a master of Your goodness, meaning I faithfully share all the goodness You have lavished on me. Amen.

DAY 365

The Gift of Choice

Morning

I will sacrifice a
voluntary offering to you;
I will praise your name,
O Lord, for it is good.
PSALM 54:6 NLT

You have been called to live in
freedom, my brothers and sisters.
But don't use your freedom
to satisfy your sinful nature.
Instead, use your freedom to
serve one another in love.
GALATIANS 5:13 NLT

Why would God give us freedom of choice? He must have known the destruction we would bring on ourselves and into the lives of others. But His motivation is clear. Fellowship that is mandated is not fellowship at all, only coerced consent.

Dear Lord, may I live my life to help others choose You too! Amen.

Evening

Jesus replied,
"All who love me will do
what I say. My Father will
love them, and we will come
and make our home with each
of them. Anyone who doesn't
love me will not obey me."
JOHN 14:23–24 NLT

Live as people who are free,
not using your freedom
as a cover-up for evil, but
living as servants of God.
1 PETER 2:16 ESV

Much more than creatures who would mindlessly obey, God wanted fellowship with those who would choose to know Him, love Him, and live in relationship with Him. What is your choice?

Dear Lord, I choose You and Your way each and every day, because there is truly nothing better than knowing You and serving You. Amen.

TOPICAL INDEX AND SCRIPTURE INDEX

Topical Index

Scripture Index

Galatians

Ephesians

Philippians

Colossians

1 Thessalonians

2 Thessalonians

1 Timothy